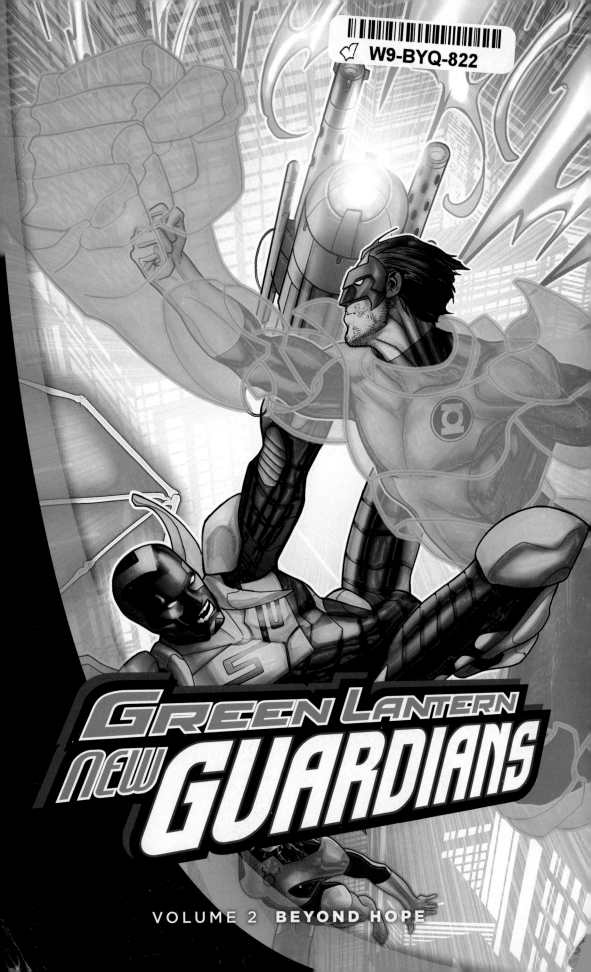

GREEN LANTERN NEW GUARDIANS

VOLUME 2 · BEYOND HOPE

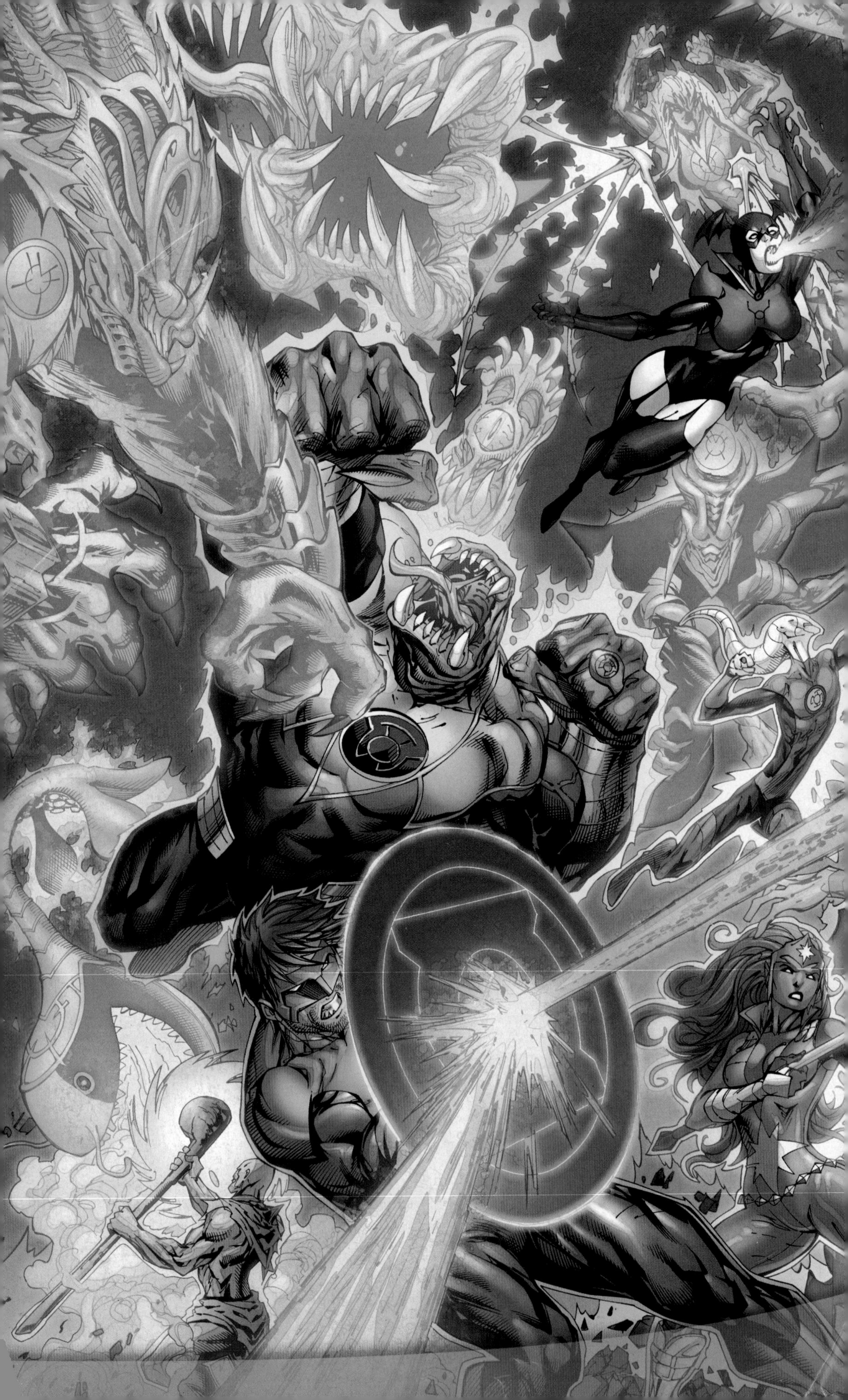

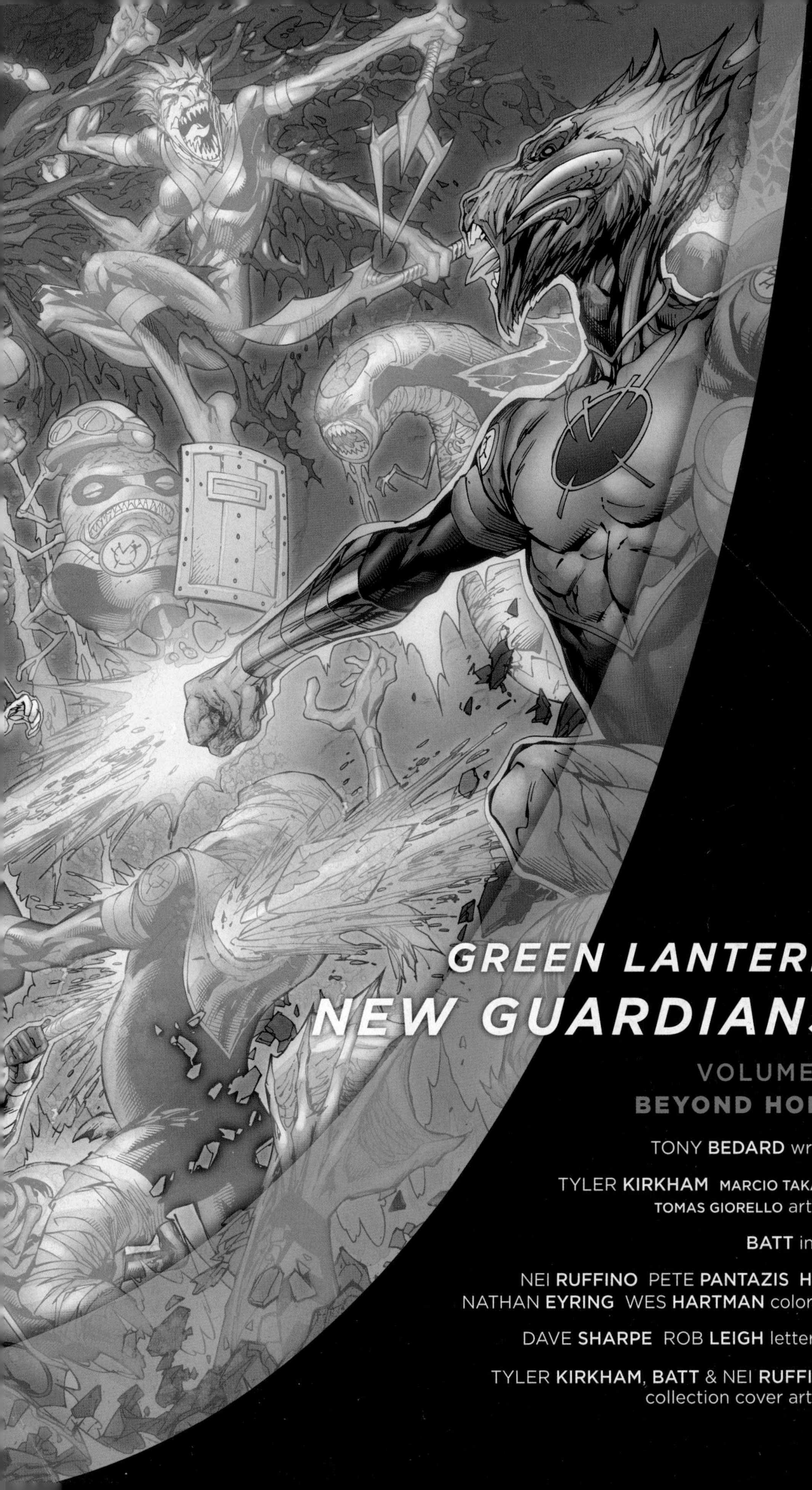

GREEN LANTERN
NEW GUARDIANS

VOLUME 2
BEYOND HOPE

TONY **BEDARD** writer

TYLER **KIRKHAM** MARCIO TAKARA
TOMAS GIORELLO artists

BATT inker

NEI **RUFFINO** PETE **PANTAZIS** **HI-FI**
NATHAN **EYRING** WES **HARTMAN** colorists

DAVE **SHARPE** ROB **LEIGH** letterers

TYLER **KIRKHAM**, **BATT** & NEI **RUFFINO**
collection cover artists

PAT McCALLUM Editor – Original Series SEAN MACKIEWICZ Assistant Editor – Original Series
ROWENA YOW Editor ROBBIN BROSTERMAN Design Director – Books
ROBBIE BIEDERMAN Publication Design

BOB HARRAS Senior VP – Editor-in-Chief, DC Comics

DIANE NELSON President DAN DIDIO and JIM LEE Co-Publishers
GEOFF JOHNS Chief Creative Officer
JOHN ROOD Executive VP – Sales, Marketing and Business Development
AMY GENKINS Senior VP – Business and Legal Affairs NAIRI GARDINER Senior VP – Finance
JEFF BOISON VP – Publishing Planning MARK CHIARELLO VP – Art Direction and Design
JOHN CUNNINGHAM VP – Marketing TERRI CUNNINGHAM VP – Editorial Administration
ALISON GILL Senior VP – Manufacturing and Operations HANK KANALZ Senior VP – Vertigo and Integrated Publishing
JAY KOGAN VP – Business and Legal Affairs, Publishing JACK MAHAN VP – Business Affairs, Talent
NICK NAPOLITANO VP – Manufacturing Administration SUE POHJA VP – Book Sales
COURTNEY SIMMONS Senior VP – Publicity BOB WAYNE Senior VP – Sales

GREEN LANTERN - NEW GUARDIANS VOLUME 2: BEYOND HOPE

DC Comics, 1700 Broadway, New York, NY 10019
A Warner Bros. Entertainment Company.
Printed by RR Donnelley, Salem, VA, USA. 12/20/13. First Printing.

SC ISBN: 978-1-4012-4293-0

Certified Chain of Custody
At Least 20% Certified Forest Content
www.sfiprogram.org
SFI-01042
APPLIES TO TEXT STOCK ONLY

SUSTAINABLE
FORESTRY
INITIATIVE

Library of Congress Cataloging-in-Publication Data

Bedard, Tony.
Green Lantern: New Guardians. Volume 2, Beyond hope / Tony Bedard, Tyler Kirkham, Batt.
pages cm. — (Green Lantern: New Guardians)
"Originally published in single magazine form in Green Lantern: The New Guardians 8-12, Blue Beetle 9."
ISBN 978-1-4012-4293-0
1. Graphic novels. I. Kirkham, Tyler, illustrator. II. Batt, illustrator. III. Title. IV. Title: New guardians. Volume 2. V. Title: Beyond hope.
PN6728.G74B34 2013
741.5'973—dc23
                                    2013010693

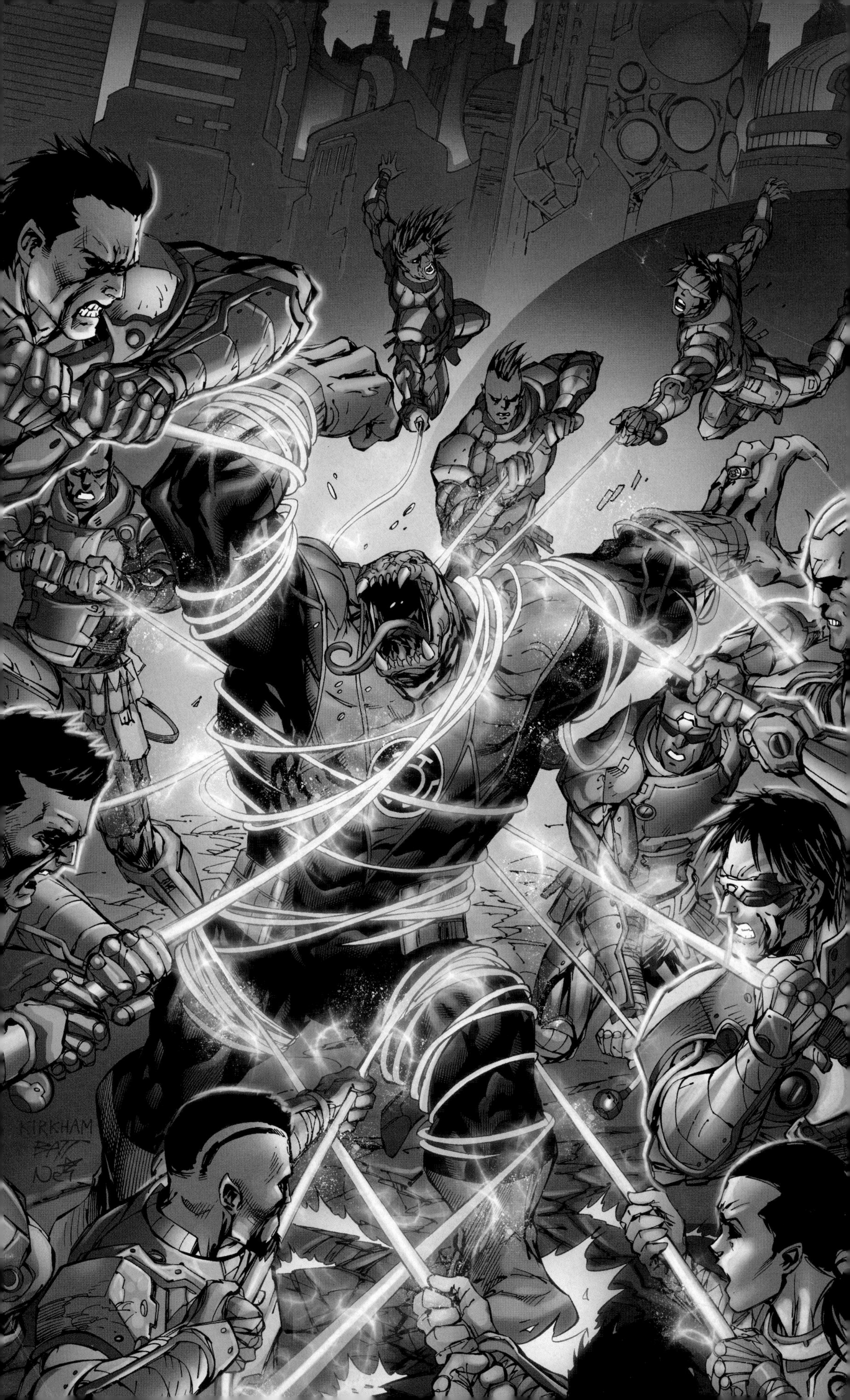
KIRKHAM

TONY BEDARD writer TYLER KIRKHAM penciller BATT inker cover by TYLER KIRKHAM, BATT & NEI RUFFINO

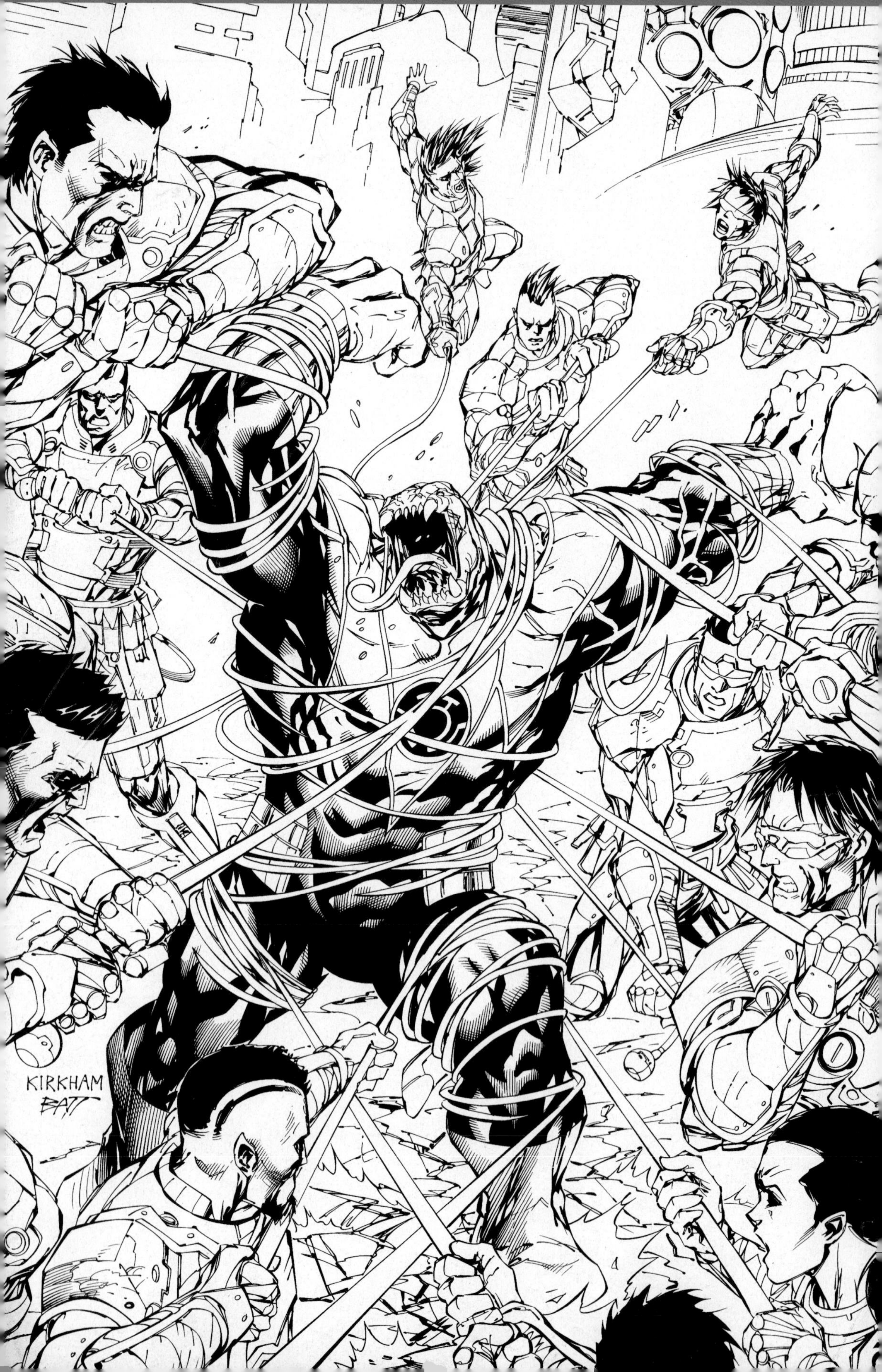
KIRKHAM
BATT

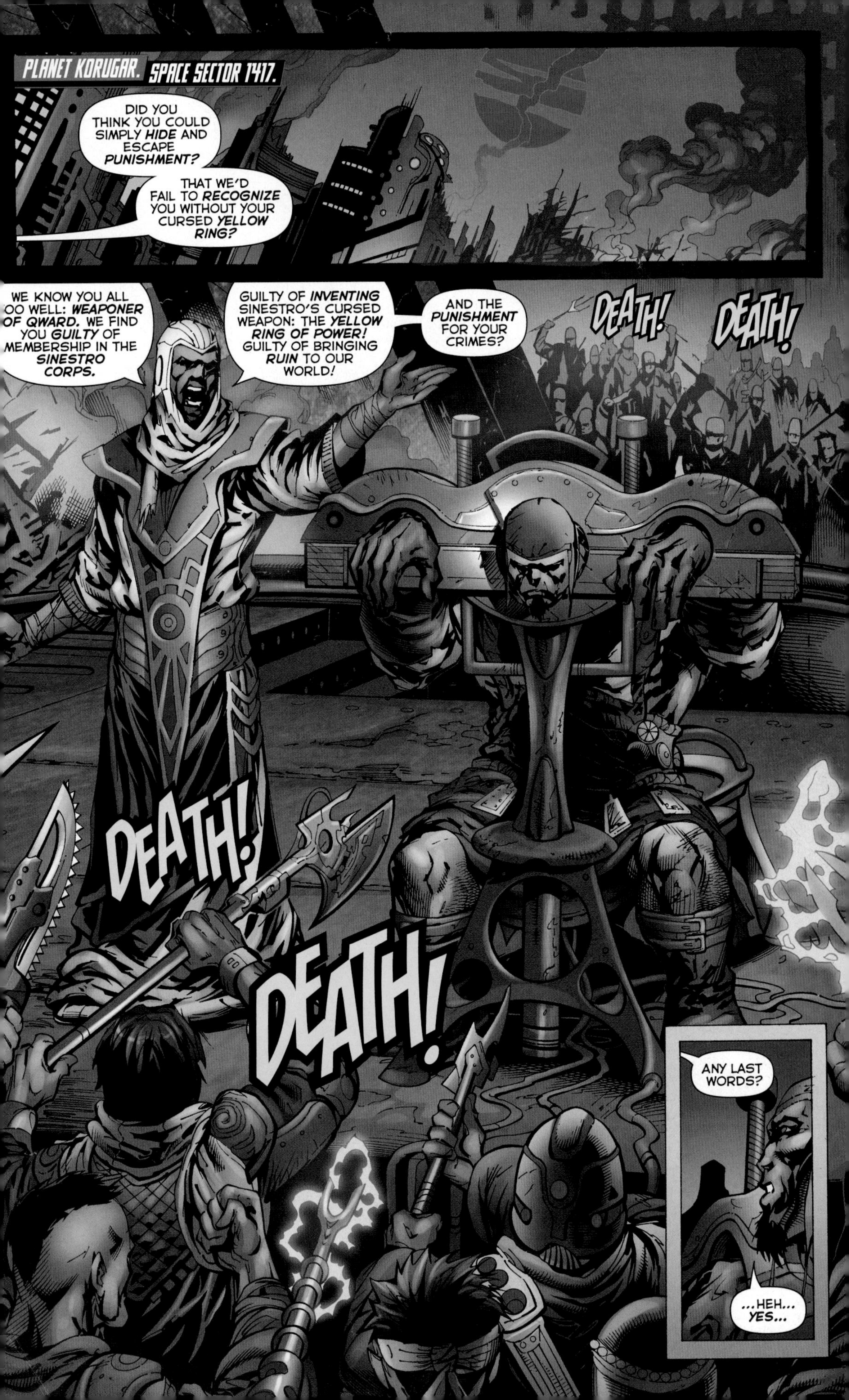

PLANET KORUGAR.
SPACE SECTOR 1417.
DID YOU THINK YOU COULD SIMPLY HIDE AND ESCAPE PUNISHMENT?
THAT WE'D FAIL TO RECOGNIZE YOU WITHOUT YOUR CURSED YELLOW RING?
WE KNOW YOU ALL OO WELL: WEAPONER OF QWARD. WE FIND YOU GUILTY OF MEMBERSHIP IN THE SINESTRO CORPS.
GUILTY OF INVENTING SINESTRO'S CURSED WEAPON: THE YELLOW RING OF POWER! GUILTY OF BRINGING RUIN TO OUR WORLD!
AND THE PUNISHMENT FOR YOUR CRIMES?
DEATH!
DEATH!
DEATH!
DEATH!
ANY LAST WORDS?
...HEH... YES...

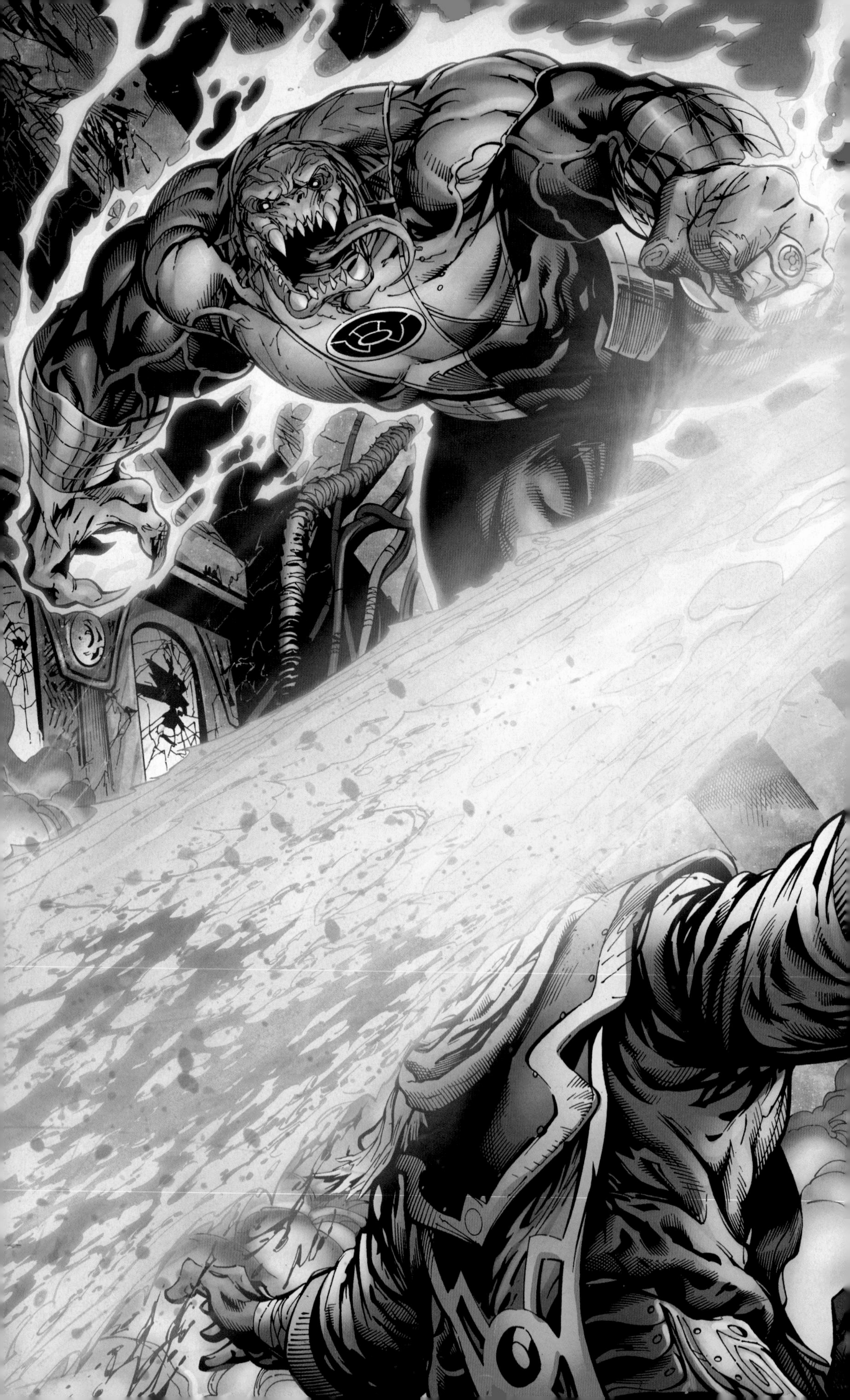

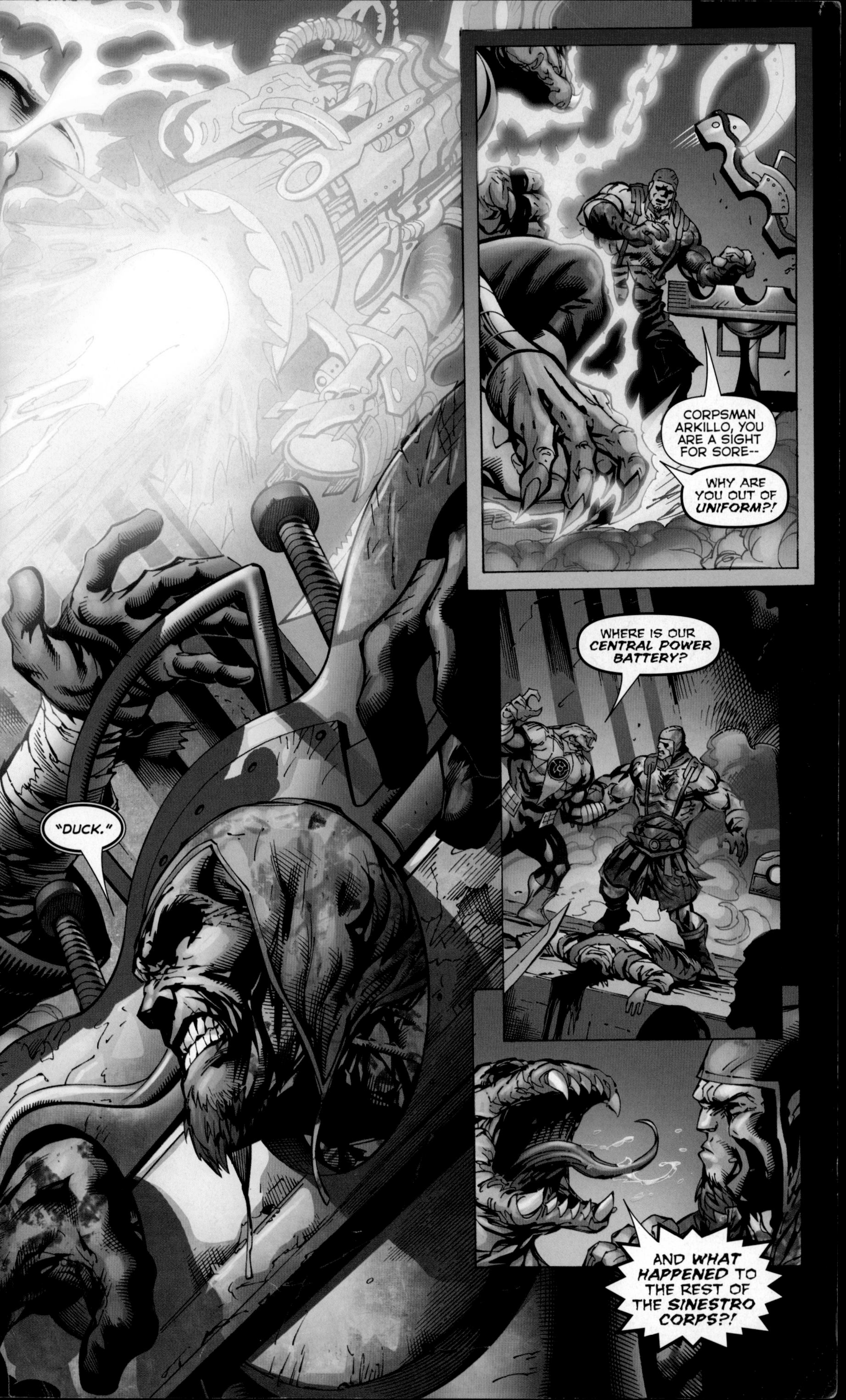
CORPSMAN ARKILLO, YOU ARE A SIGHT FOR SORE--
WHY ARE YOU OUT OF UNIFORM?!
WHERE IS OUR CENTRAL POWER BATTERY?
"DUCK."
AND WHAT HAPPENED TO THE REST OF THE SINESTRO CORPS?!

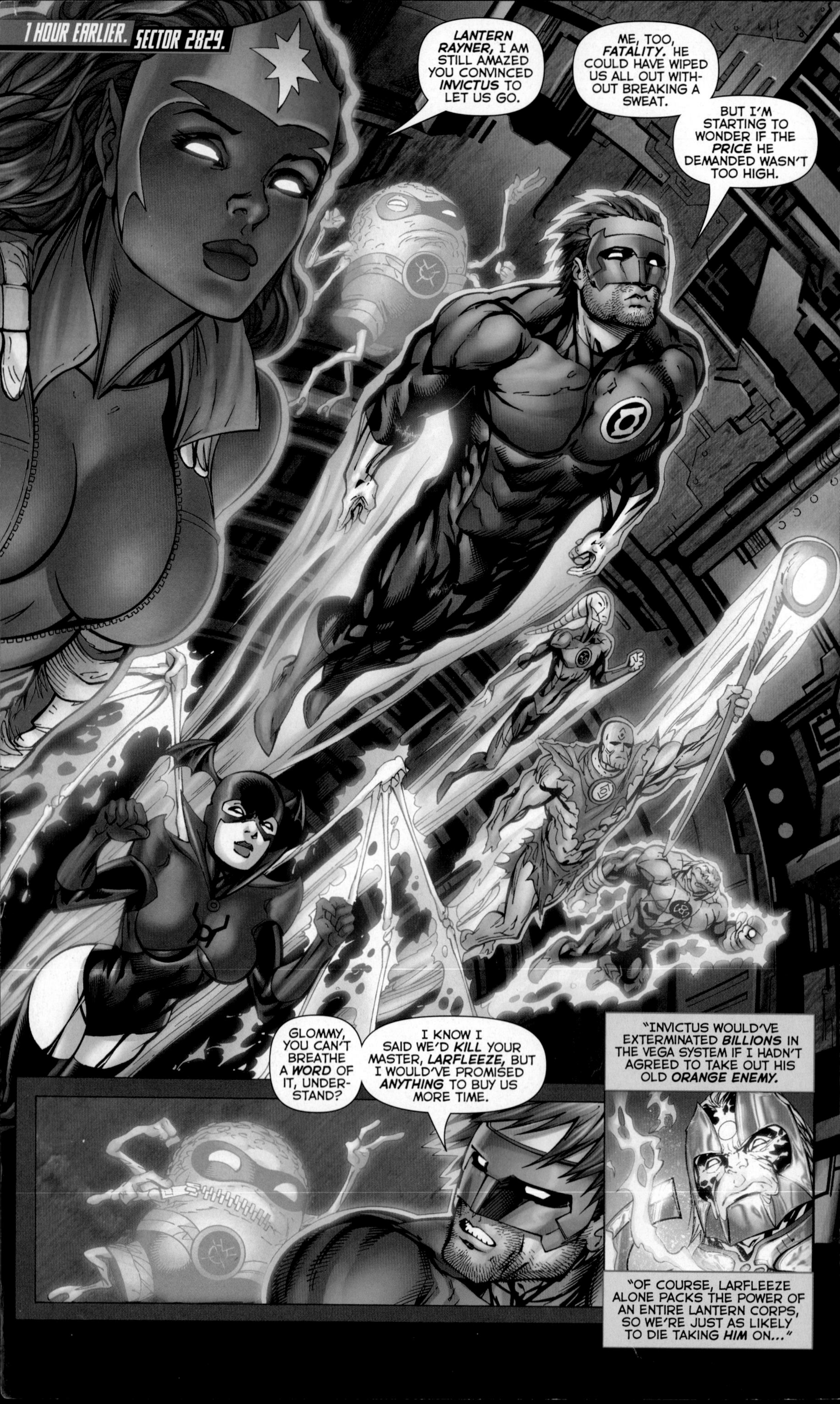
1 HOUR EARLIER.
SECTOR 2829.
LANTERN RAYNER, I AM STILL AMAZED YOU CONVINCED INVICTUS TO LET US GO.
ME, TOO, FATALITY. HE COULD HAVE WIPED US ALL OUT WITH-OUT BREAKING A SWEAT.
BUT I'M STARTING TO WONDER IF THE PRICE HE DEMANDED WASN'T TOO HIGH.
GLOMMY, YOU CAN'T BREATHE A WORD OF IT, UNDER-STAND?
I KNOW I SAID WE'D KILL YOUR MASTER, LARFLEEZE, BUT I WOULD'VE PROMISED ANYTHING TO BUY US MORE TIME.
"INVICTUS WOULD'VE EXTERMINATED BILLIONS IN THE VEGA SYSTEM IF I HADN'T AGREED TO TAKE OUT HIS OLD ORANGE ENEMY.
"OF COURSE, LARFLEEZE ALONE PACKS THE POWER OF AN ENTIRE LANTERN CORPS, SO WE'RE JUST AS LIKELY TO DIE TAKING HIM ON..."

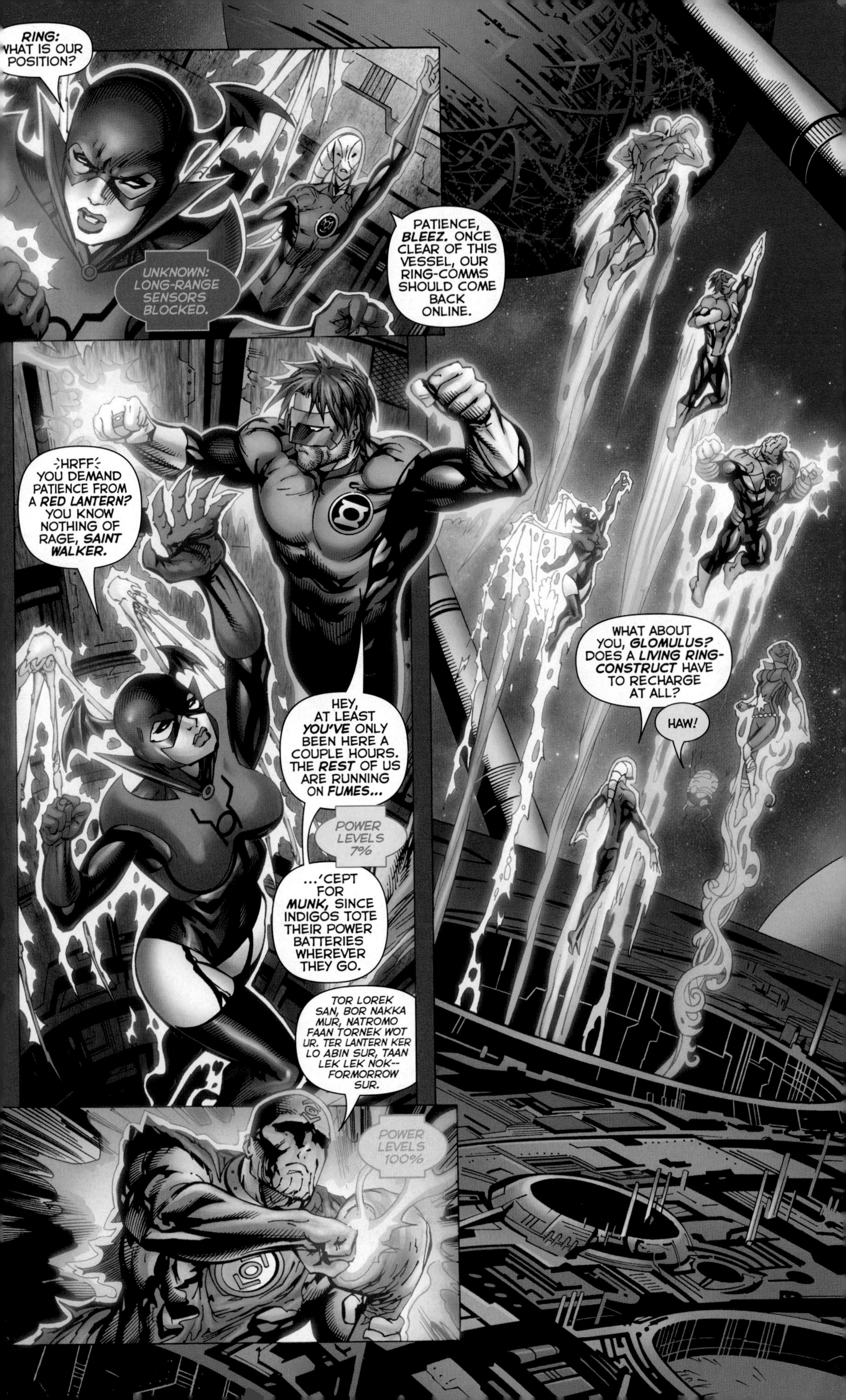

RING: WHAT IS OUR POSITION?
UNKNOWN: LONG-RANGE SENSORS BLOCKED.
PATIENCE, BLEEZ. ONCE CLEAR OF THIS VESSEL, OUR RING-COMMS SHOULD COME BACK ONLINE.
-HRFF- YOU DEMAND PATIENCE FROM A RED LANTERN? YOU KNOW NOTHING OF RAGE, SAINT WALKER.
HEY, AT LEAST YOU'VE ONLY BEEN HERE A COUPLE HOURS. THE REST OF US ARE RUNNING ON FUMES...
POWER LEVELS 7%
...'CEPT FOR MUNK, SINCE INDIGOS TOTE THEIR POWER BATTERIES WHEREVER THEY GO.
WHAT ABOUT YOU, GLOMULUS? DOES A LIVING RING-CONSTRUCT HAVE TO RECHARGE AT ALL?
HAW!
TOR LOREK SAN, BOR NAKKA MUR, NATROMO FAAN TORNEK WOT UR. TER LANTERN KER LO ABIN SUR, TAAN LEK LEK NOK-- FORMORROW SUR.
POWER LEVELS 100%

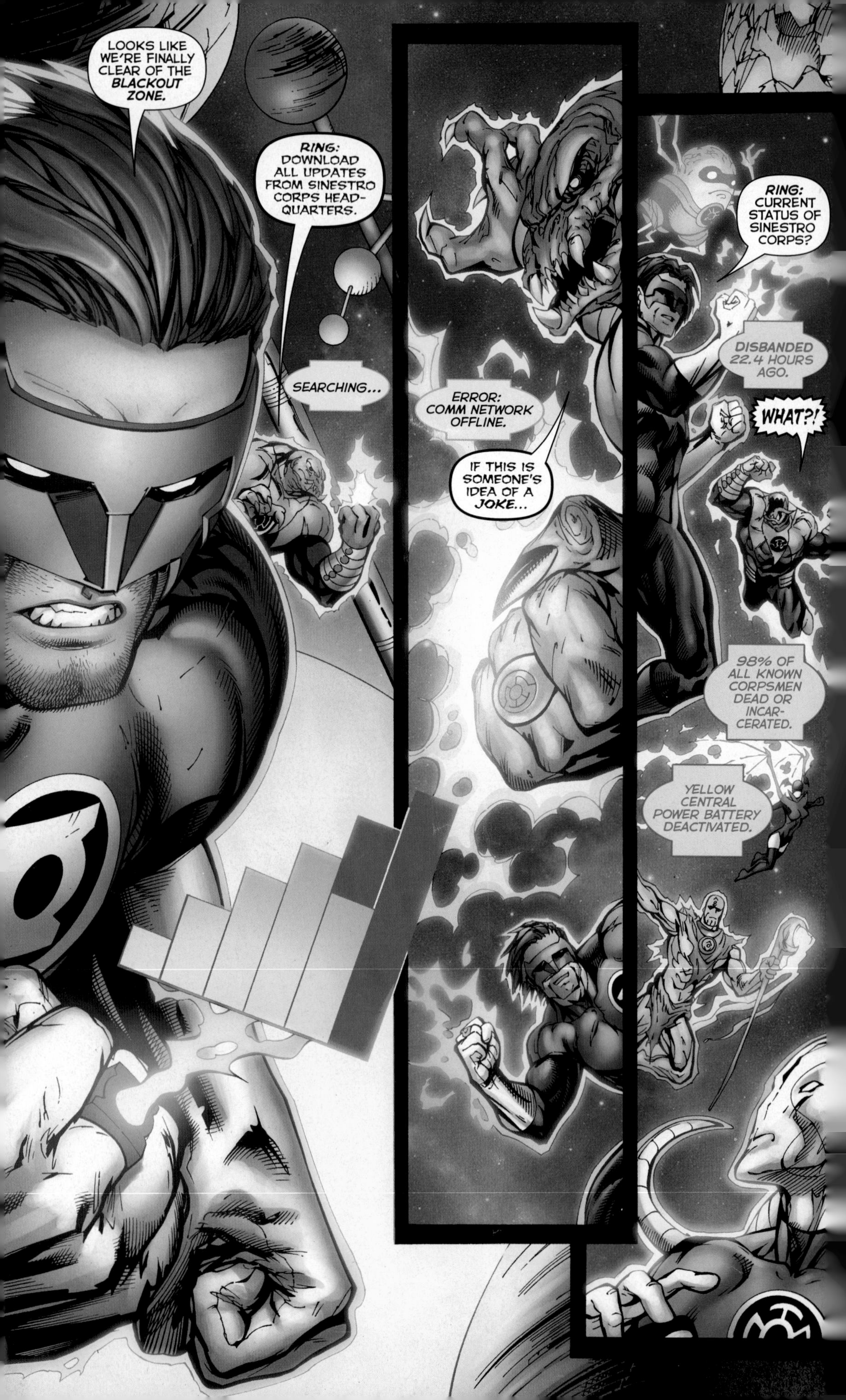

LOOKS LIKE WE'RE FINALLY CLEAR OF THE BLACKOUT ZONE.
RING: DOWNLOAD ALL UPDATES FROM SINESTRO CORPS HEAD-QUARTERS.
SEARCHING...
ERROR: COMM NETWORK OFFLINE.
IF THIS IS SOMEONE'S IDEA OF A JOKE...
RING: CURRENT STATUS OF SINESTRO CORPS?
DISBANDED 22.4 HOURS AGO.
WHAT?!
98% OF ALL KNOWN CORPSMEN DEAD OR INCAR-CERATED.
YELLOW CENTRAL POWER BATTERY DEACTIVATED.

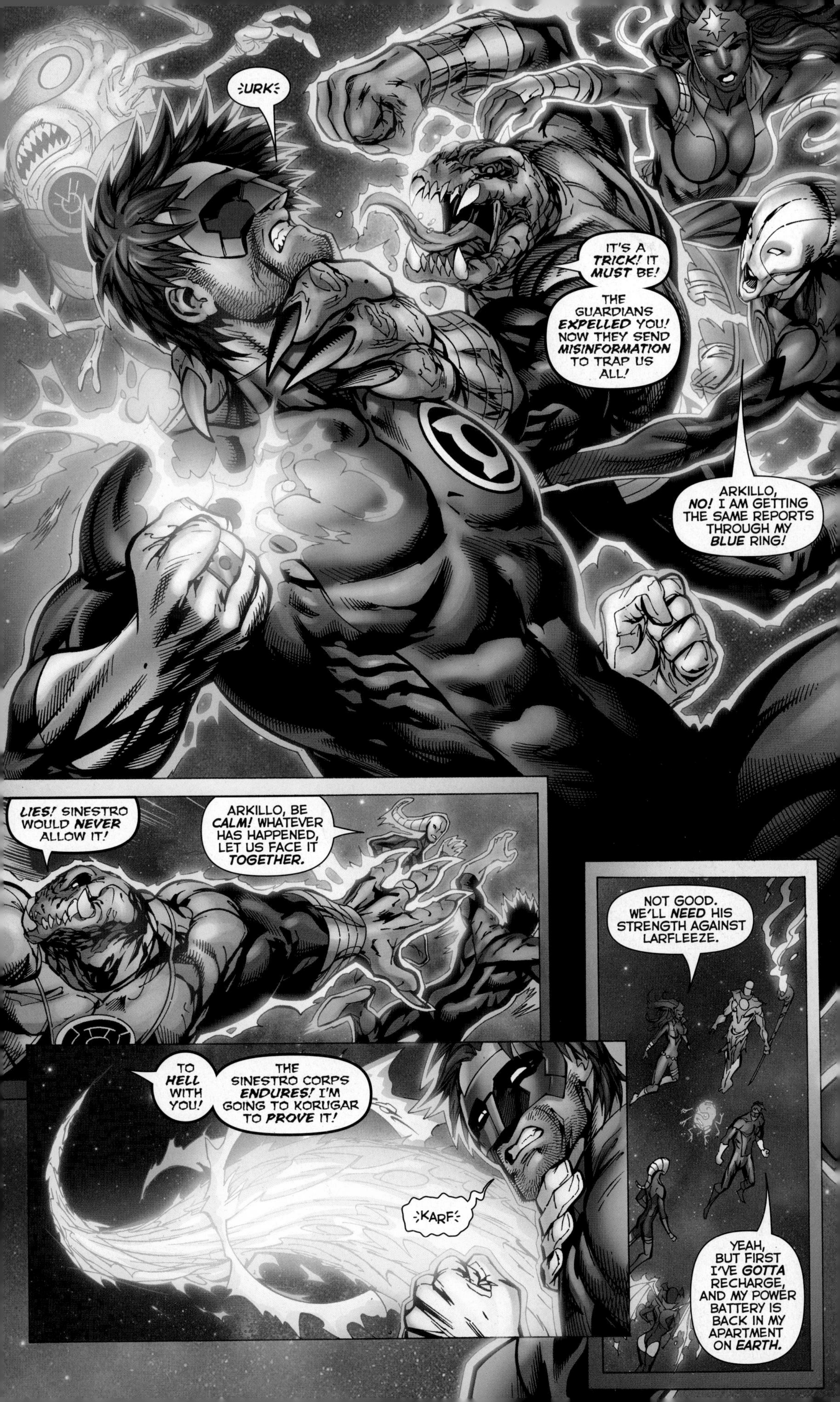
URK
IT'S A TRICK! IT MUST BE!
THE GUARDIANS EXPELLED YOU! NOW THEY SEND MISINFORMATION TO TRAP US ALL!
ARKILLO, NO! I AM GETTING THE SAME REPORTS THROUGH MY BLUE RING!
LIES! SINESTRO WOULD NEVER ALLOW IT!
ARKILLO, BE CALM! WHATEVER HAS HAPPENED, LET US FACE IT TOGETHER.
TO HELL WITH YOU!
THE SINESTRO CORPS ENDURES! I'M GOING TO KORUGAR TO PROVE IT!
KARF
NOT GOOD. WE'LL NEED HIS STRENGTH AGAINST LARFLEEZE.
YEAH, BUT FIRST I'VE GOTTA RECHARGE, AND MY POWER BATTERY IS BACK IN MY APARTMENT ON EARTH.

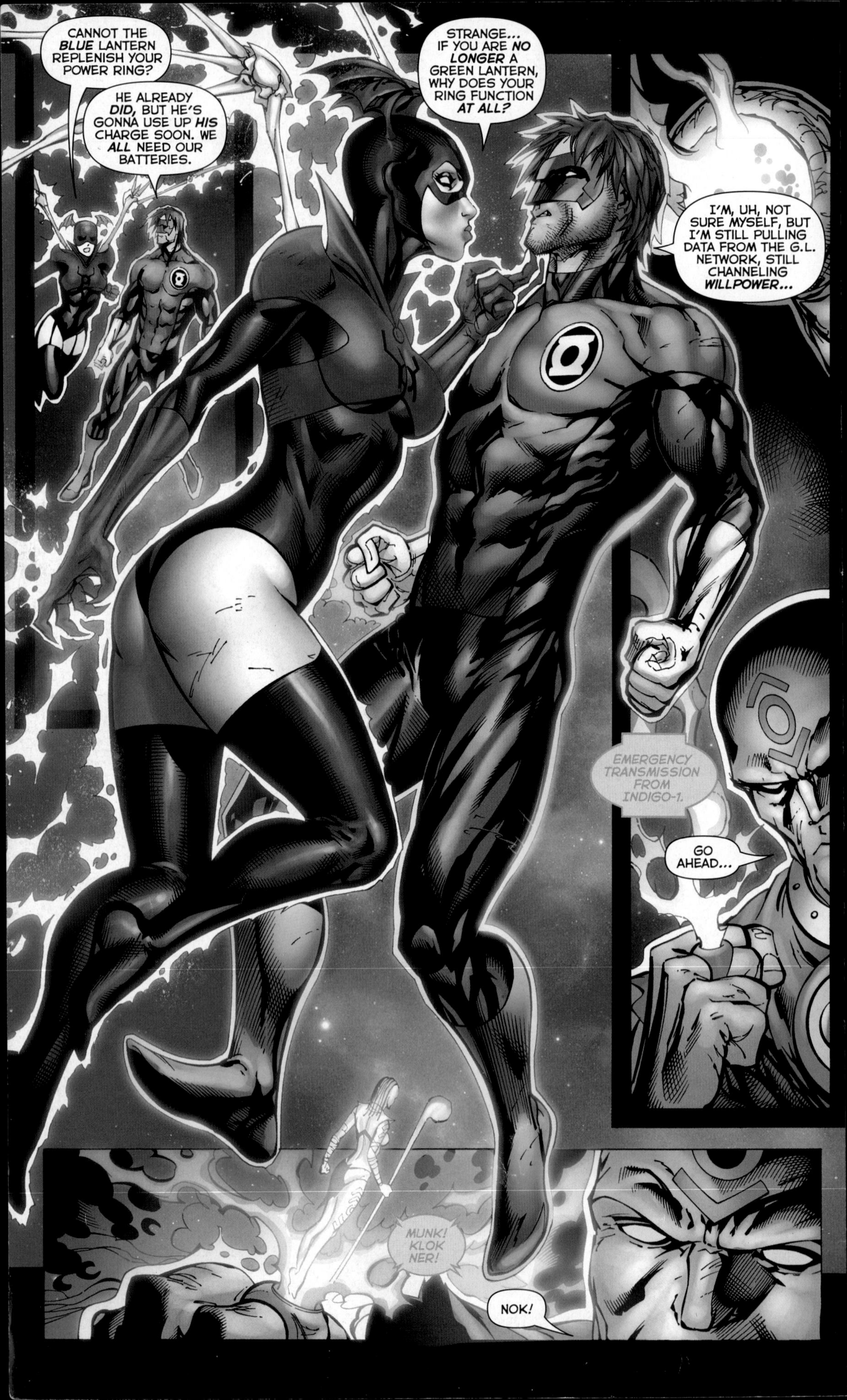
CANNOT THE BLUE LANTERN REPLENISH YOUR POWER RING?
HE ALREADY DID, BUT HE'S GONNA USE UP HIS CHARGE SOON. WE ALL NEED OUR BATTERIES.
STRANGE... IF YOU ARE NO LONGER A GREEN LANTERN, WHY DOES YOUR RING FUNCTION AT ALL?
I'M, UH, NOT SURE MYSELF, BUT I'M STILL PULLING DATA FROM THE G.L. NETWORK, STILL CHANNELING WILLPOWER...
EMERGENCY TRANSMISSION FROM INDIGO-1.
GO AHEAD...
MUNK! KLOK NER!
NOK!

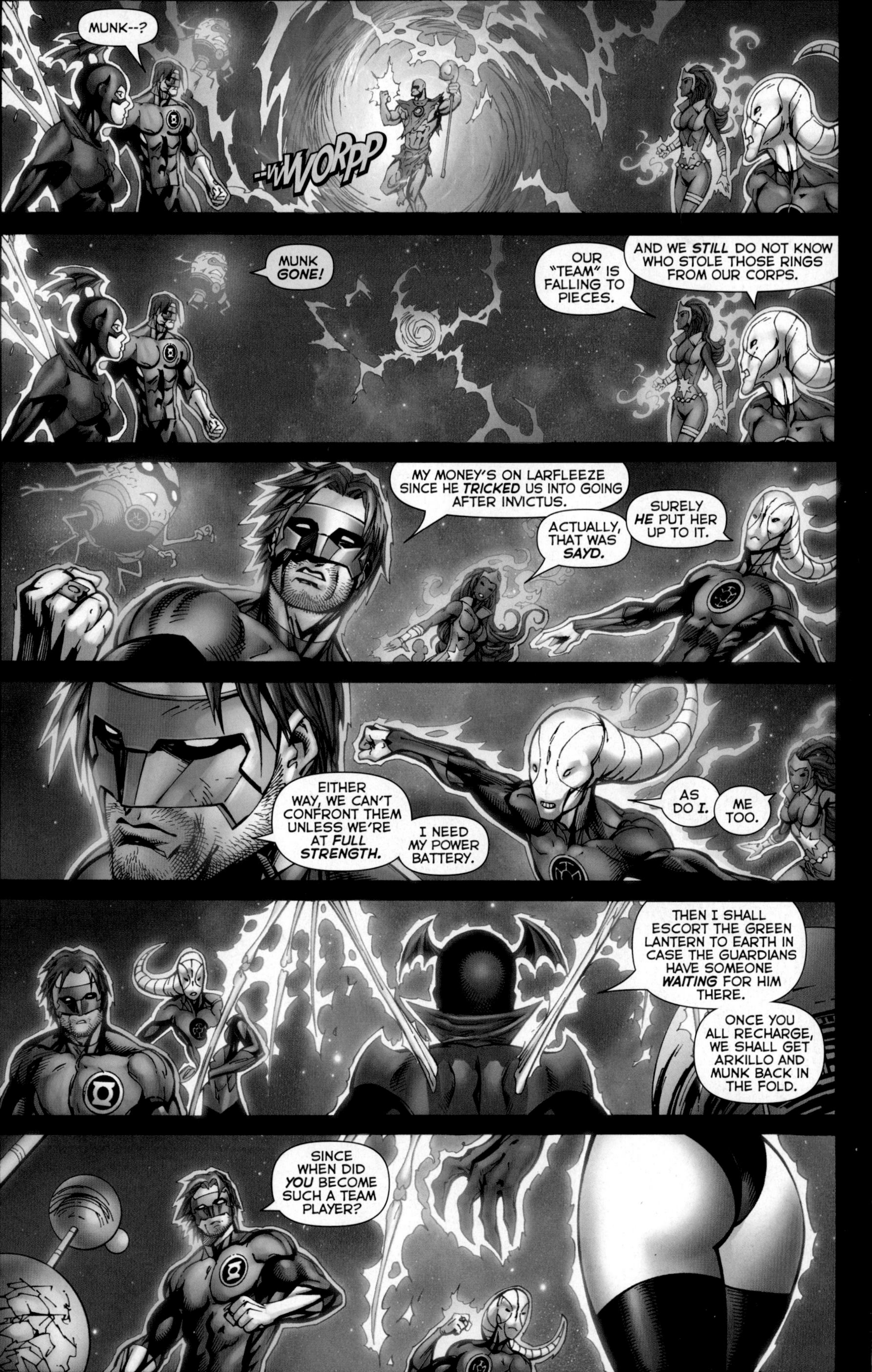

MUNK--?
-VVVWORPP
MUNK GONE!
OUR "TEAM" IS FALLING TO PIECES.
AND WE STILL DO NOT KNOW WHO STOLE THOSE RINGS FROM OUR CORPS.
MY MONEY'S ON LARFLEEZE SINCE HE TRICKED US INTO GOING AFTER INVICTUS.
ACTUALLY, THAT WAS SAYD.
SURELY HE PUT HER UP TO IT.
EITHER WAY, WE CAN'T CONFRONT THEM UNLESS WE'RE AT FULL STRENGTH.
I NEED MY POWER BATTERY.
AS DO I.
ME TOO.
THEN I SHALL ESCORT THE GREEN LANTERN TO EARTH IN CASE THE GUARDIANS HAVE SOMEONE WAITING FOR HIM THERE.
ONCE YOU ALL RECHARGE, WE SHALL GET ARKILLO AND MUNK BACK IN THE FOLD.
SINCE WHEN DID YOU BECOME SUCH A TEAM PLAYER?

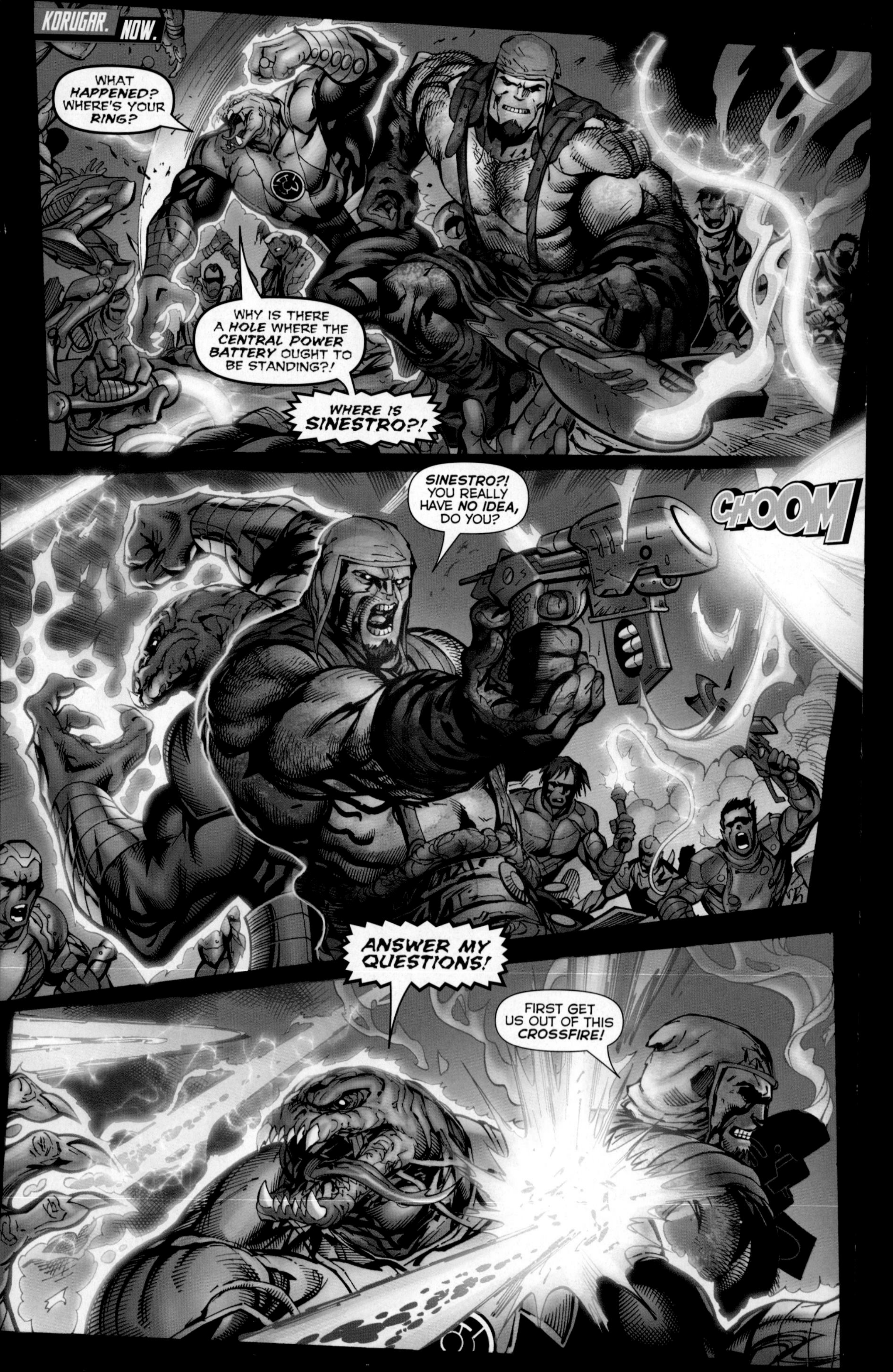
KORUGAR. NOW.
WHAT HAPPENED? WHERE'S YOUR RING?
WHY IS THERE A HOLE WHERE THE CENTRAL POWER BATTERY OUGHT TO BE STANDING?!
WHERE IS SINESTRO?!
SINESTRO?! YOU REALLY HAVE NO IDEA, DO YOU?
CHOOM
ANSWER MY QUESTIONS!
FIRST GET US OUT OF THIS CROSSFIRE!

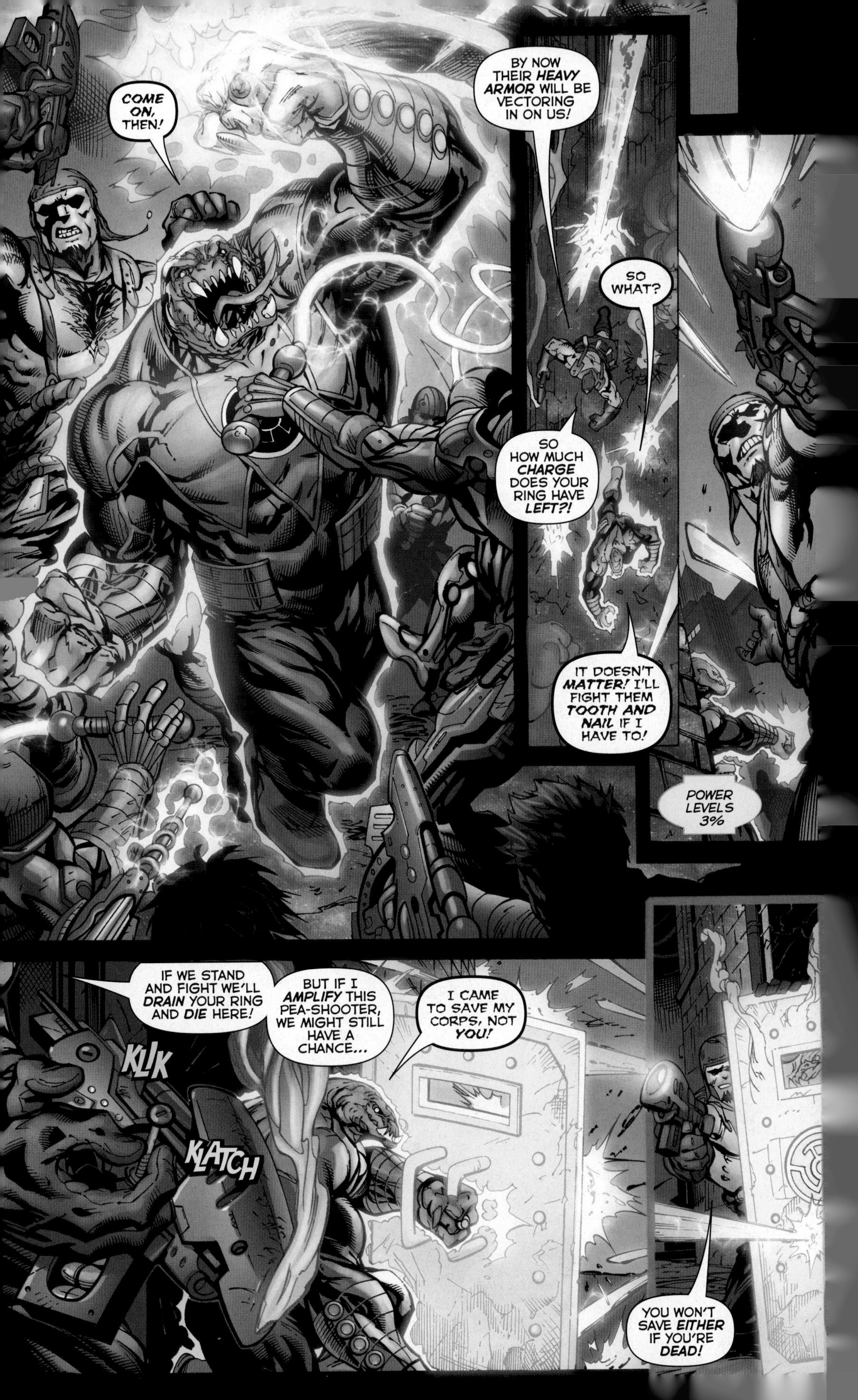
COME ON, THEN!
BY NOW THEIR HEAVY ARMOR WILL BE VECTORING IN ON US!
SO WHAT?
SO HOW MUCH CHARGE DOES YOUR RING HAVE LEFT?!
IT DOESN'T MATTER! I'LL FIGHT THEM TOOTH AND NAIL IF I HAVE TO!
POWER LEVELS 3%
IF WE STAND AND FIGHT WE'LL DRAIN YOUR RING AND DIE HERE!
BUT IF I AMPLIFY THIS PEA-SHOOTER, WE MIGHT STILL HAVE A CHANCE...
I CAME TO SAVE MY CORPS, NOT YOU!
KLIK
KLATCH
YOU WON'T SAVE EITHER IF YOU'RE DEAD!

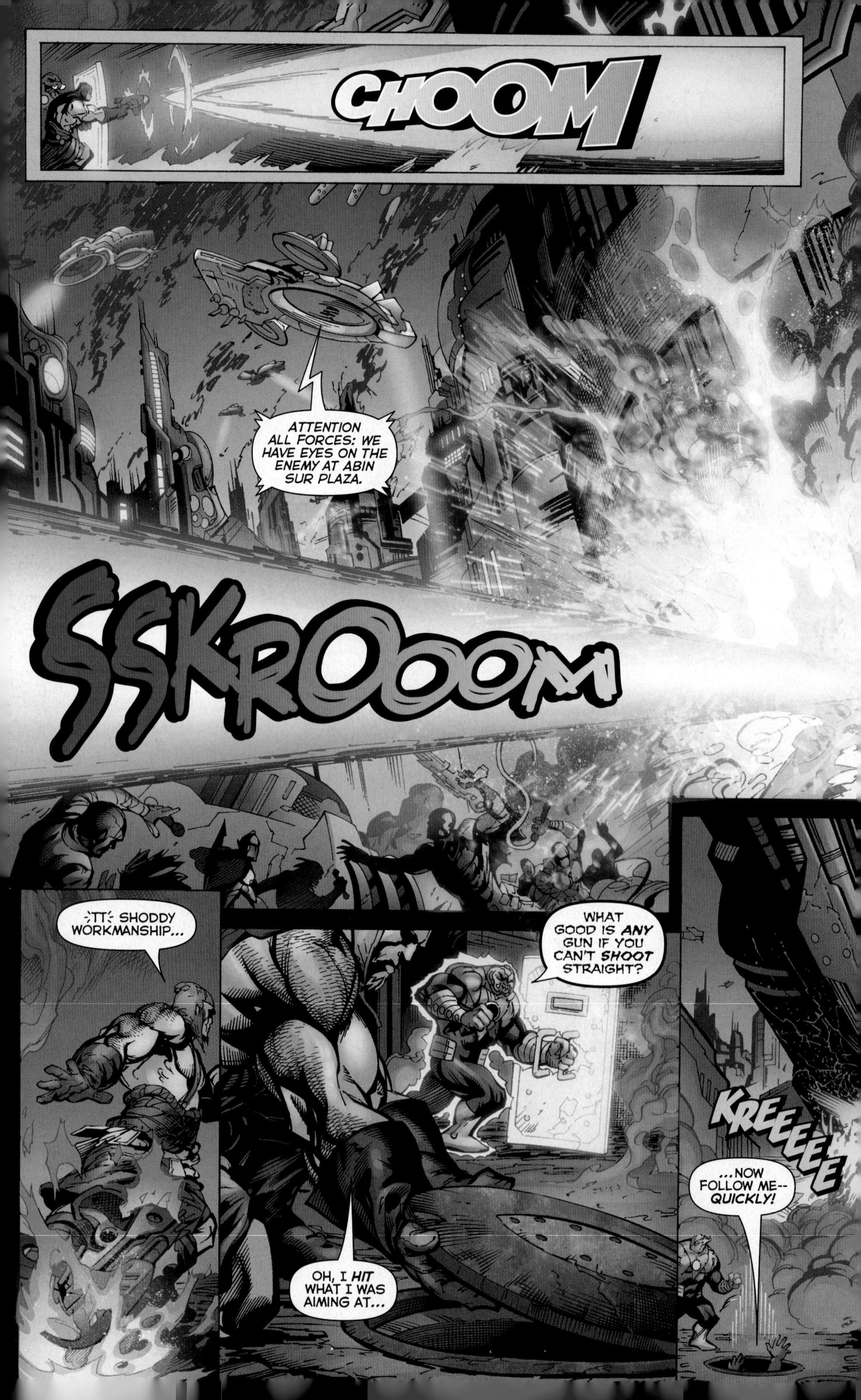
CHOOM
ATTENTION ALL FORCES: WE HAVE EYES ON THE ENEMY AT ABIN SUR PLAZA.
SSKROOOOM
TT SHODDY WORKMANSHIP...
WHAT GOOD IS ANY GUN IF YOU CAN'T SHOOT STRAIGHT?
OH, I HIT WHAT I WAS AIMING AT...
KREEEEEE
...NOW FOLLOW ME-- QUICKLY!

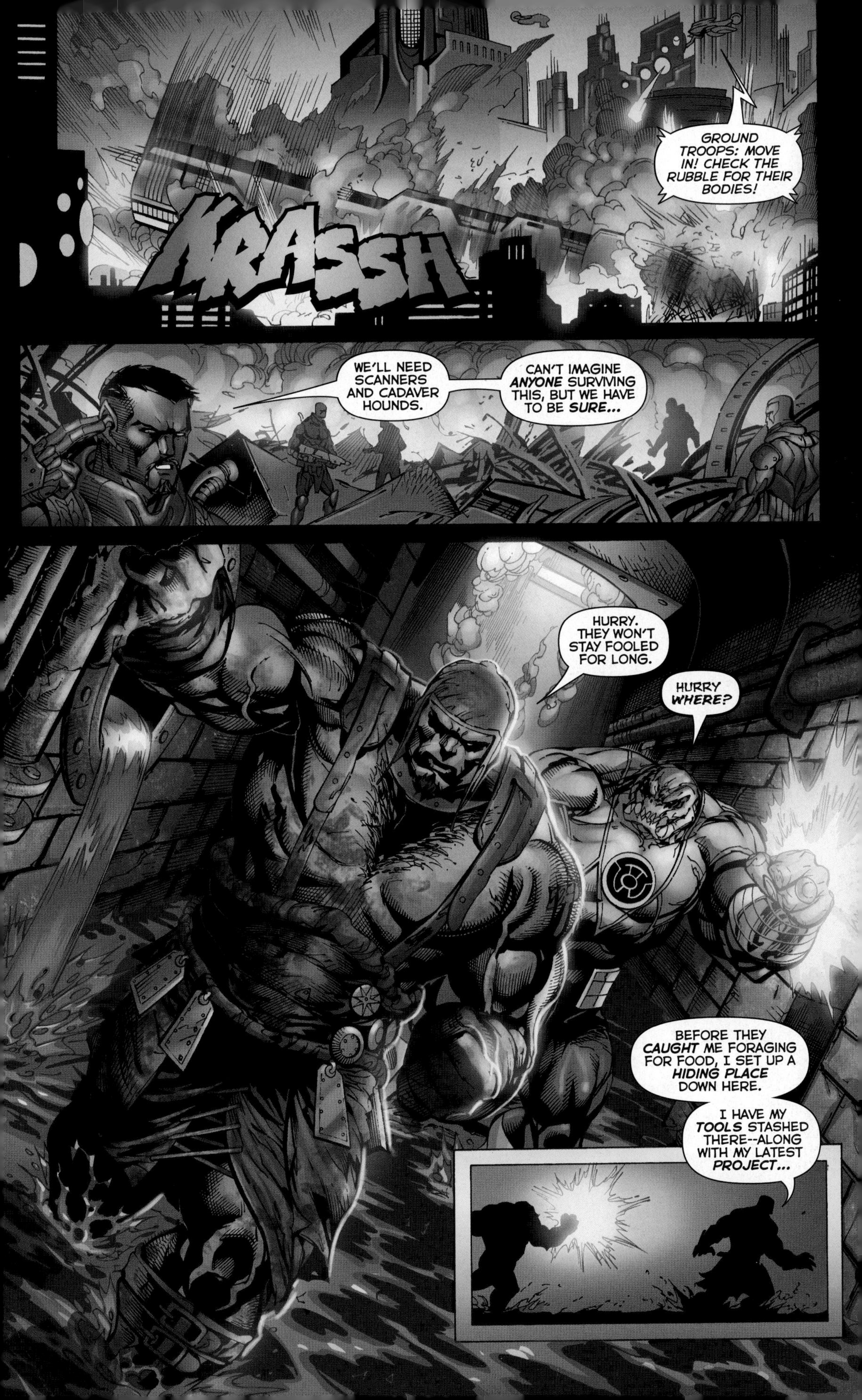
GROUND TROOPS: MOVE IN! CHECK THE RUBBLE FOR THEIR BODIES!
KRASSH
WE'LL NEED SCANNERS AND CADAVER HOUNDS.
CAN'T IMAGINE ANYONE SURVIVING THIS, BUT WE HAVE TO BE SURE...
HURRY. THEY WON'T STAY FOOLED FOR LONG.
HURRY WHERE?
BEFORE THEY CAUGHT ME FORAGING FOR FOOD, I SET UP A HIDING PLACE DOWN HERE.
I HAVE MY TOOLS STASHED THERE--ALONG WITH MY LATEST PROJECT...

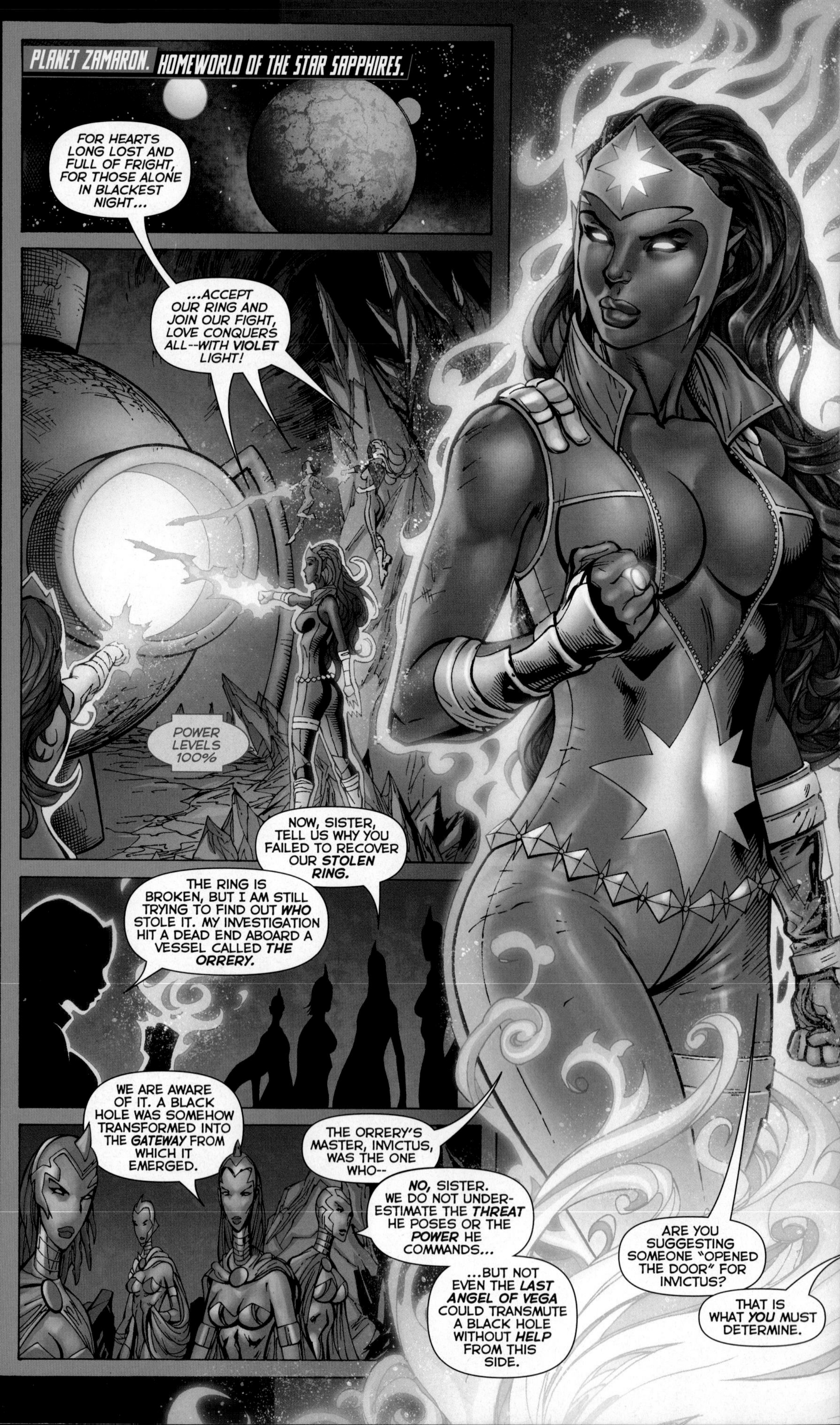
PLANET ZAMARON. HOMEWORLD OF THE STAR SAPPHIRES.
FOR HEARTS LONG LOST AND FULL OF FRIGHT, FOR THOSE ALONE IN BLACKEST NIGHT...
...ACCEPT OUR RING AND JOIN OUR FIGHT, LOVE CONQUERS ALL--WITH VIOLET LIGHT!
POWER LEVELS 100%
NOW, SISTER, TELL US WHY YOU FAILED TO RECOVER OUR STOLEN RING.
THE RING IS BROKEN, BUT I AM STILL TRYING TO FIND OUT WHO STOLE IT. MY INVESTIGATION HIT A DEAD END ABOARD A VESSEL CALLED THE ORRERY.
WE ARE AWARE OF IT. A BLACK HOLE WAS SOMEHOW TRANSFORMED INTO THE GATEWAY FROM WHICH IT EMERGED.
THE ORRERY'S MASTER, INVICTUS, WAS THE ONE WHO--
NO, SISTER. WE DO NOT UNDER-ESTIMATE THE THREAT HE POSES OR THE POWER HE COMMANDS...
...BUT NOT EVEN THE LAST ANGEL OF VEGA COULD TRANSMUTE A BLACK HOLE WITHOUT HELP FROM THIS SIDE.
ARE YOU SUGGESTING SOMEONE "OPENED THE DOOR" FOR INVICTUS?
THAT IS WHAT YOU MUST DETERMINE.

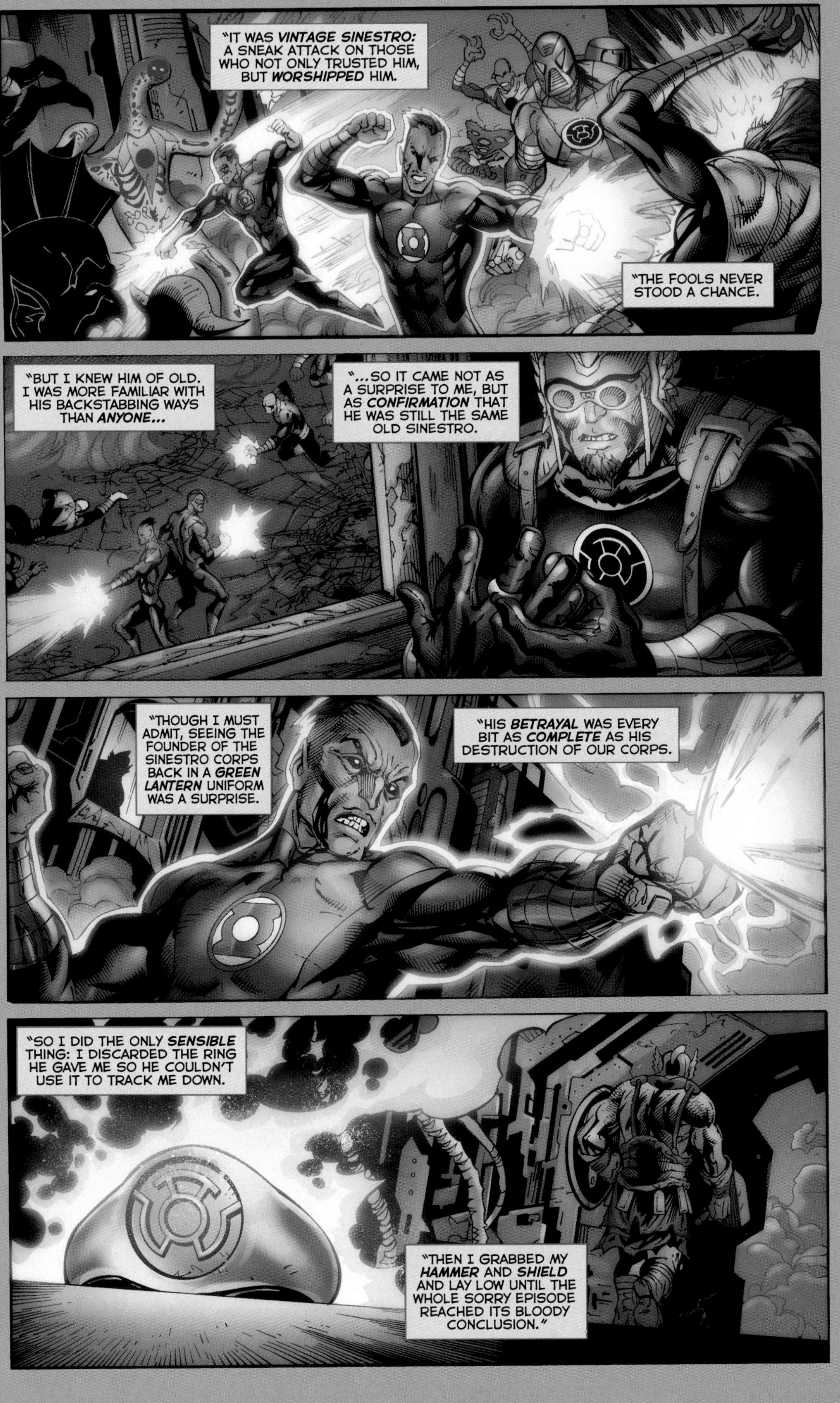
"IT WAS VINTAGE SINESTRO: A SNEAK ATTACK ON THOSE WHO NOT ONLY TRUSTED HIM, BUT WORSHIPPED HIM.
"THE FOOLS NEVER STOOD A CHANCE.
"BUT I KNEW HIM OF OLD. I WAS MORE FAMILIAR WITH HIS BACKSTABBING WAYS THAN ANYONE...
"...SO IT CAME NOT AS A SURPRISE TO ME, BUT AS CONFIRMATION THAT HE WAS STILL THE SAME OLD SINESTRO.
"THOUGH I MUST ADMIT, SEEING THE FOUNDER OF THE SINESTRO CORPS BACK IN A GREEN LANTERN UNIFORM WAS A SURPRISE.
"HIS BETRAYAL WAS EVERY BIT AS COMPLETE AS HIS DESTRUCTION OF OUR CORPS.
"SO I DID THE ONLY SENSIBLE THING: I DISCARDED THE RING HE GAVE ME SO HE COULDN'T USE IT TO TRACK ME DOWN.
"THEN I GRABBED MY HAMMER AND SHIELD AND LAY LOW UNTIL THE WHOLE SORRY EPISODE REACHED ITS BLOODY CONCLUSION."

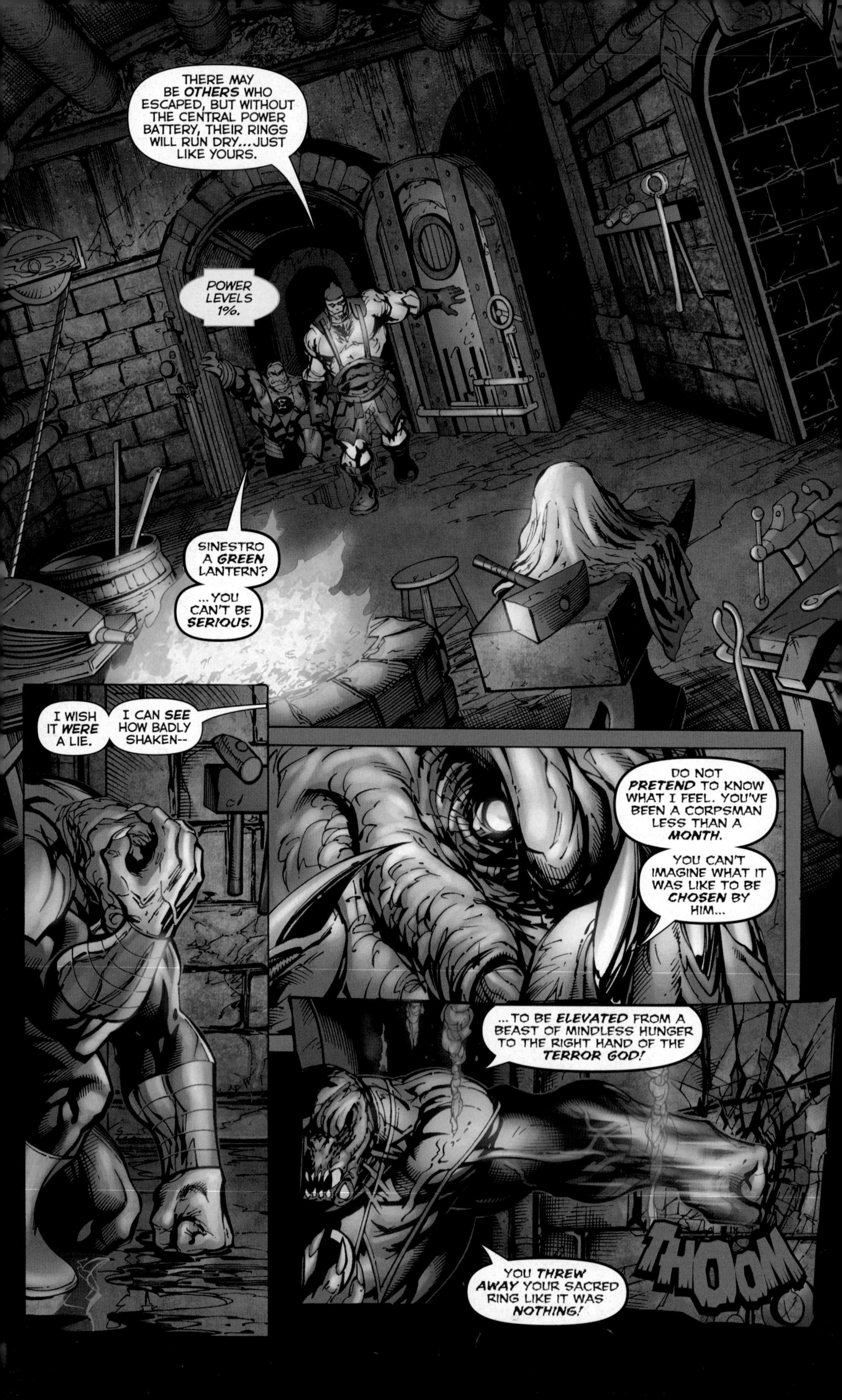
THERE MAY BE OTHERS WHO ESCAPED, BUT WITHOUT THE CENTRAL POWER BATTERY, THEIR RINGS WILL RUN DRY...JUST LIKE YOURS.
POWER LEVELS 1%.
SINESTRO A GREEN LANTERN?
...YOU CAN'T BE SERIOUS.
I WISH IT WERE A LIE.
I CAN SEE HOW BADLY SHAKEN--
DO NOT PRETEND TO KNOW WHAT I FEEL. YOU'VE BEEN A CORPSMAN LESS THAN A MONTH.
YOU CAN'T IMAGINE WHAT IT WAS LIKE TO BE CHOSEN BY HIM...
...TO BE ELEVATED FROM A BEAST OF MINDLESS HUNGER TO THE RIGHT HAND OF THE TERROR GOD!
THOOM
YOU THREW AWAY YOUR SACRED RING LIKE IT WAS NOTHING!

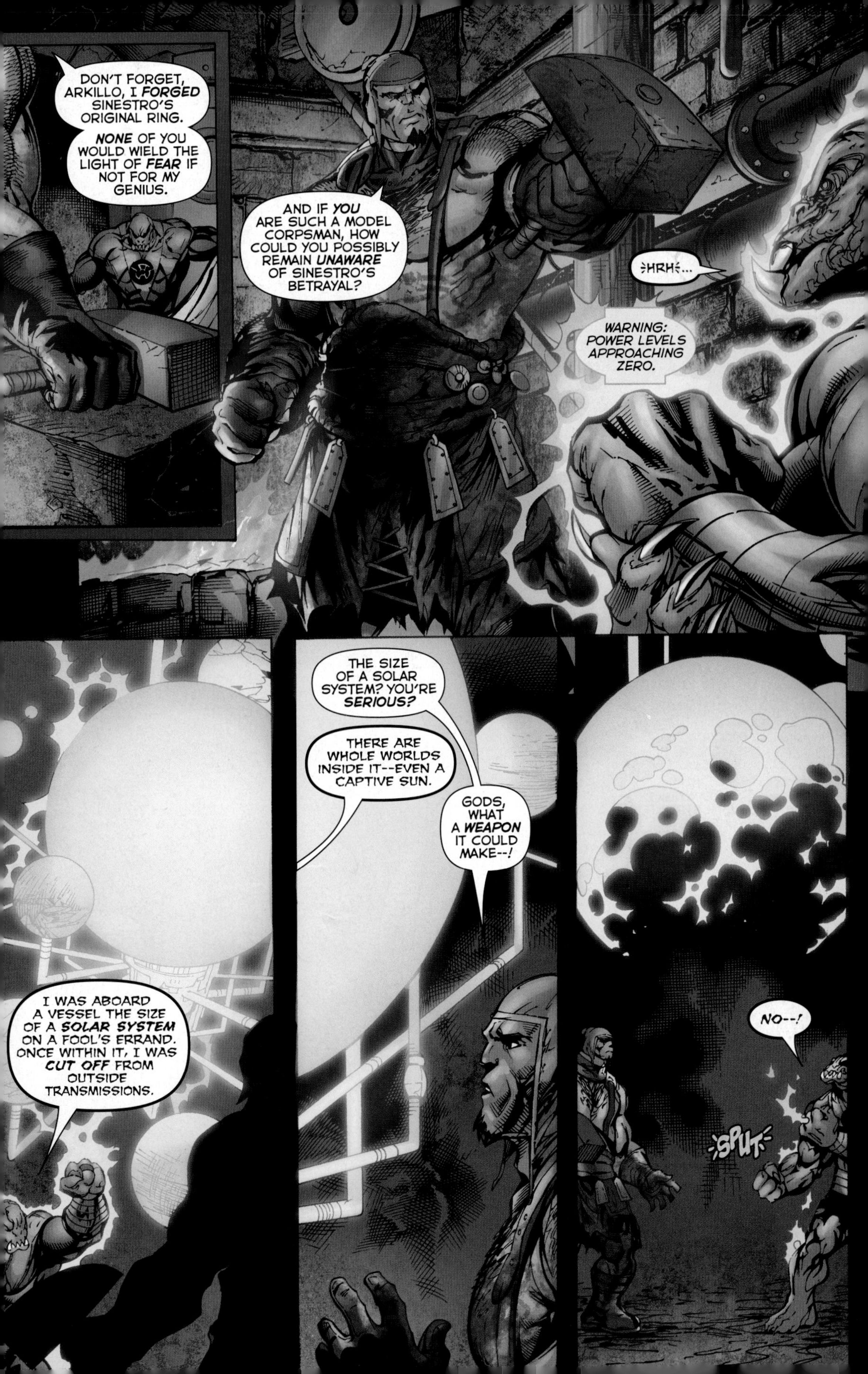
DON'T FORGET, ARKILLO, I FORGED SINESTRO'S ORIGINAL RING.
NONE OF YOU WOULD WIELD THE LIGHT OF FEAR IF NOT FOR MY GENIUS.
AND IF YOU ARE SUCH A MODEL CORPSMAN, HOW COULD YOU POSSIBLY REMAIN UNAWARE OF SINESTRO'S BETRAYAL?
HRH...
WARNING: POWER LEVELS APPROACHING ZERO.
I WAS ABOARD A VESSEL THE SIZE OF A SOLAR SYSTEM ON A FOOL'S ERRAND. ONCE WITHIN IT, I WAS CUT OFF FROM OUTSIDE TRANSMISSIONS.
THE SIZE OF A SOLAR SYSTEM? YOU'RE SERIOUS?
THERE ARE WHOLE WORLDS INSIDE IT--EVEN A CAPTIVE SUN.
GODS, WHAT A WEAPON IT COULD MAKE--!
NO--!
SPUT

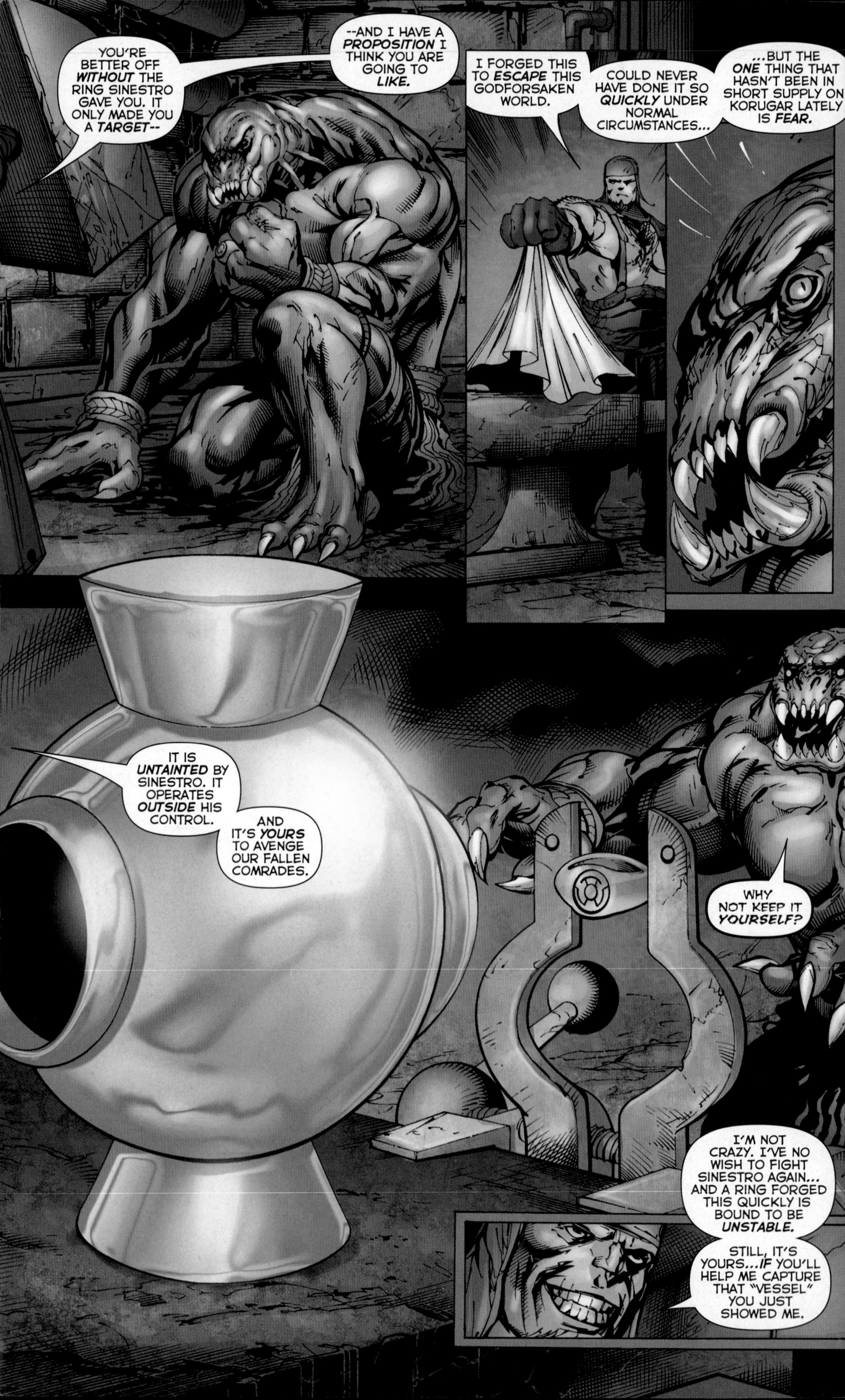
YOU'RE BETTER OFF WITHOUT THE RING SINESTRO GAVE YOU. IT ONLY MADE YOU A TARGET--
--AND I HAVE A PROPOSITION I THINK YOU ARE GOING TO LIKE.
I FORGED THIS TO ESCAPE THIS GODFORSAKEN WORLD.
COULD NEVER HAVE DONE IT SO QUICKLY UNDER NORMAL CIRCUMSTANCES...
...BUT THE ONE THING THAT HASN'T BEEN IN SHORT SUPPLY ON KORUGAR LATELY IS FEAR.
IT IS UNTAINTED BY SINESTRO. IT OPERATES OUTSIDE HIS CONTROL.
AND IT'S YOURS TO AVENGE OUR FALLEN COMRADES.
WHY NOT KEEP IT YOURSELF?
I'M NOT CRAZY. I'VE NO WISH TO FIGHT SINESTRO AGAIN... AND A RING FORGED THIS QUICKLY IS BOUND TO BE UNSTABLE.
STILL, IT'S YOURS...IF YOU'LL HELP ME CAPTURE THAT "VESSEL" YOU JUST SHOWED ME.

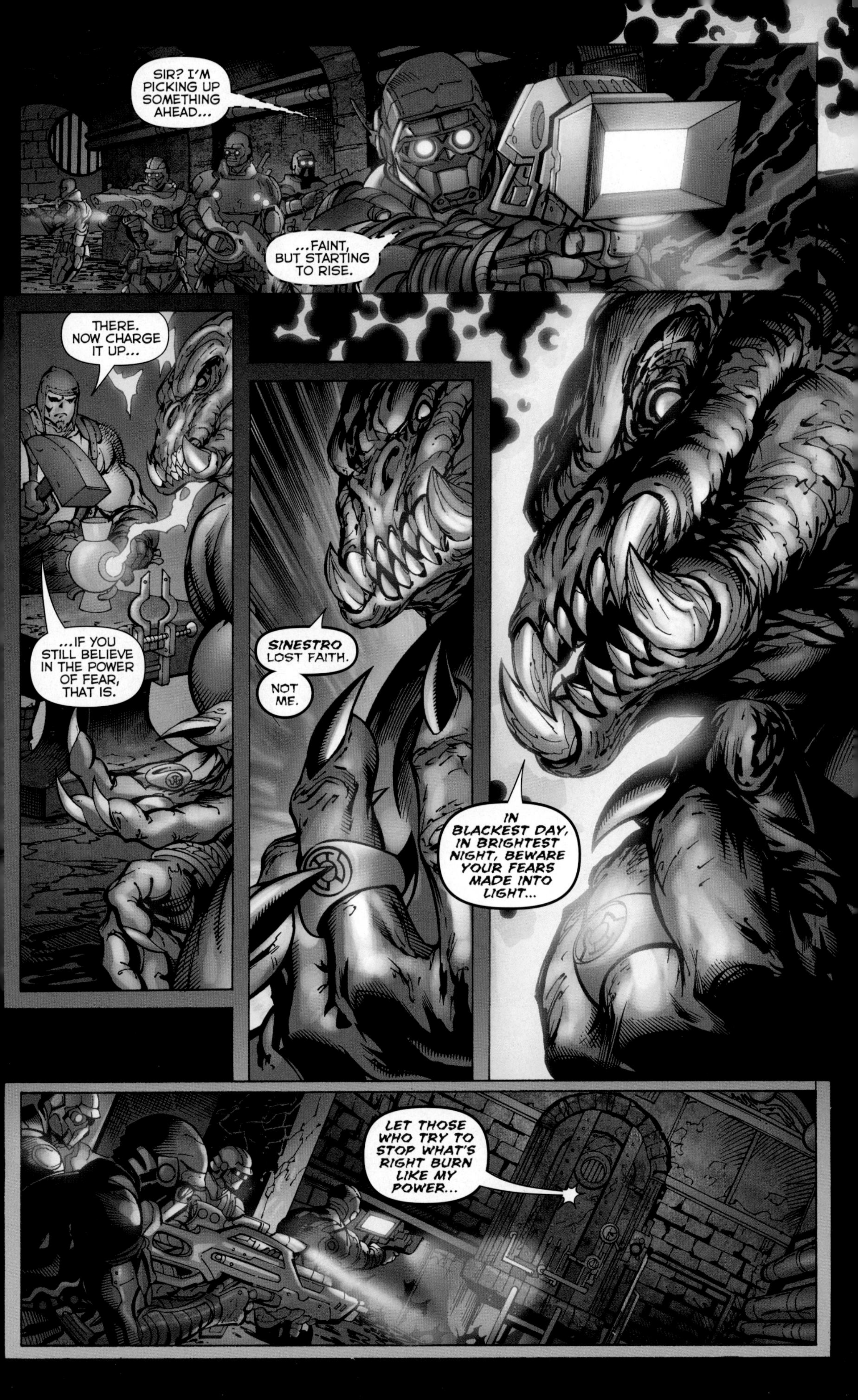
SIR? I'M PICKING UP SOMETHING AHEAD...
...FAINT, BUT STARTING TO RISE.
THERE. NOW CHARGE IT UP...
...IF YOU STILL BELIEVE IN THE POWER OF FEAR, THAT IS.
SINESTRO LOST FAITH.
NOT ME.
IN BLACKEST DAY, IN BRIGHTEST NIGHT, BEWARE YOUR FEARS MADE INTO LIGHT...
LET THOSE WHO TRY TO STOP WHAT'S RIGHT BURN LIKE MY POWER...

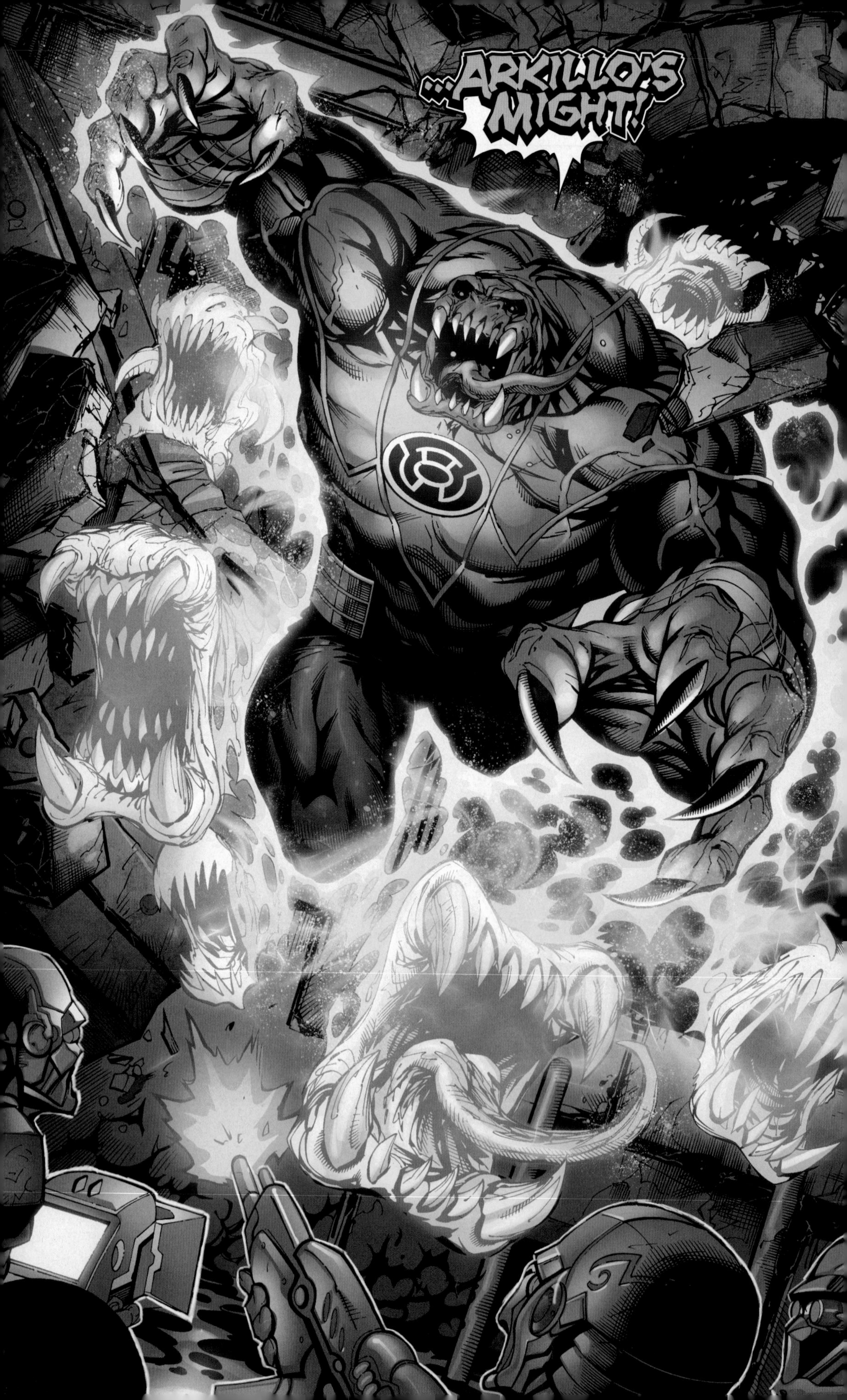
...ARKILLO'S MIGHT!

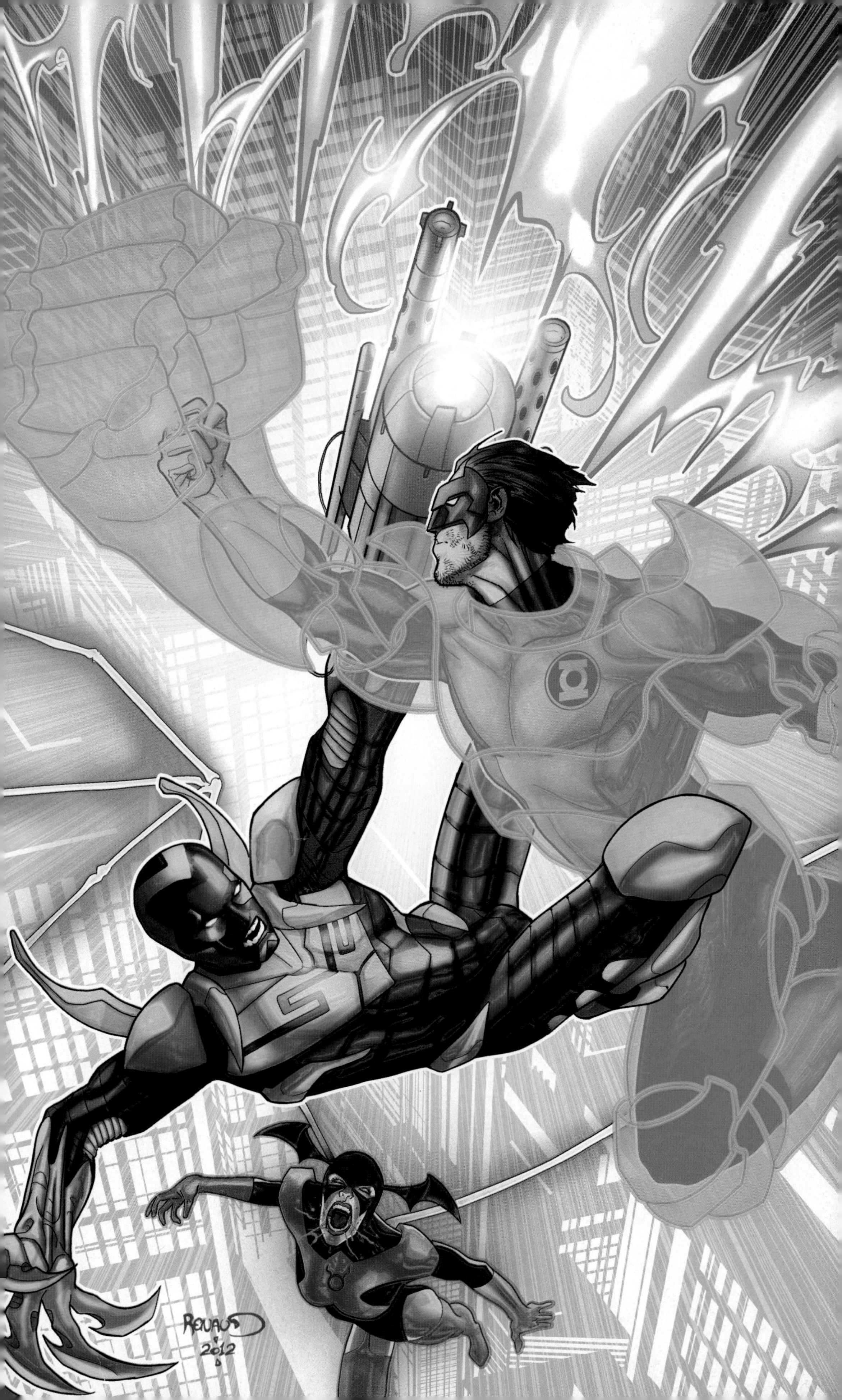

THE ENEMY OF MY ENEMY

TONY BEDARD writer **MARCIO TAKARA** artist cover by **PAUL RENAUD**

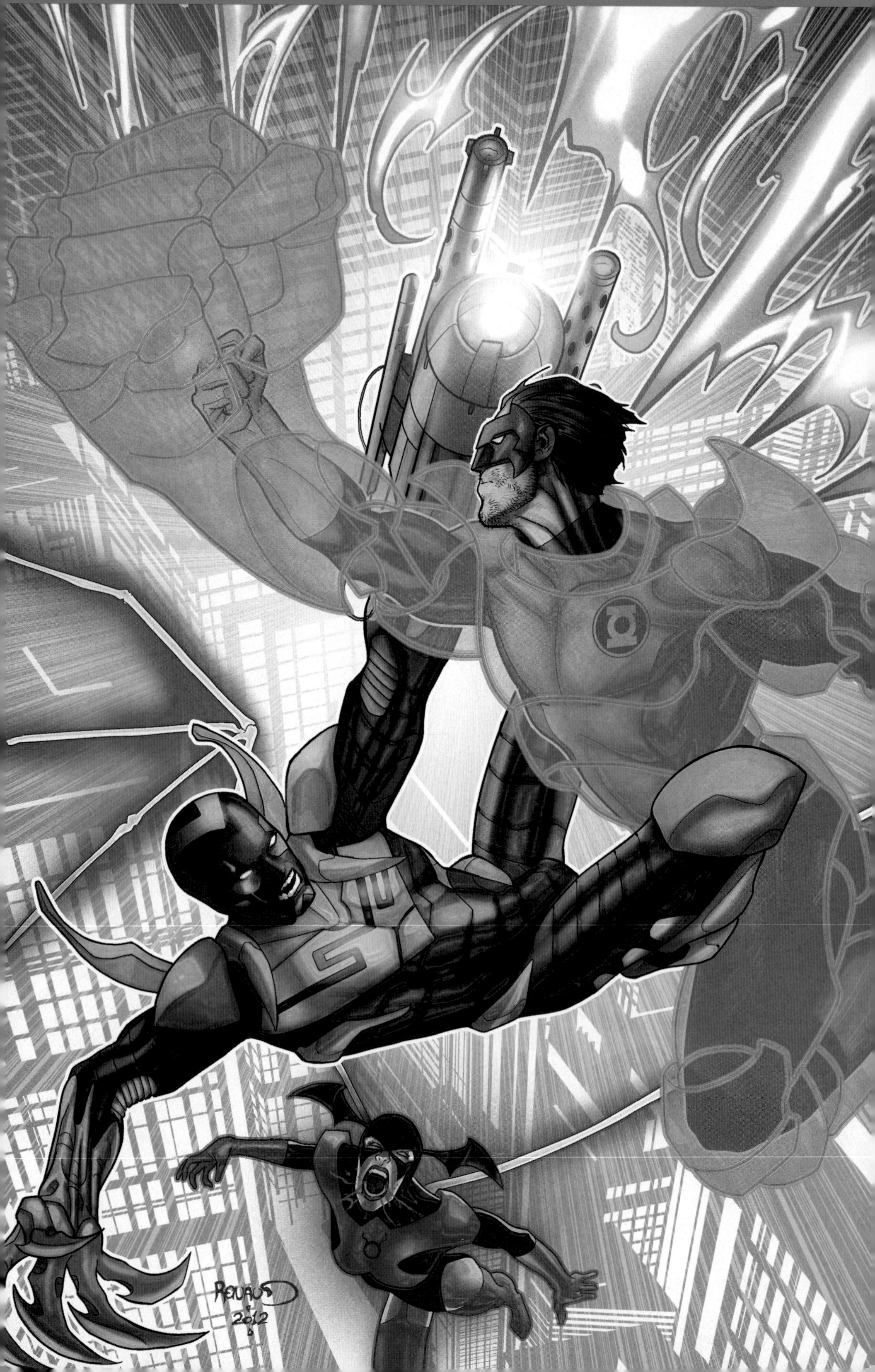
RENAUD
2012

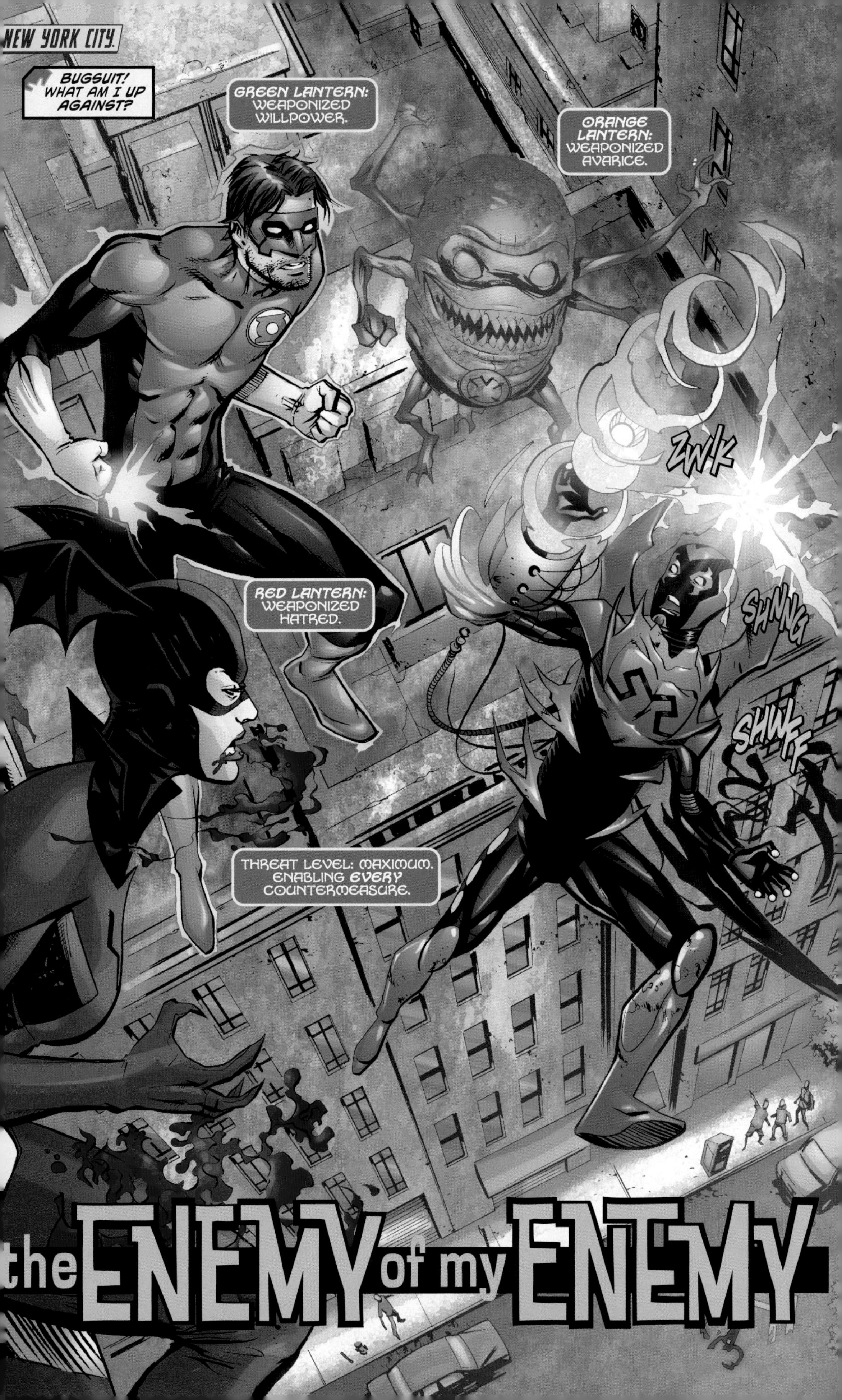

NEW YORK CITY.
BUGSUIT! WHAT AM I UP AGAINST?
GREEN LANTERN: WEAPONIZED WILLPOWER.
ORANGE LANTERN: WEAPONIZED AVARICE.
ZWIK
RED LANTERN: WEAPONIZED HATRED.
SHNNG
SHWFF
THREAT LEVEL: MAXIMUM. ENABLING EVERY COUNTERMEASURE.
the ENEMY of my ENEMY

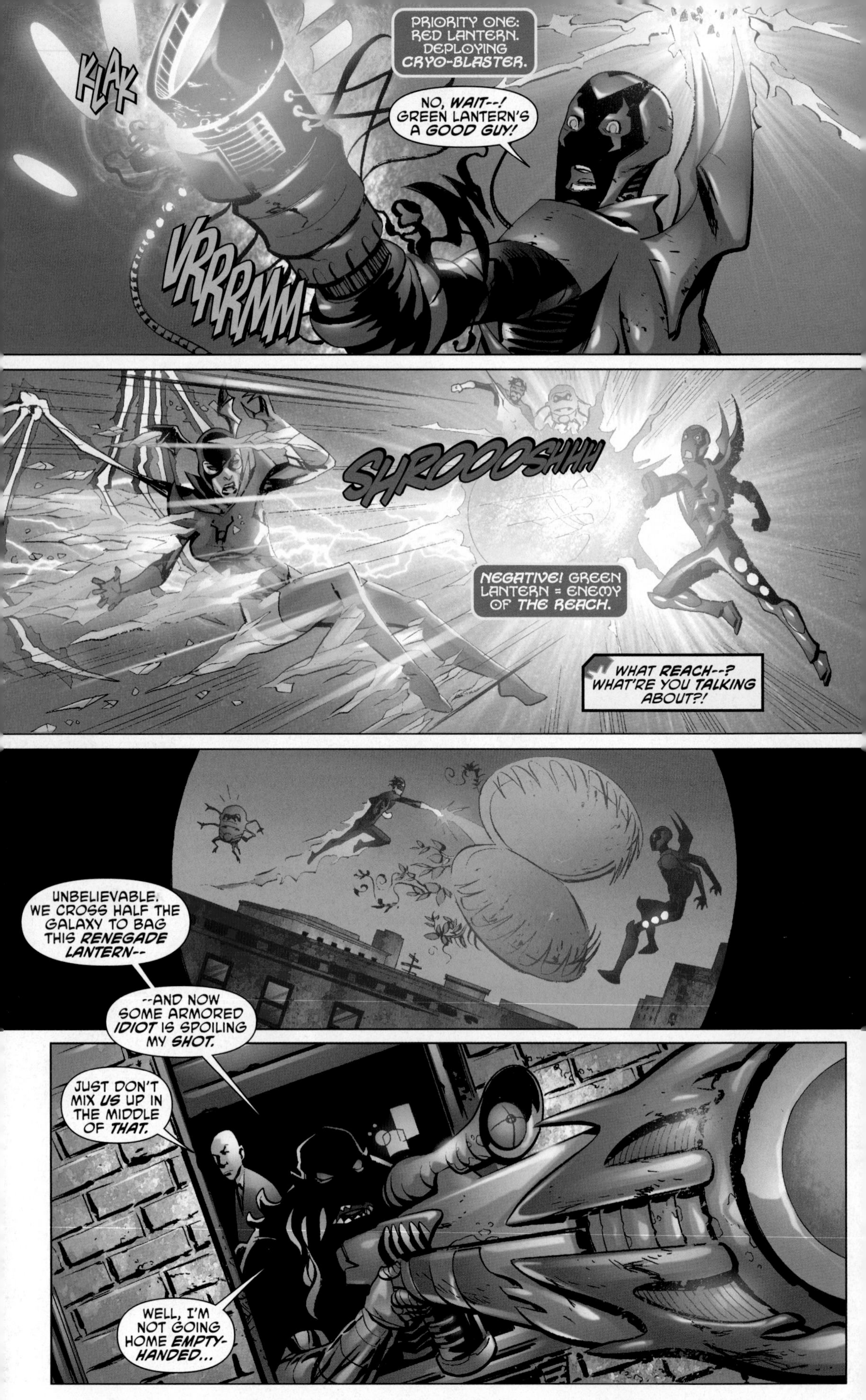
KLAK
PRIORITY ONE: RED LANTERN. DEPLOYING CRYO-BLASTER.
NO, WAIT--! GREEN LANTERN'S A GOOD GUY!
VRRRMM
SHROOOOSHHH
NEGATIVE! GREEN LANTERN = ENEMY OF THE REACH.
WHAT REACH--? WHAT'RE YOU TALKING ABOUT?!
UNBELIEVABLE. WE CROSS HALF THE GALAXY TO BAG THIS RENEGADE LANTERN--
--AND NOW SOME ARMORED IDIOT IS SPOILING MY SHOT.
JUST DON'T MIX US UP IN THE MIDDLE OF THAT.
WELL, I'M NOT GOING HOME EMPTY-HANDED...

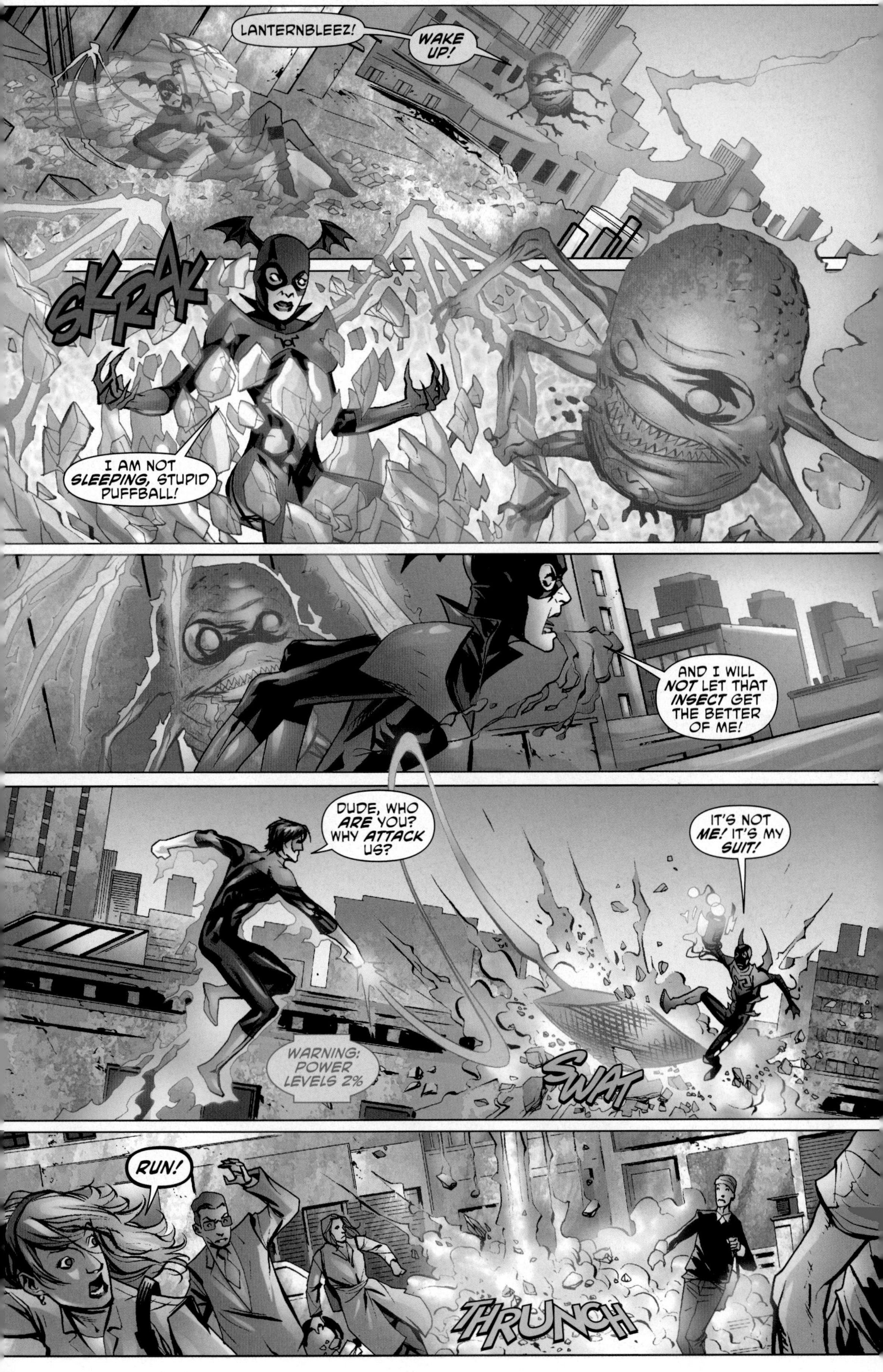
LANTERNBLEEZ!
WAKE UP!
SKRAK
I AM NOT SLEEPING, STUPID PUFFBALL!
AND I WILL NOT LET THAT INSECT GET THE BETTER OF ME!
DUDE, WHO ARE YOU? WHY ATTACK US?
IT'S NOT ME! IT'S MY SUIT!
WARNING: POWER LEVELS 2%
SWAT
RUN!
THRUNCH

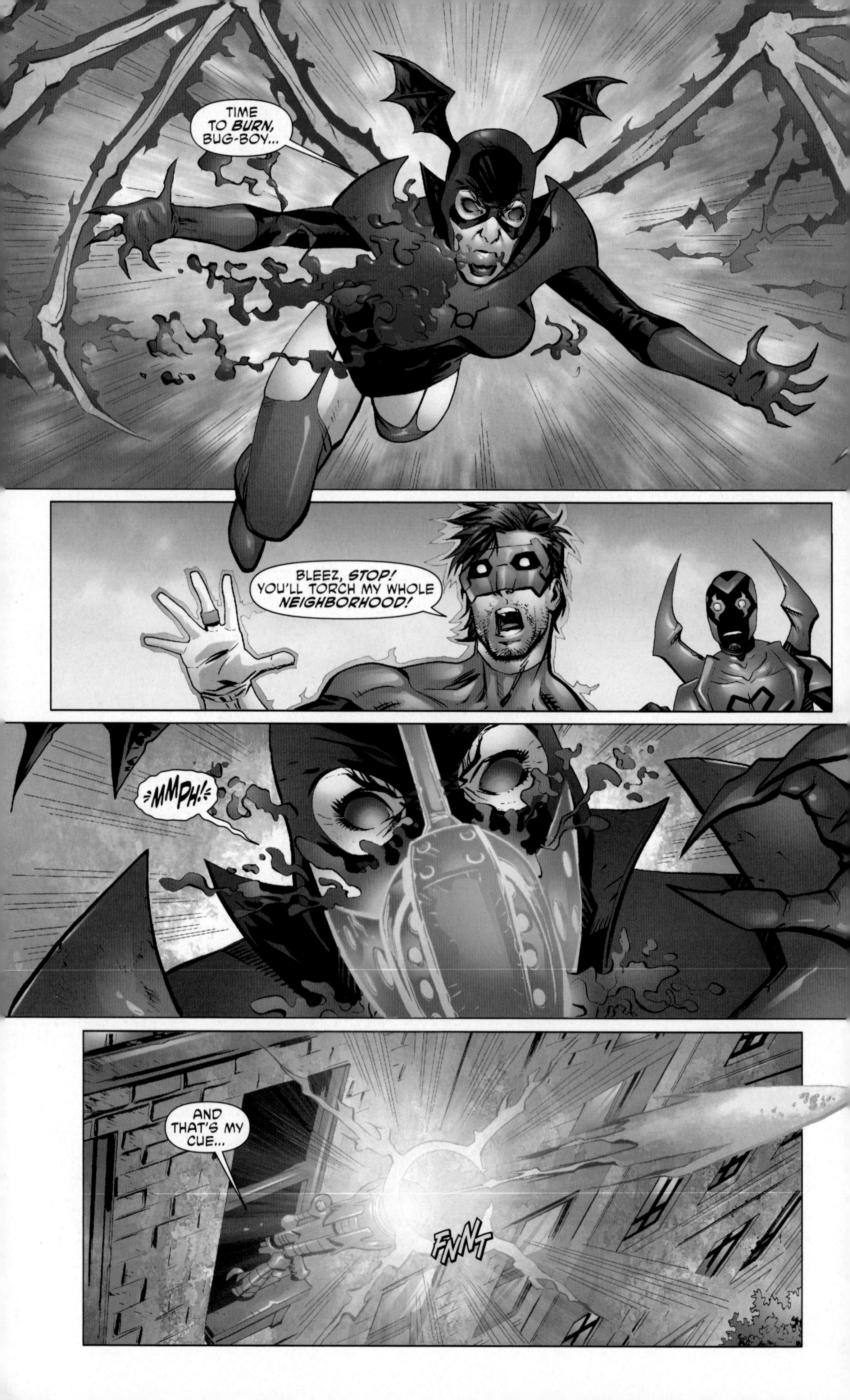
TIME TO BURN, BUG-BOY...
BLEEZ, STOP! YOU'LL TORCH MY WHOLE NEIGHBORHOOD!
MMPH!
AND THAT'S MY CUE...
FNNT

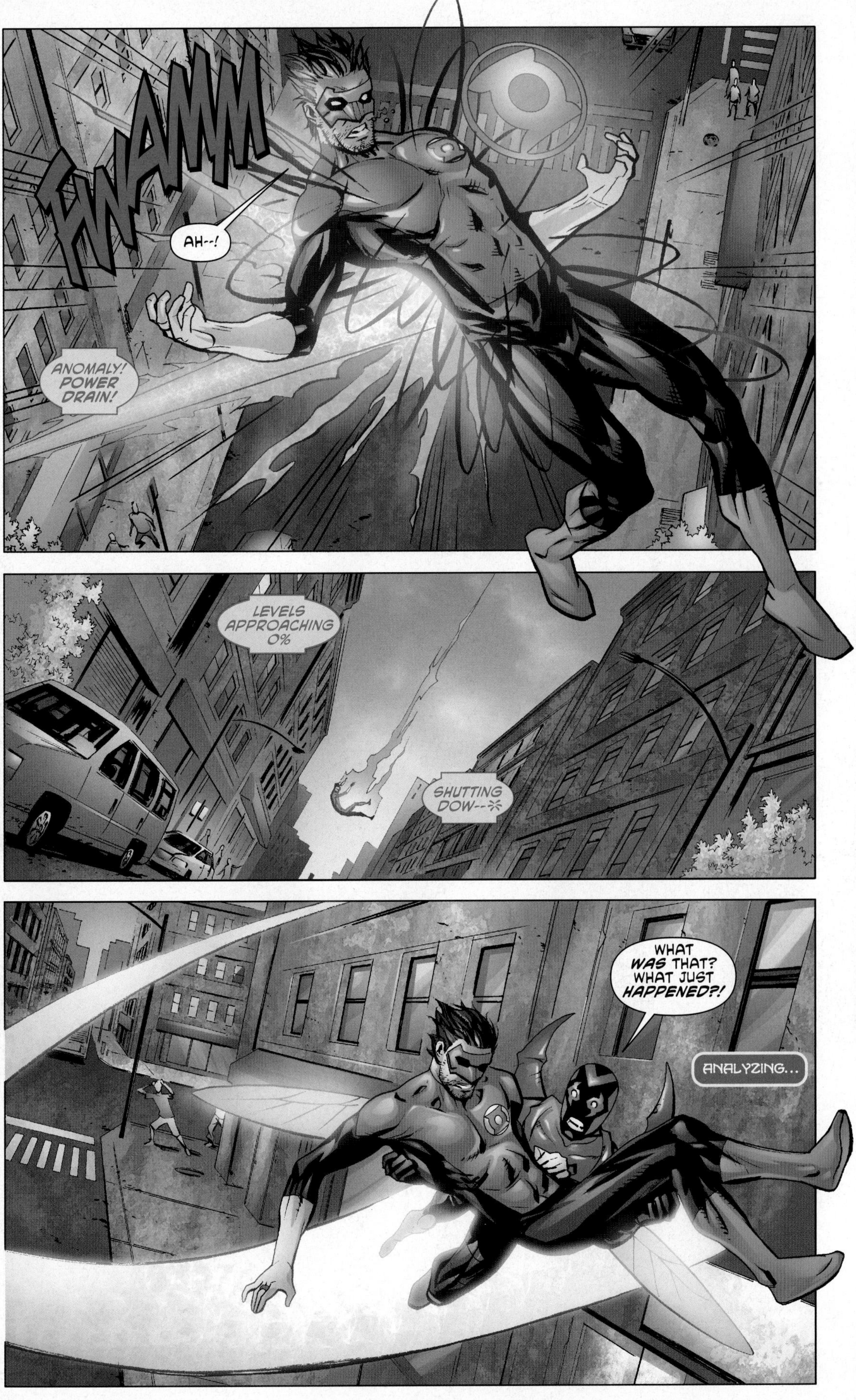
FWAMM
AH--!
ANOMALY! POWER DRAIN!
LEVELS APPROACHING 0%
SHUTTING DOW--
WHAT WAS THAT? WHAT JUST HAPPENED?!
ANALYZING...

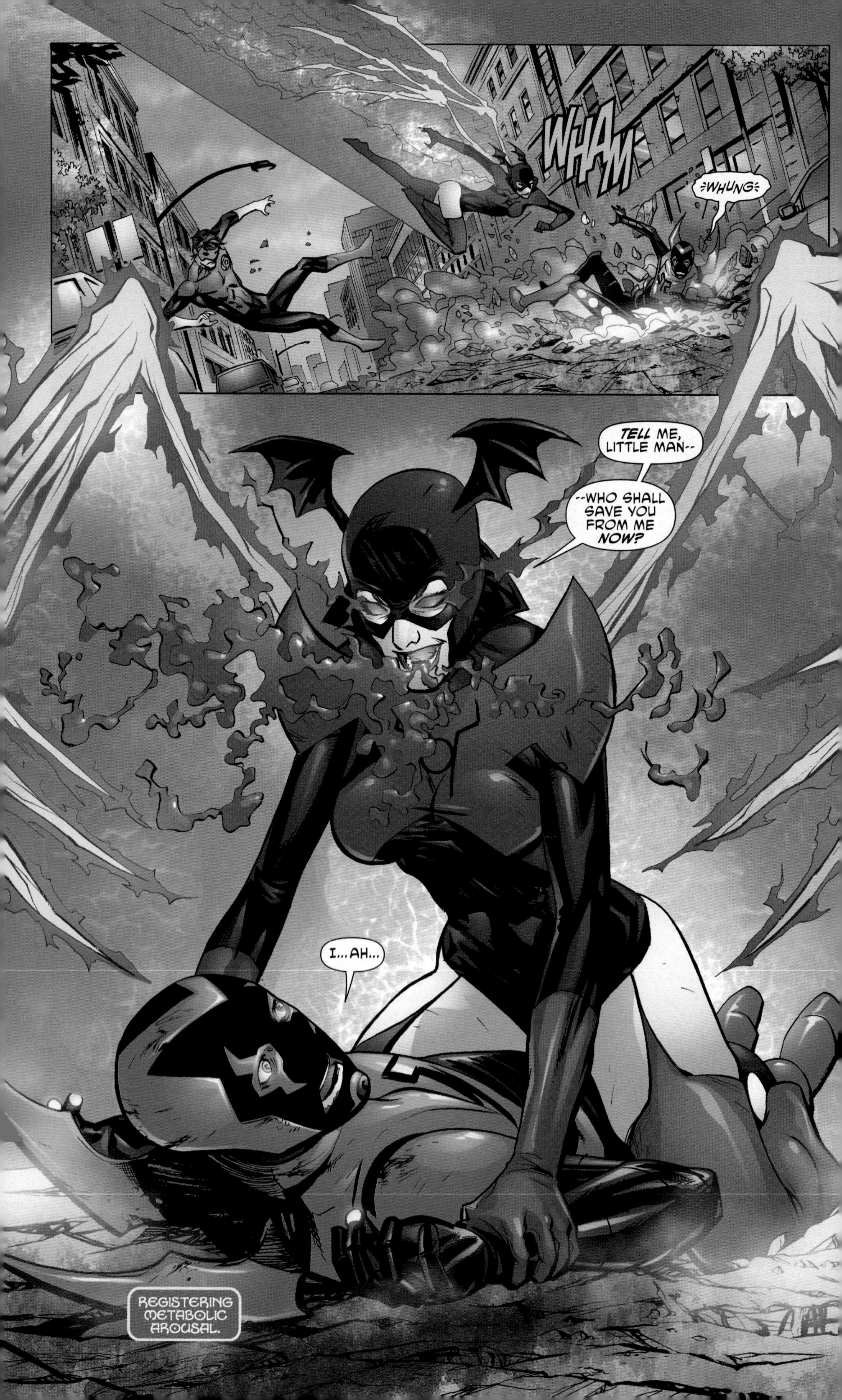

WHAM
WHUNG
TELL ME, LITTLE MAN--
--WHO SHALL SAVE YOU FROM ME NOW?
I...AH...
REGISTERING METABOLIC AROUSAL.

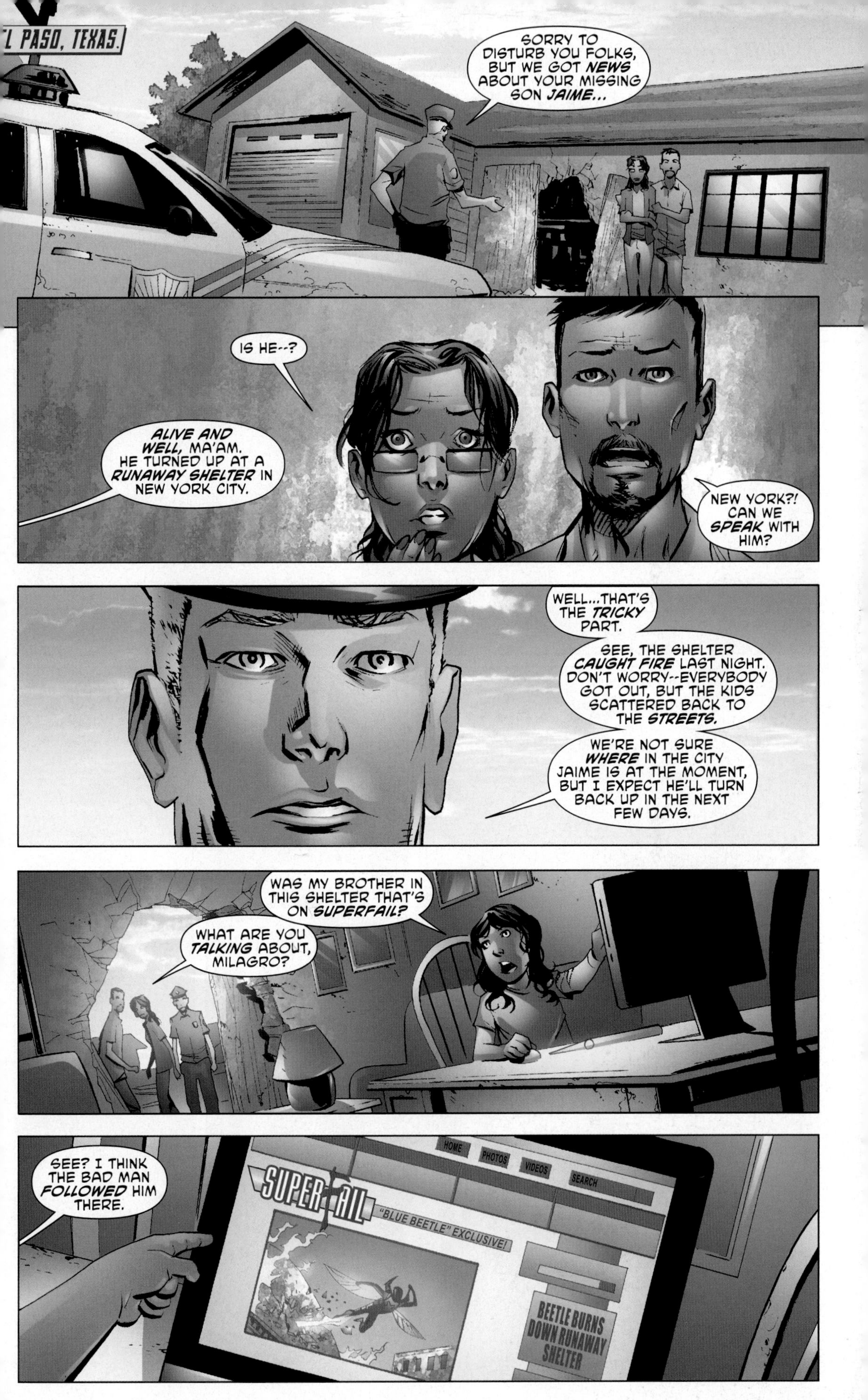
L PASO, TEXAS.
SORRY TO DISTURB YOU FOLKS, BUT WE GOT NEWS ABOUT YOUR MISSING SON JAIME...
IS HE--?
ALIVE AND WELL, MA'AM. HE TURNED UP AT A RUNAWAY SHELTER IN NEW YORK CITY.
NEW YORK?! CAN WE SPEAK WITH HIM?
WELL...THAT'S THE TRICKY PART.
SEE, THE SHELTER CAUGHT FIRE LAST NIGHT. DON'T WORRY--EVERYBODY GOT OUT, BUT THE KIDS SCATTERED BACK TO THE STREETS.
WE'RE NOT SURE WHERE IN THE CITY JAIME IS AT THE MOMENT, BUT I EXPECT HE'LL TURN BACK UP IN THE NEXT FEW DAYS.
WAS MY BROTHER IN THIS SHELTER THAT'S ON SUPERFAIL?
WHAT ARE YOU TALKING ABOUT, MILAGRO?
SEE? I THINK THE BAD MAN FOLLOWED HIM THERE.
HOME
PHOTOS
VIDEOS
SEARCH
SUPERFAIL
"BLUE BEETLE" EXCLUSIVE!
BEETLE BURNS DOWN RUNAWAY SHELTER

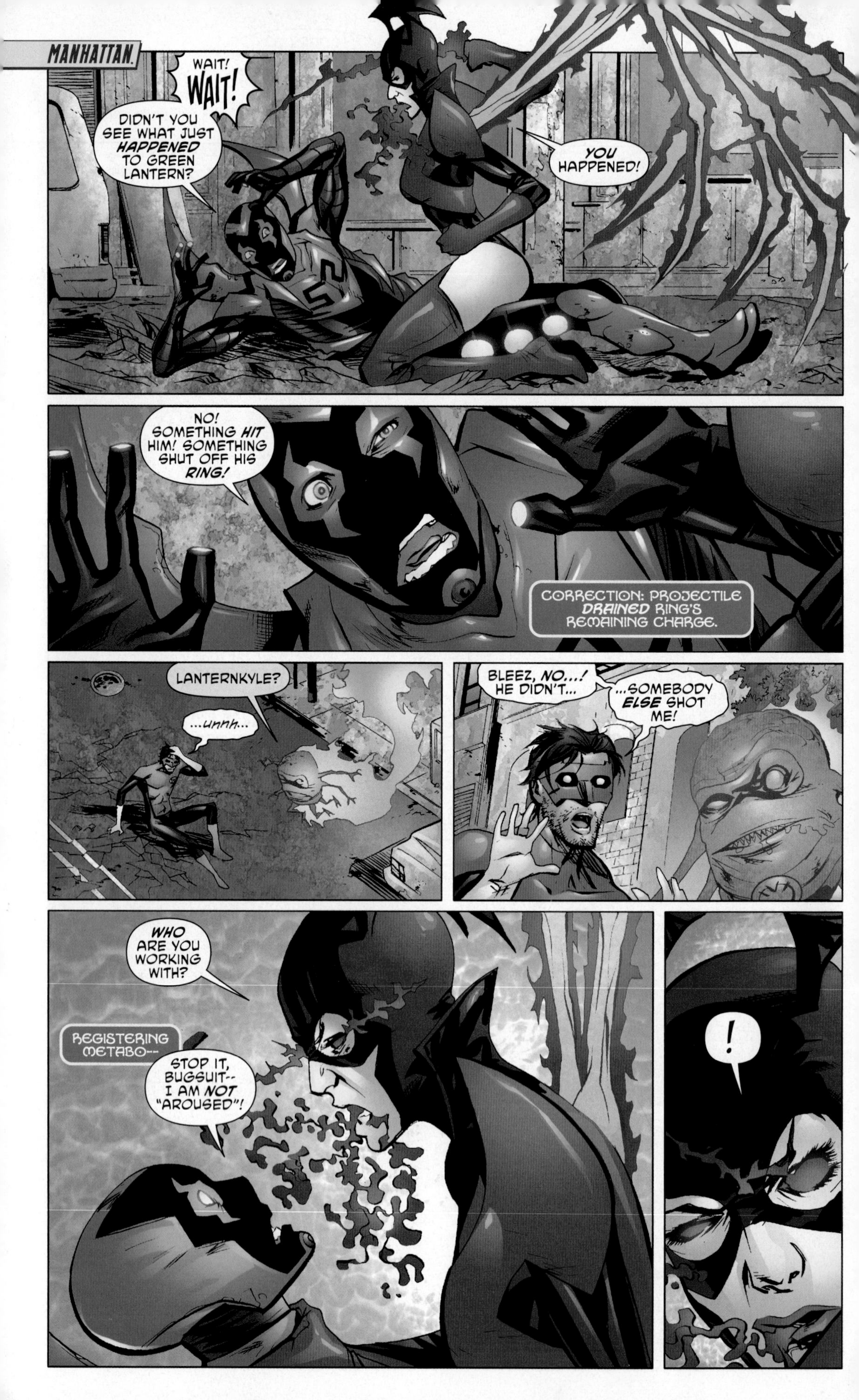
MANHATTAN.
WAIT! WAIT!
DIDN'T YOU SEE WHAT JUST *HAPPENED* TO GREEN LANTERN?
YOU HAPPENED!
NO! SOMETHING *HIT* HIM! SOMETHING SHUT OFF HIS *RING!*
CORRECTION: PROJECTILE *DRAINED* RING'S REMAINING CHARGE.
LANTERNKYLE?
...unnh...
BLEEZ, *NO...!* HE DIDN'T...
...SOMEBODY *ELSE* SHOT ME!
WHO ARE YOU WORKING WITH?
REGISTERING METABO--
STOP IT, BUGSUIT-- I AM *NOT* "AROUSED"!
!

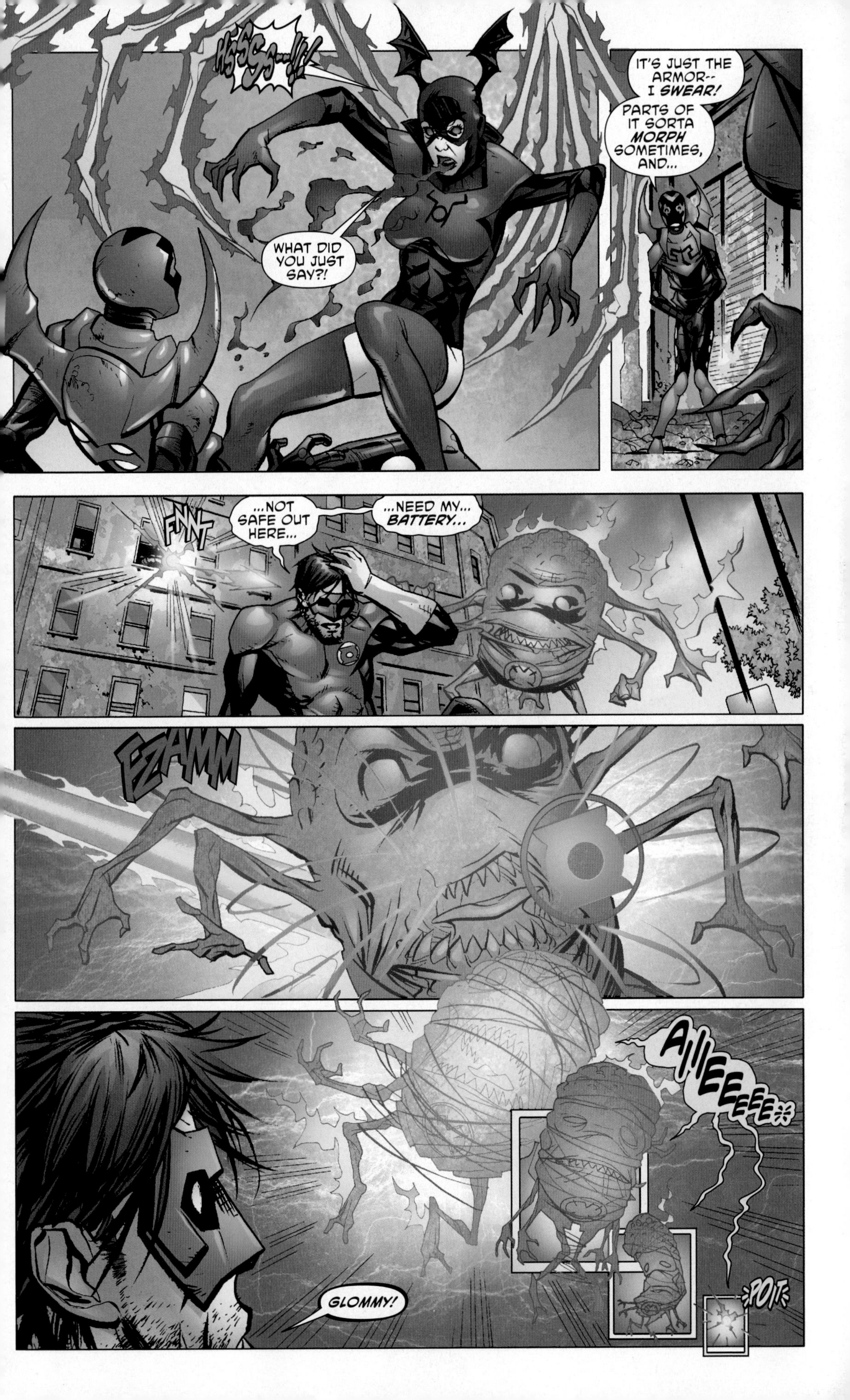
HSSSS--!!
WHAT DID YOU JUST SAY?!
IT'S JUST THE ARMOR-- I SWEAR!
PARTS OF IT SORTA MORPH SOMETIMES, AND...
FNNT
...NOT SAFE OUT HERE...
...NEED MY... BATTERY...
FZAMM
AIIEEEEEE!
GLOMMY!
POIT

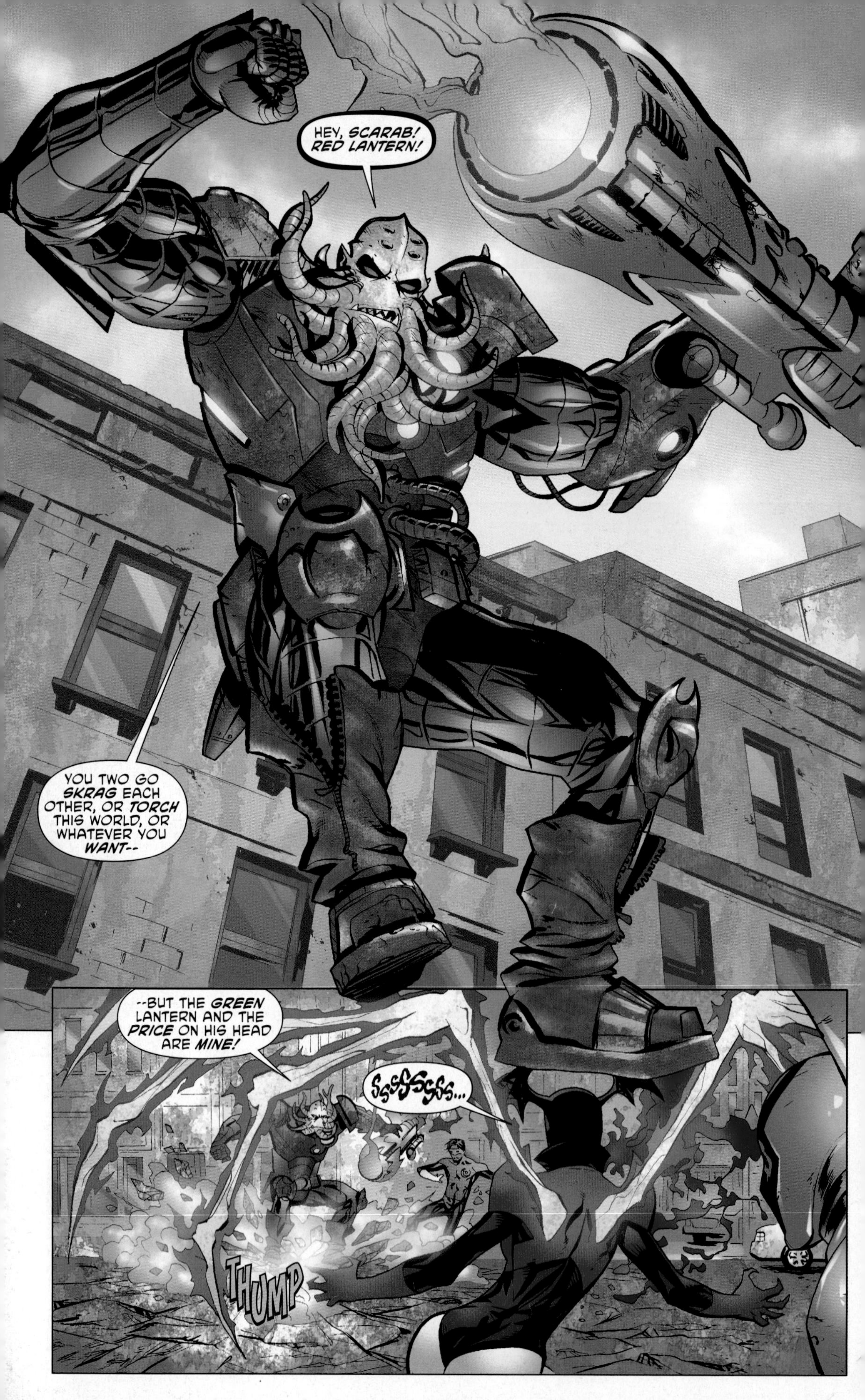
HEY, SCARAB! RED LANTERN!
YOU TWO GO SKRAG EACH OTHER, OR TORCH THIS WORLD, OR WHATEVER YOU WANT--
--BUT THE GREEN LANTERN AND THE PRICE ON HIS HEAD ARE MINE!
SsSSSsSs...
THUMP

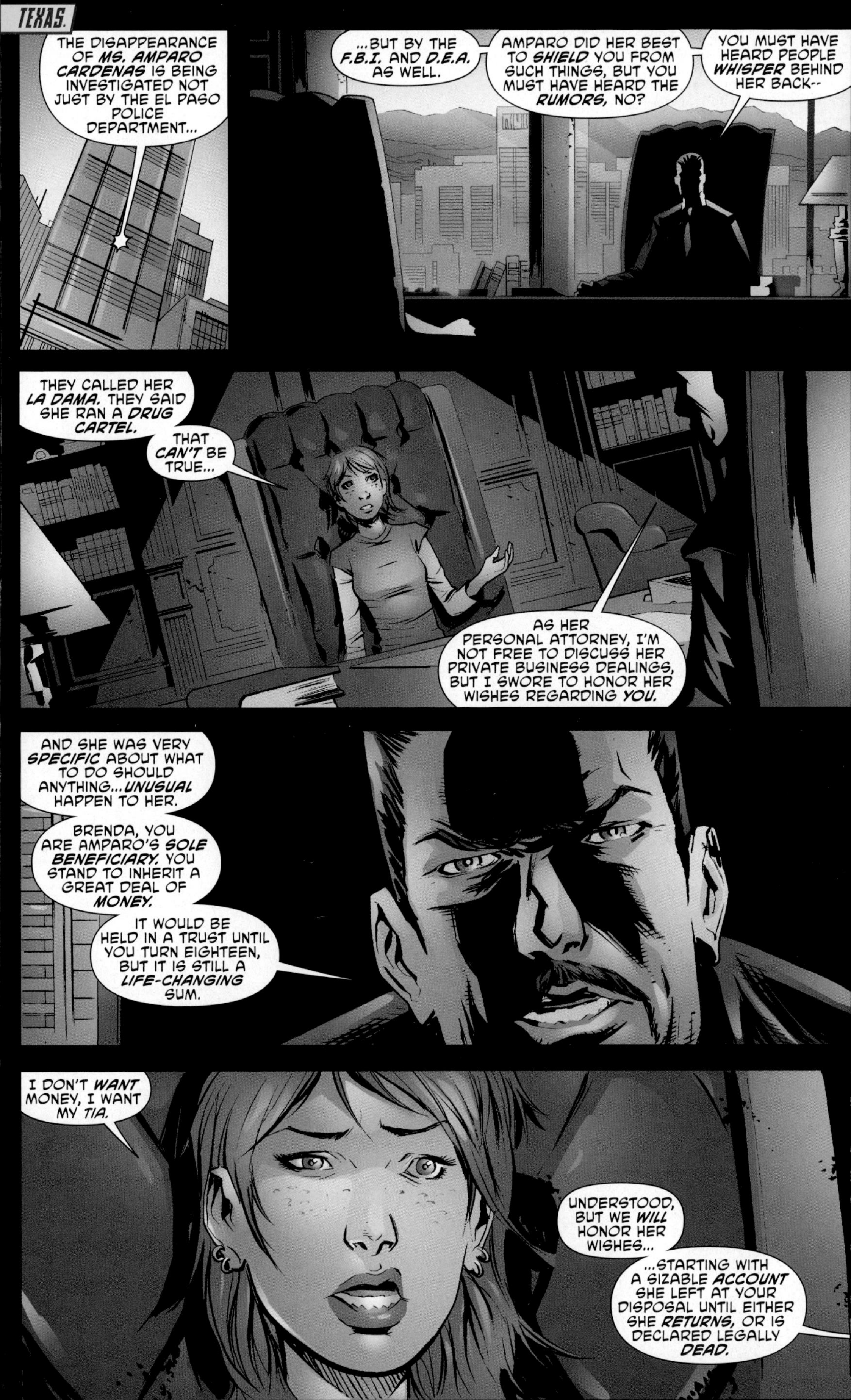
TEXAS.
THE DISAPPEARANCE OF MS. AMPARO CARDENAS IS BEING INVESTIGATED NOT JUST BY THE EL PASO POLICE DEPARTMENT...
...BUT BY THE F.B.I. AND D.E.A. AS WELL.
AMPARO DID HER BEST TO SHIELD YOU FROM SUCH THINGS, BUT YOU MUST HAVE HEARD THE RUMORS, NO?
YOU MUST HAVE HEARD PEOPLE WHISPER BEHIND HER BACK--
THEY CALLED HER LA DAMA. THEY SAID SHE RAN A DRUG CARTEL.
THAT CAN'T BE TRUE...
AS HER PERSONAL ATTORNEY, I'M NOT FREE TO DISCUSS HER PRIVATE BUSINESS DEALINGS, BUT I SWORE TO HONOR HER WISHES REGARDING YOU.
AND SHE WAS VERY SPECIFIC ABOUT WHAT TO DO SHOULD ANYTHING...UNUSUAL HAPPEN TO HER.
BRENDA, YOU ARE AMPARO'S SOLE BENEFICIARY. YOU STAND TO INHERIT A GREAT DEAL OF MONEY.
IT WOULD BE HELD IN A TRUST UNTIL YOU TURN EIGHTEEN, BUT IT IS STILL A LIFE-CHANGING SUM.
I DON'T WANT MONEY, I WANT MY TIA.
UNDERSTOOD, BUT WE WILL HONOR HER WISHES...
...STARTING WITH A SIZABLE ACCOUNT SHE LEFT AT YOUR DISPOSAL UNTIL EITHER SHE RETURNS, OR IS DECLARED LEGALLY DEAD.

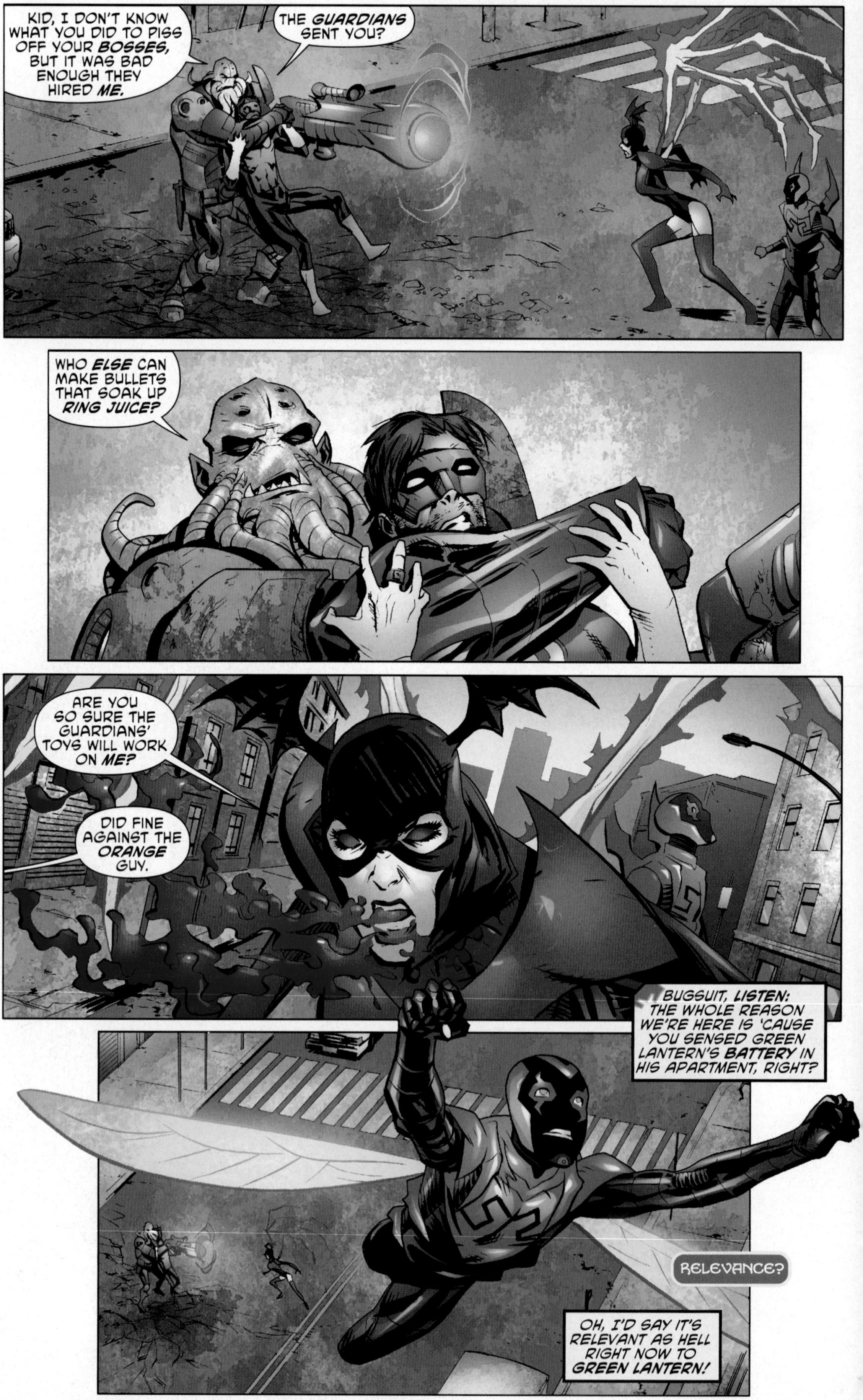
KID, I DON'T KNOW WHAT YOU DID TO PISS OFF YOUR BOSSES, BUT IT WAS BAD ENOUGH THEY HIRED ME.
THE GUARDIANS SENT YOU?
WHO ELSE CAN MAKE BULLETS THAT SOAK UP RING JUICE?
ARE YOU SO SURE THE GUARDIANS' TOYS WILL WORK ON ME?
DID FINE AGAINST THE ORANGE GUY.
BUGSUIT, LISTEN: THE WHOLE REASON WE'RE HERE IS 'CAUSE YOU SENSED GREEN LANTERN'S BATTERY IN HIS APARTMENT, RIGHT?
RELEVANCE?
OH, I'D SAY IT'S RELEVANT AS HELL RIGHT NOW TO GREEN LANTERN!

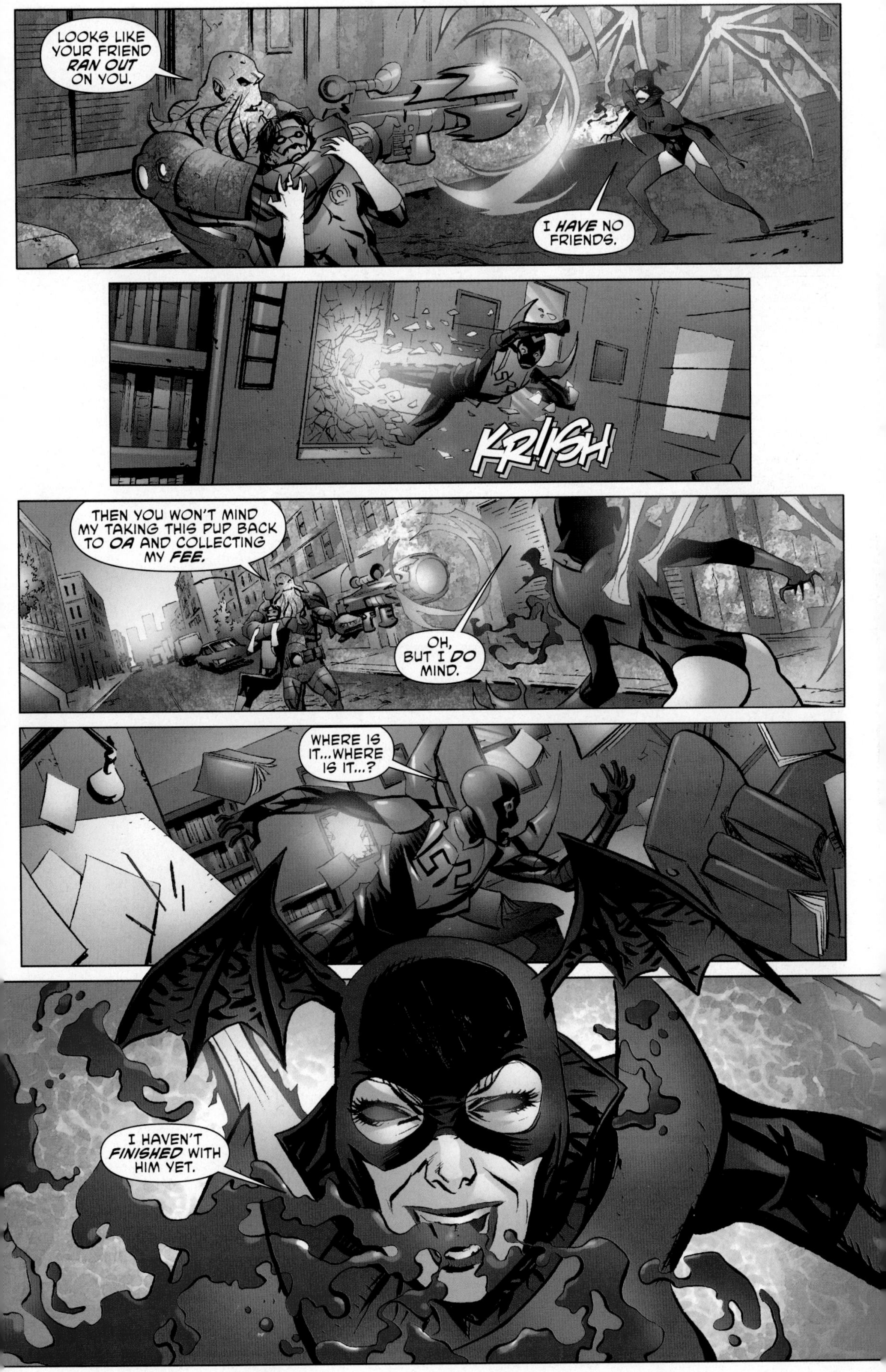
LOOKS LIKE YOUR FRIEND *RAN OUT* ON YOU.
I *HAVE* NO FRIENDS.
KRISH
THEN YOU WON'T MIND MY TAKING THIS PUP BACK TO *OA* AND COLLECTING MY *FEE.*
OH, BUT I *DO* MIND.
WHERE IS IT...WHERE IS IT...?
I HAVEN'T *FINISHED* WITH HIM YET.

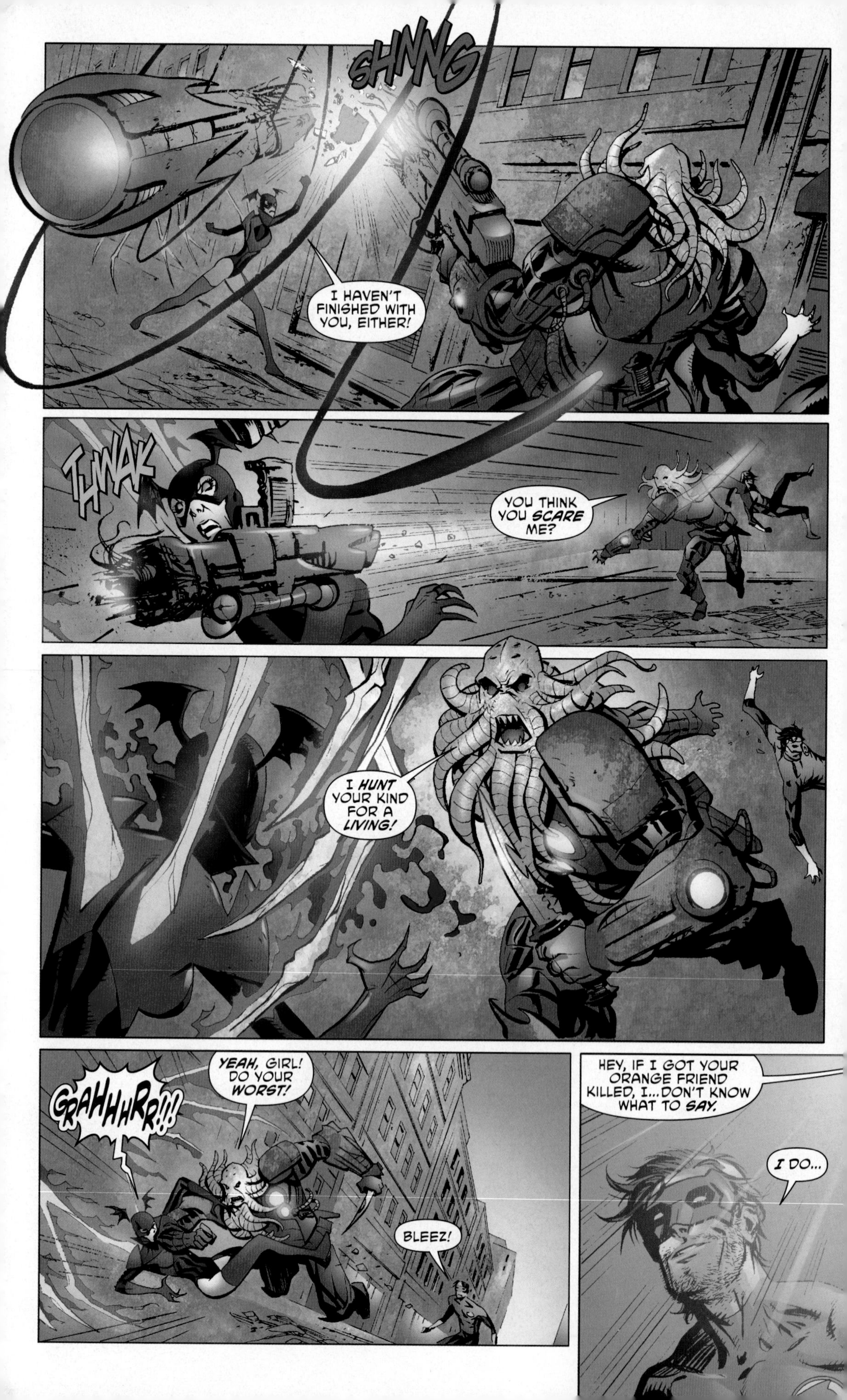
SHNNG
I HAVEN'T FINISHED WITH YOU, EITHER!
THWAK
YOU THINK YOU SCARE ME?
I HUNT YOUR KIND FOR A LIVING!
GRAHHHRR!!!
YEAH, GIRL! DO YOUR WORST!
BLEEZ!
HEY, IF I GOT YOUR ORANGE FRIEND KILLED, I...DON'T KNOW WHAT TO SAY.
I DO...

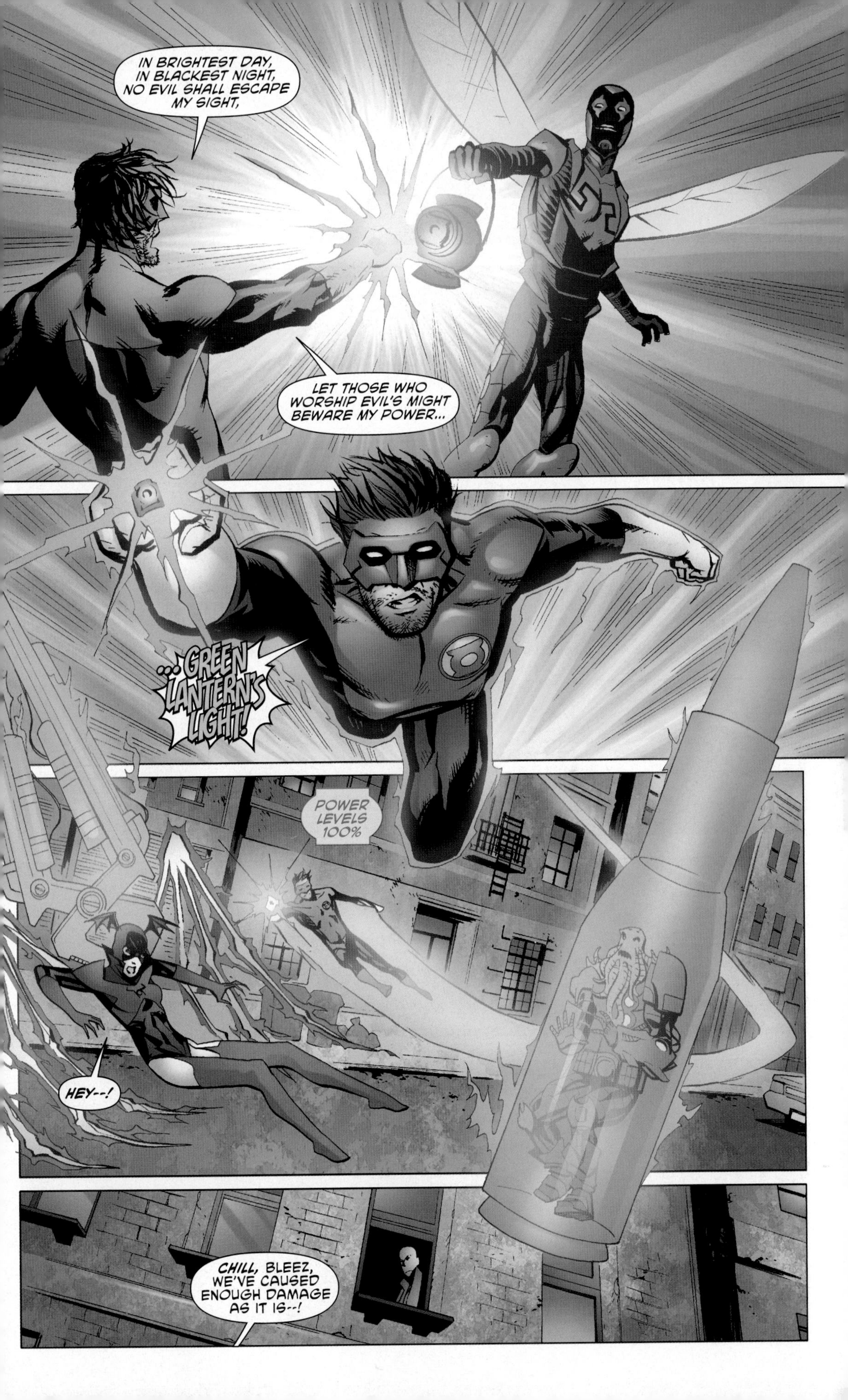
IN BRIGHTEST DAY, IN BLACKEST NIGHT, NO EVIL SHALL ESCAPE MY SIGHT,
LET THOSE WHO WORSHIP EVIL'S MIGHT BEWARE MY POWER...
...GREEN LANTERN'S LIGHT!
POWER LEVELS 100%
HEY--!
CHILL, BLEEZ, WE'VE CAUSED ENOUGH DAMAGE AS IT IS--!

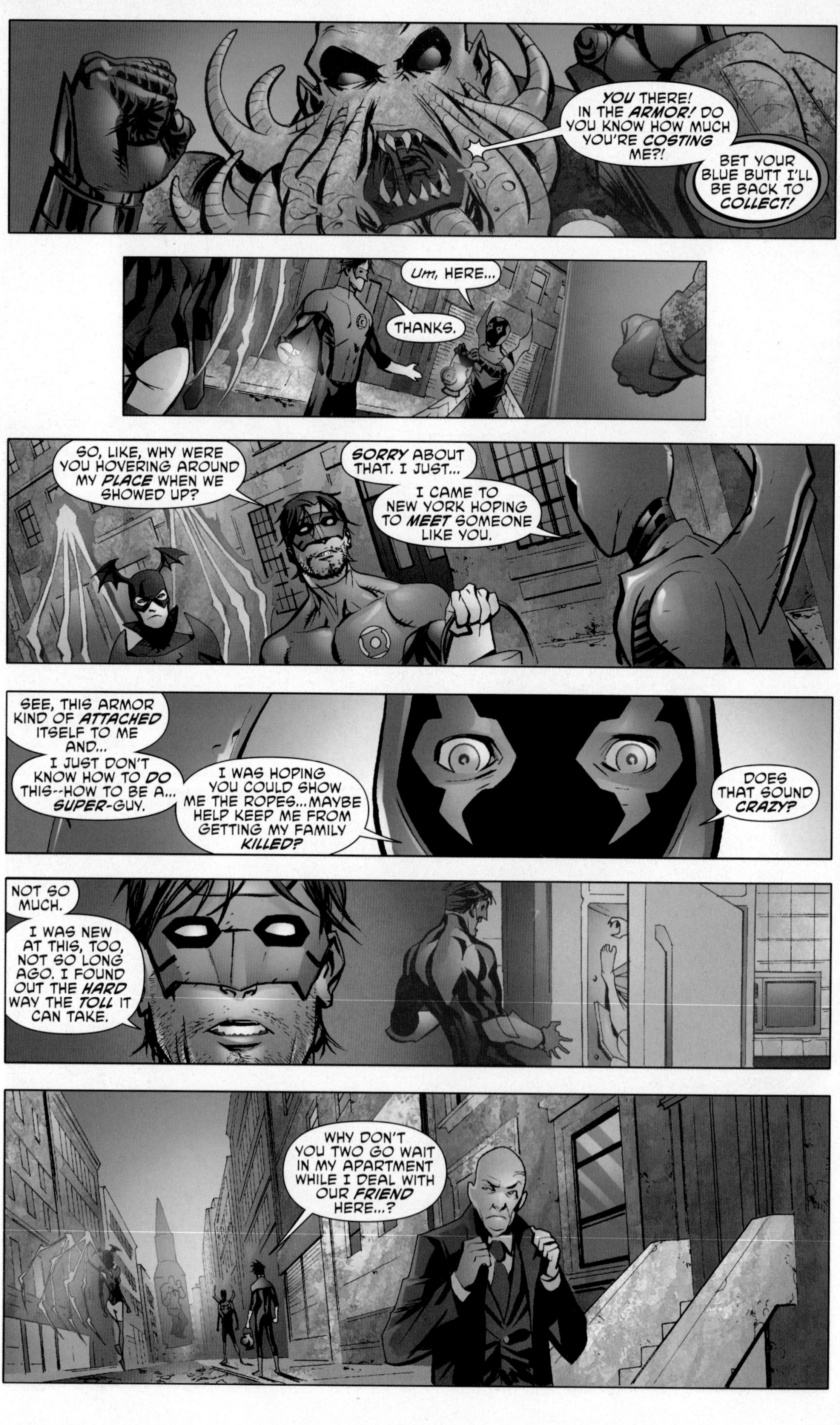

YOU THERE! IN THE ARMOR! DO YOU KNOW HOW MUCH YOU'RE COSTING ME?!
BET YOUR BLUE BUTT I'LL BE BACK TO COLLECT!
Um, HERE...
THANKS.
SO, LIKE, WHY WERE YOU HOVERING AROUND MY PLACE WHEN WE SHOWED UP?
SORRY ABOUT THAT. I JUST...
I CAME TO NEW YORK HOPING TO MEET SOMEONE LIKE YOU.
SEE, THIS ARMOR KIND OF ATTACHED ITSELF TO ME AND...
I JUST DON'T KNOW HOW TO DO THIS--HOW TO BE A... SUPER-GUY.
I WAS HOPING YOU COULD SHOW ME THE ROPES...MAYBE HELP KEEP ME FROM GETTING MY FAMILY KILLED?
DOES THAT SOUND CRAZY?
NOT SO MUCH.
I WAS NEW AT THIS, TOO, NOT SO LONG AGO. I FOUND OUT THE HARD WAY THE TOLL IT CAN TAKE.
WHY DON'T YOU TWO GO WAIT IN MY APARTMENT WHILE I DEAL WITH OUR FRIEND HERE...?

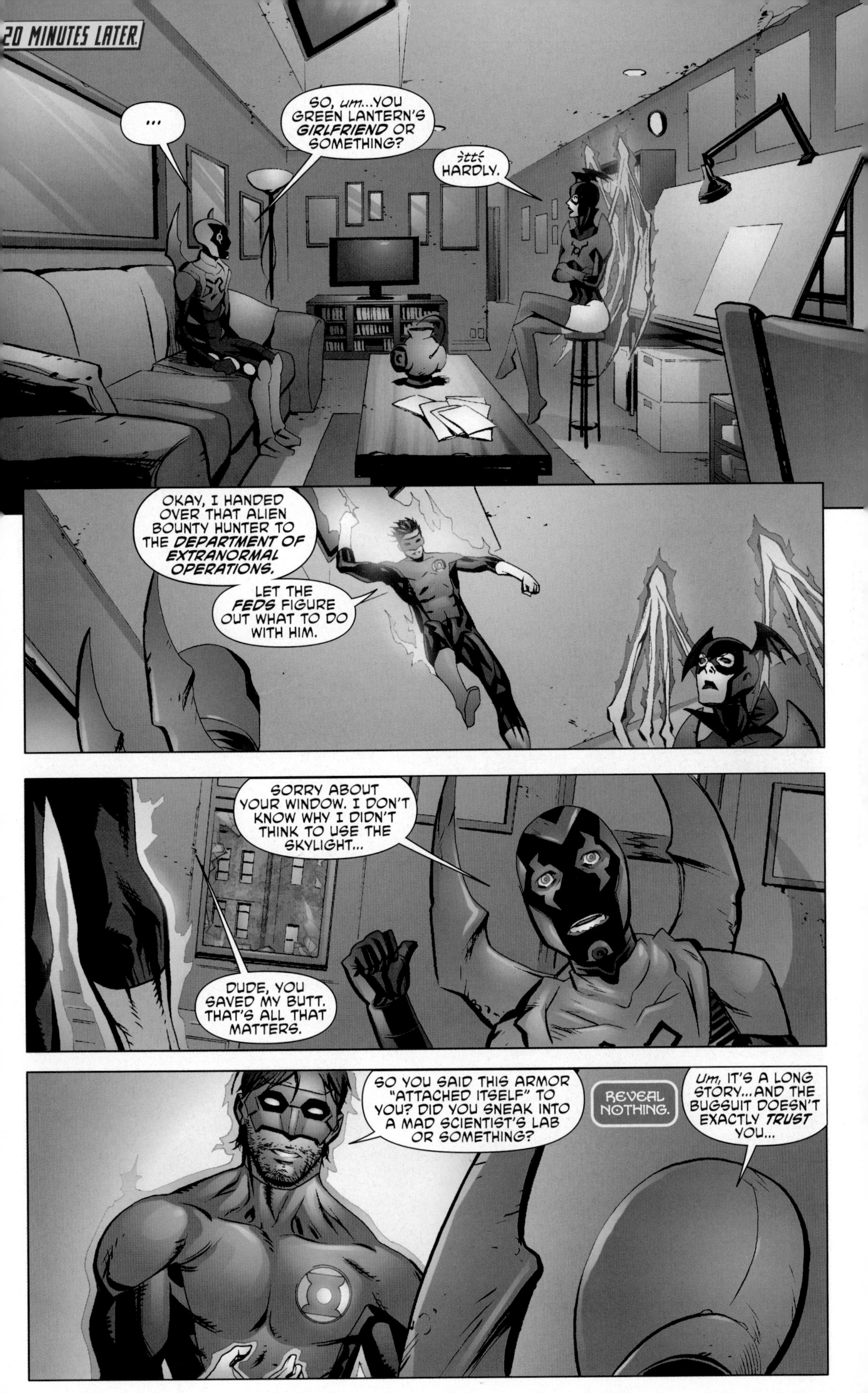

20 MINUTES LATER.
...
SO, um...YOU GREEN LANTERN'S GIRLFRIEND OR SOMETHING?
tt HARDLY.
OKAY, I HANDED OVER THAT ALIEN BOUNTY HUNTER TO THE DEPARTMENT OF EXTRANORMAL OPERATIONS.
LET THE FEDS FIGURE OUT WHAT TO DO WITH HIM.
SORRY ABOUT YOUR WINDOW. I DON'T KNOW WHY I DIDN'T THINK TO USE THE SKYLIGHT...
DUDE, YOU SAVED MY BUTT. THAT'S ALL THAT MATTERS.
SO YOU SAID THIS ARMOR "ATTACHED ITSELF" TO YOU? DID YOU SNEAK INTO A MAD SCIENTIST'S LAB OR SOMETHING?
REVEAL NOTHING.
Um, IT'S A LONG STORY...AND THE BUGSUIT DOESN'T EXACTLY TRUST YOU...

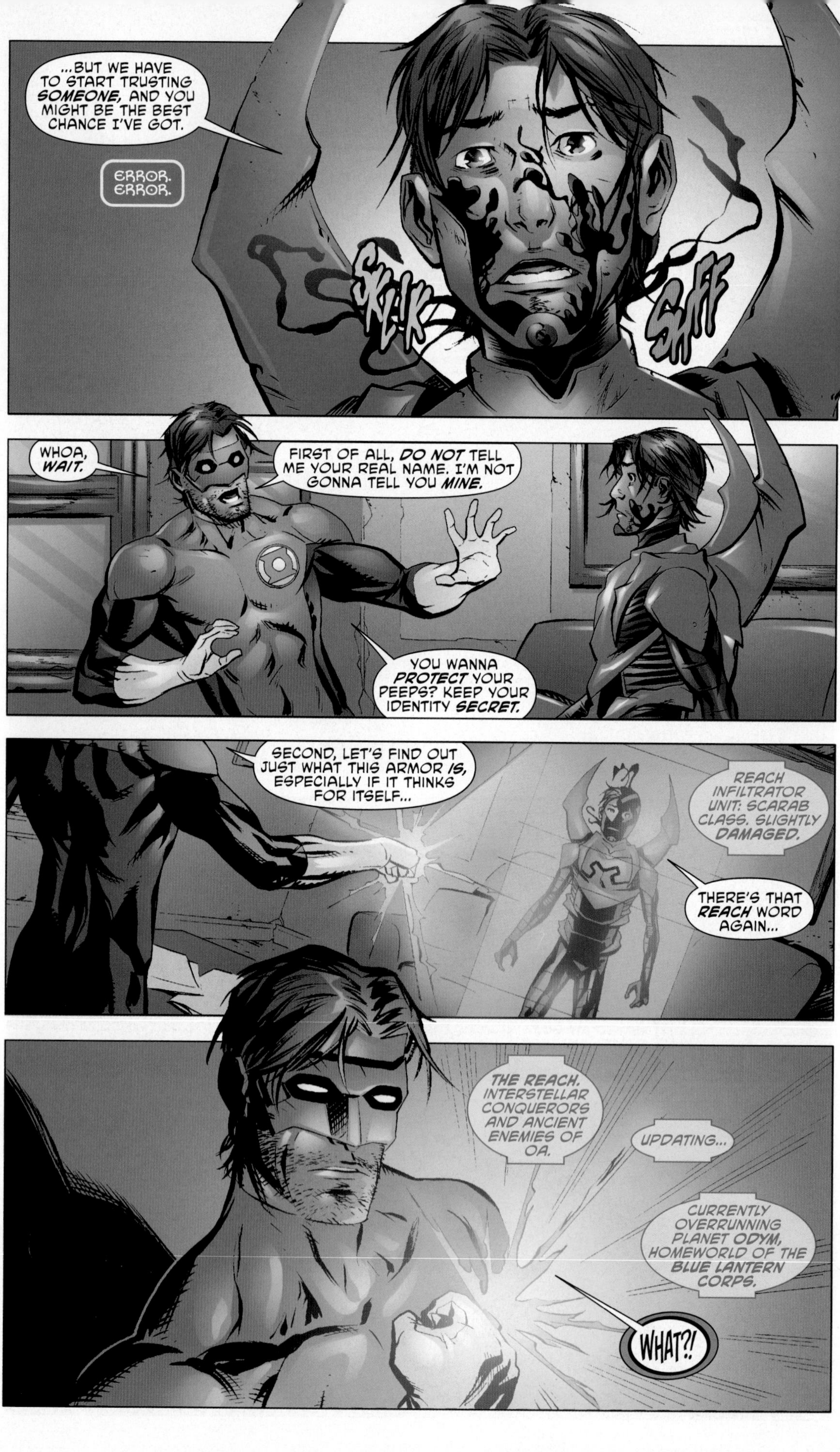
...BUT WE HAVE TO START TRUSTING SOMEONE, AND YOU MIGHT BE THE BEST CHANCE I'VE GOT.
ERROR. ERROR.
SKLIK
SHFF
WHOA, WAIT.
FIRST OF ALL, DO NOT TELL ME YOUR REAL NAME. I'M NOT GONNA TELL YOU MINE.
YOU WANNA PROTECT YOUR PEEPS? KEEP YOUR IDENTITY SECRET.
SECOND, LET'S FIND OUT JUST WHAT THIS ARMOR IS, ESPECIALLY IF IT THINKS FOR ITSELF...
REACH INFILTRATOR UNIT: SCARAB CLASS. SLIGHTLY DAMAGED.
THERE'S THAT REACH WORD AGAIN...
THE REACH. INTERSTELLAR CONQUERORS AND ANCIENT ENEMIES OF OA.
UPDATING...
CURRENTLY OVERRUNNING PLANET ODYM, HOMEWORLD OF THE BLUE LANTERN CORPS.
WHAT?!

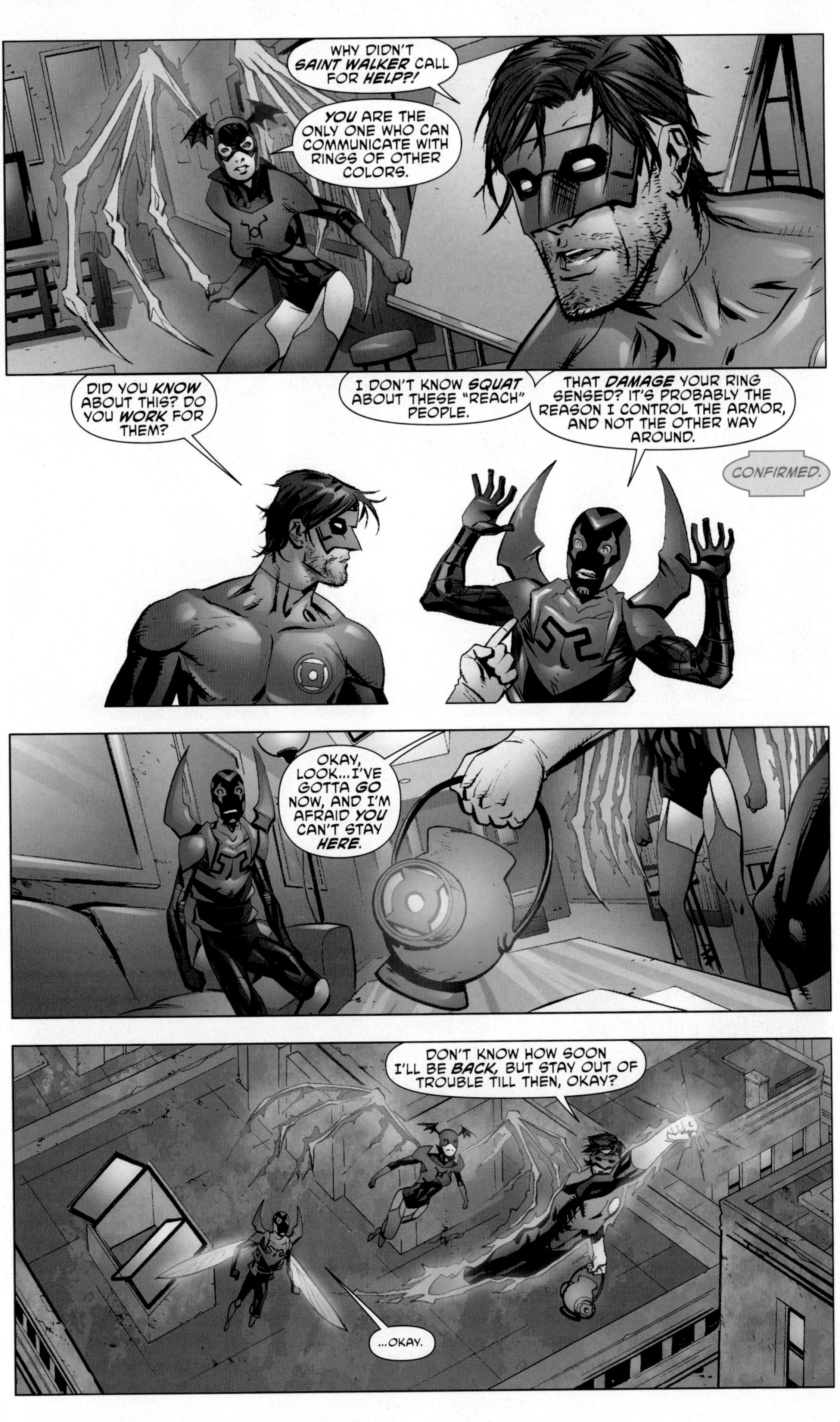
WHY DIDN'T SAINT WALKER CALL FOR HELP?!
YOU ARE THE ONLY ONE WHO CAN COMMUNICATE WITH RINGS OF OTHER COLORS.
DID YOU KNOW ABOUT THIS? DO YOU WORK FOR THEM?
I DON'T KNOW SQUAT ABOUT THESE "REACH" PEOPLE.
THAT DAMAGE YOUR RING SENSED? IT'S PROBABLY THE REASON I CONTROL THE ARMOR, AND NOT THE OTHER WAY AROUND.
CONFIRMED.
OKAY, LOOK...I'VE GOTTA GO NOW, AND I'M AFRAID YOU CAN'T STAY HERE.
DON'T KNOW HOW SOON I'LL BE BACK, BUT STAY OUT OF TROUBLE TILL THEN, OKAY?
...OKAY.

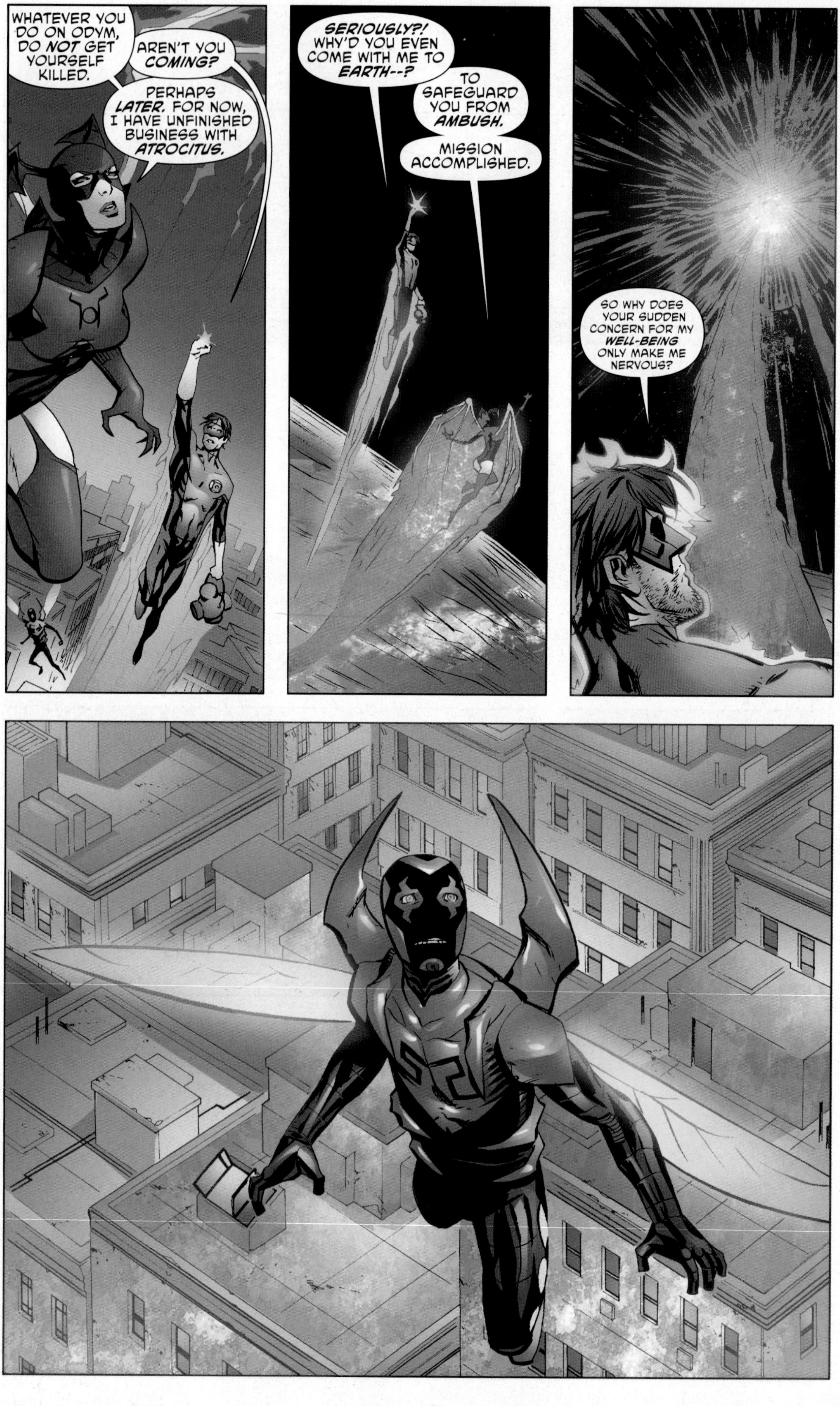
WHATEVER YOU DO ON ODYM, DO NOT GET YOURSELF KILLED.
AREN'T YOU COMING?
PERHAPS LATER. FOR NOW, I HAVE UNFINISHED BUSINESS WITH ATROCITUS.
SERIOUSLY?! WHY'D YOU EVEN COME WITH ME TO EARTH--?
TO SAFEGUARD YOU FROM AMBUSH.
MISSION ACCOMPLISHED.
SO WHY DOES YOUR SUDDEN CONCERN FOR MY WELL-BEING ONLY MAKE ME NERVOUS?

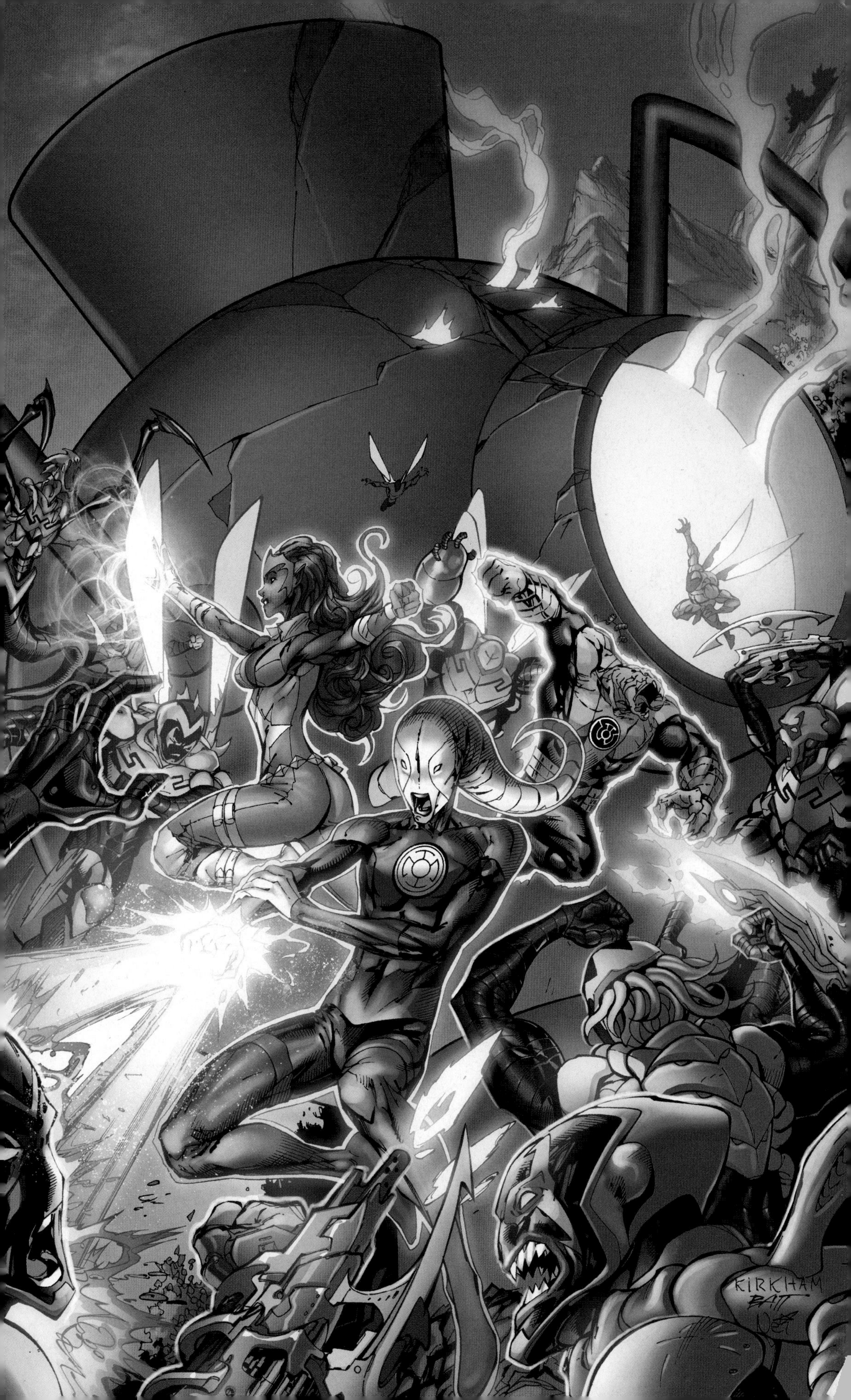
KIRKHAM
BATT

BEYOND HOPE

TONY BEDARD writer TYLER KIRKHAM – pgs 1-9, 12-15, 17-20 TOMAS GIORELLO – pgs 10, 11 & 16 pencillers BATT inker cover by TYLER KIRKHAM, BATT & NEI RUFFINC

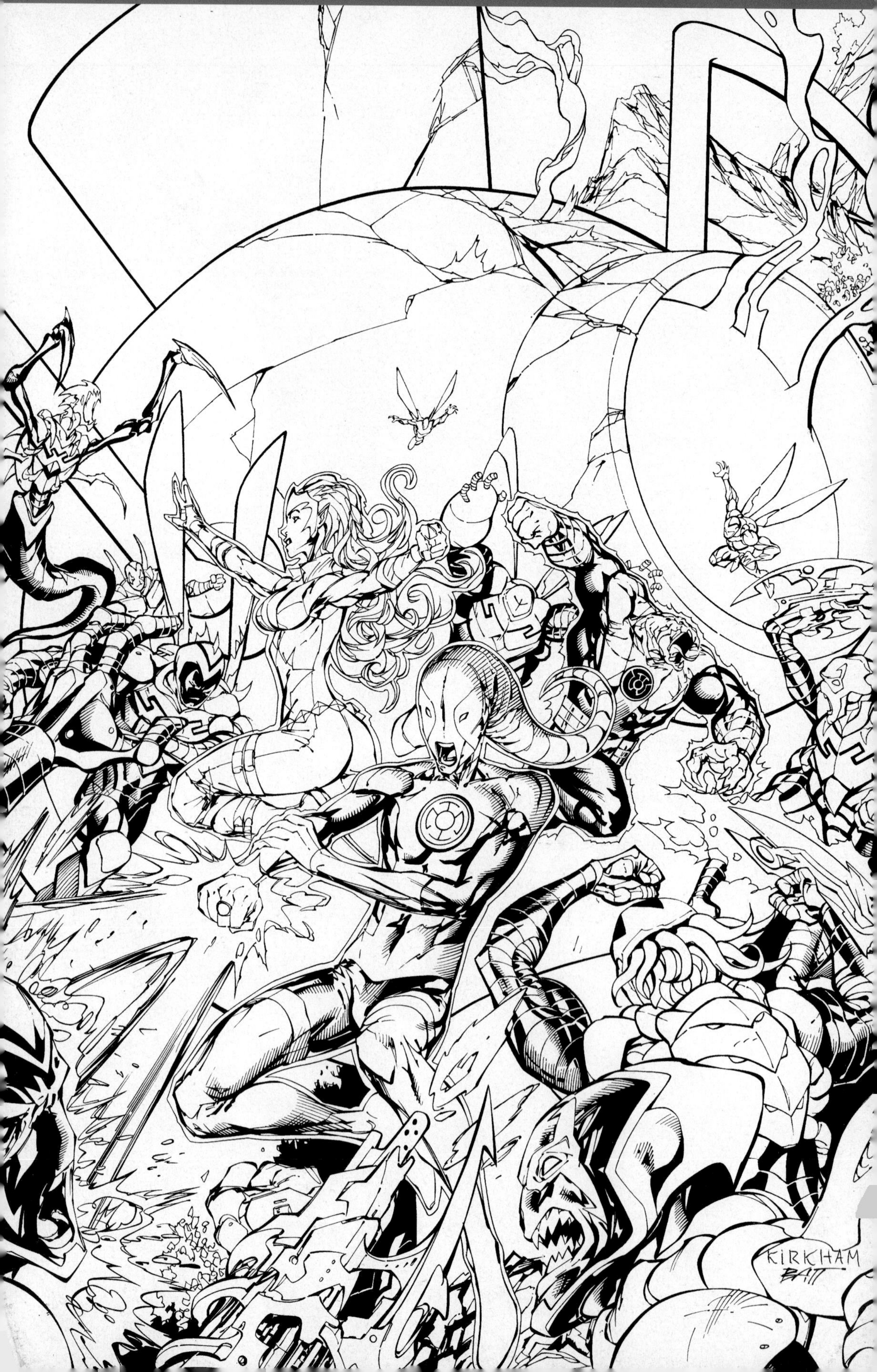
KIRKHAM
BATT

BEYOND HOPE

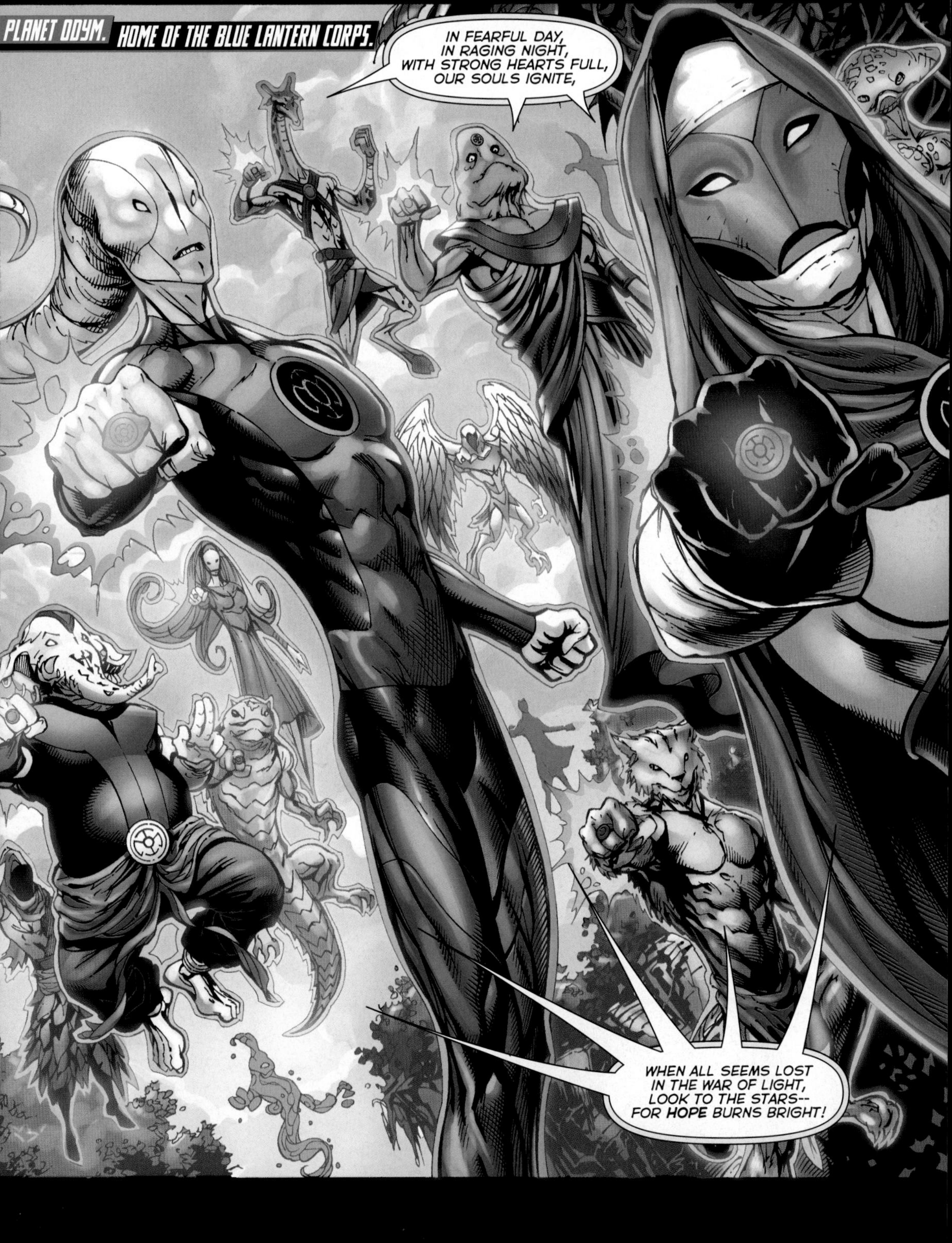
PLANET ODYM. HOME OF THE BLUE LANTERN CORPS.
IN FEARFUL DAY, IN RAGING NIGHT, WITH STRONG HEARTS FULL, OUR SOULS IGNITE,
WHEN ALL SEEMS LOST IN THE WAR OF LIGHT, LOOK TO THE STARS-- FOR **HOPE** BURNS BRIGHT!

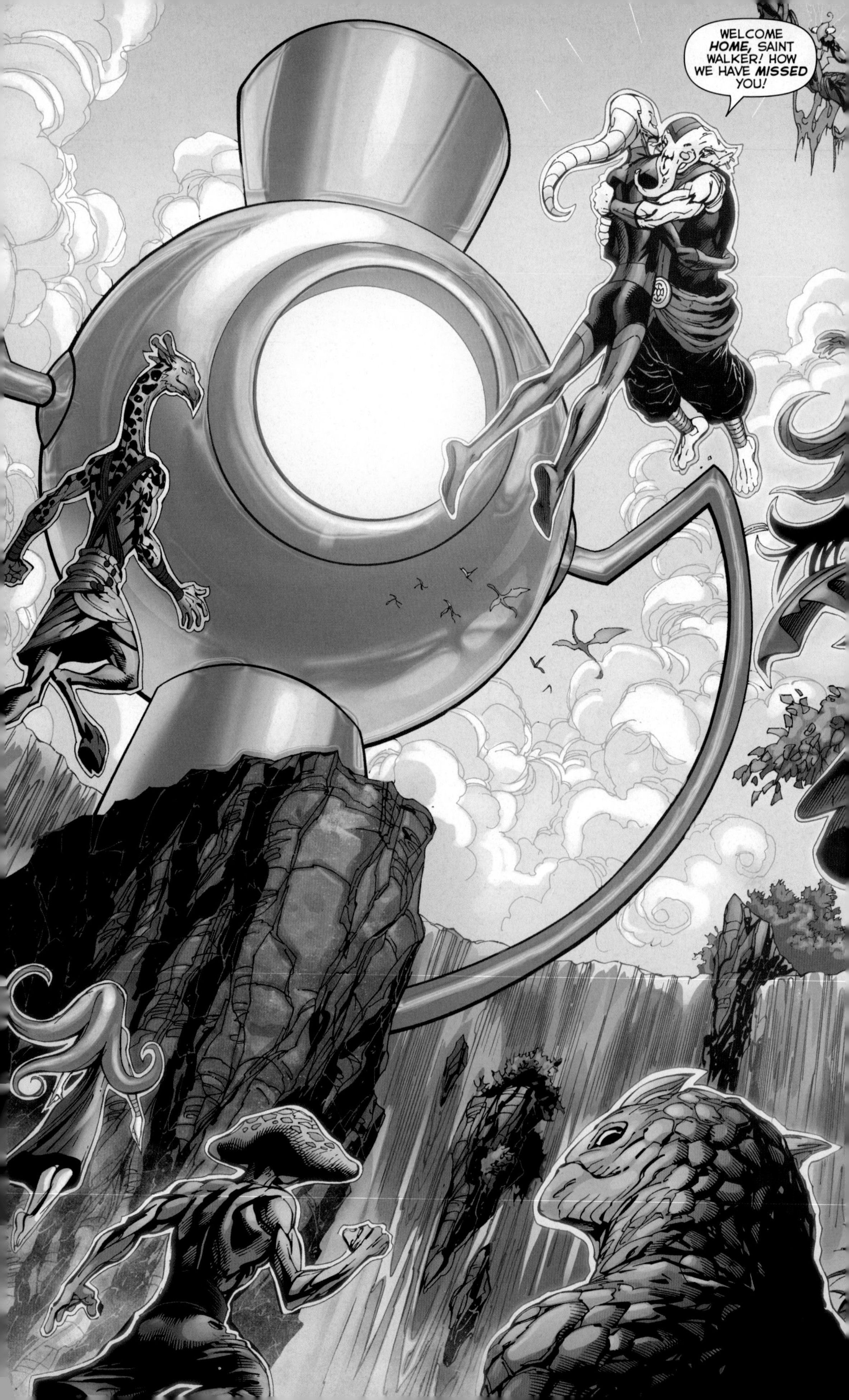
WELCOME HOME, SAINT WALKER! HOW WE HAVE MISSED YOU!

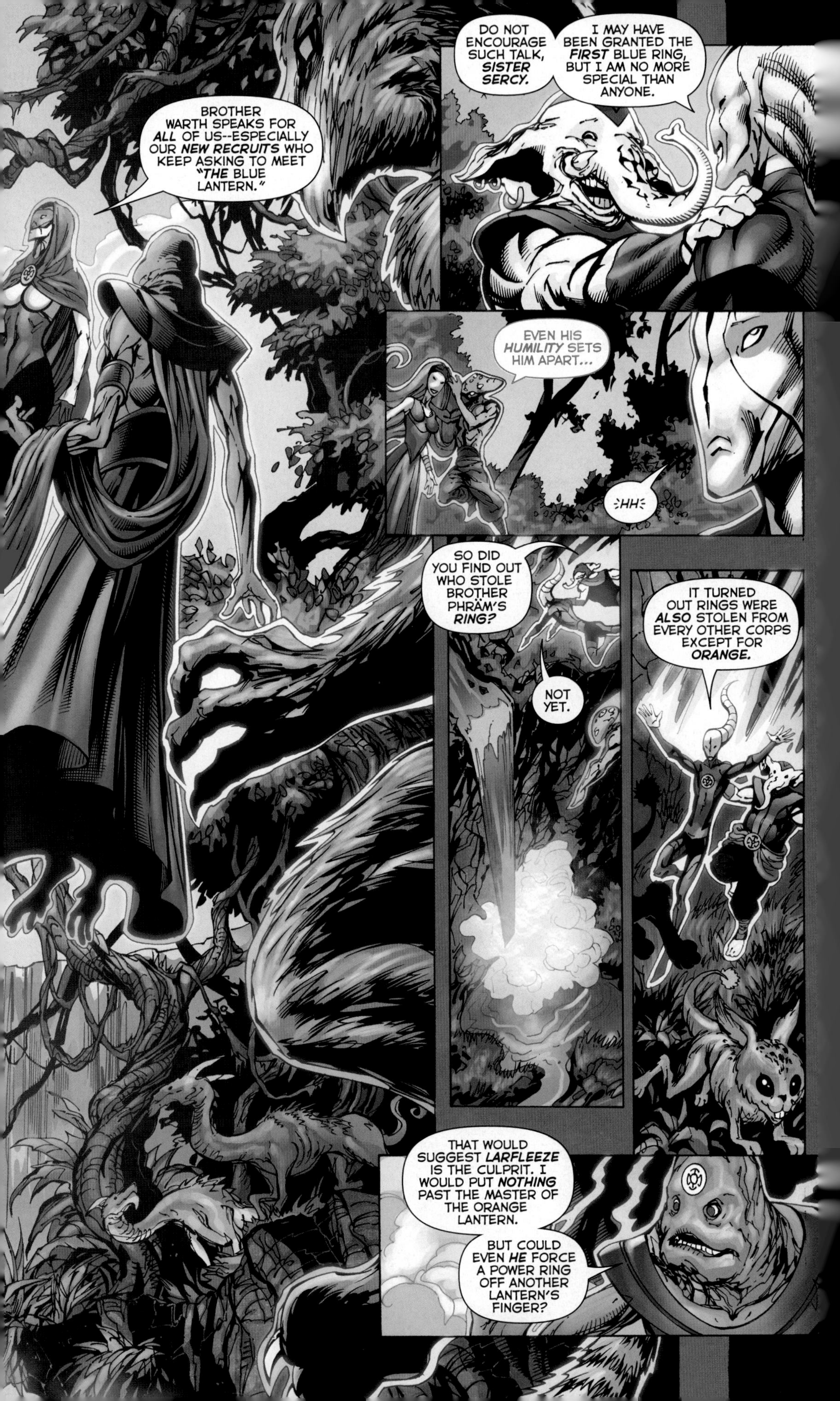
BROTHER WARTH SPEAKS FOR ALL OF US--ESPECIALLY OUR NEW RECRUITS WHO KEEP ASKING TO MEET "THE BLUE LANTERN."
DO NOT ENCOURAGE SUCH TALK, SISTER SERCY.
I MAY HAVE BEEN GRANTED THE FIRST BLUE RING, BUT I AM NO MORE SPECIAL THAN ANYONE.
EVEN HIS HUMILITY SETS HIM APART...
HH
SO DID YOU FIND OUT WHO STOLE BROTHER PHRÄM'S RING?
NOT YET.
IT TURNED OUT RINGS WERE ALSO STOLEN FROM EVERY OTHER CORPS EXCEPT FOR ORANGE.
THAT WOULD SUGGEST LARFLEEZE IS THE CULPRIT. I WOULD PUT NOTHING PAST THE MASTER OF THE ORANGE LANTERN.
BUT COULD EVEN HE FORCE A POWER RING OFF ANOTHER LANTERN'S FINGER?

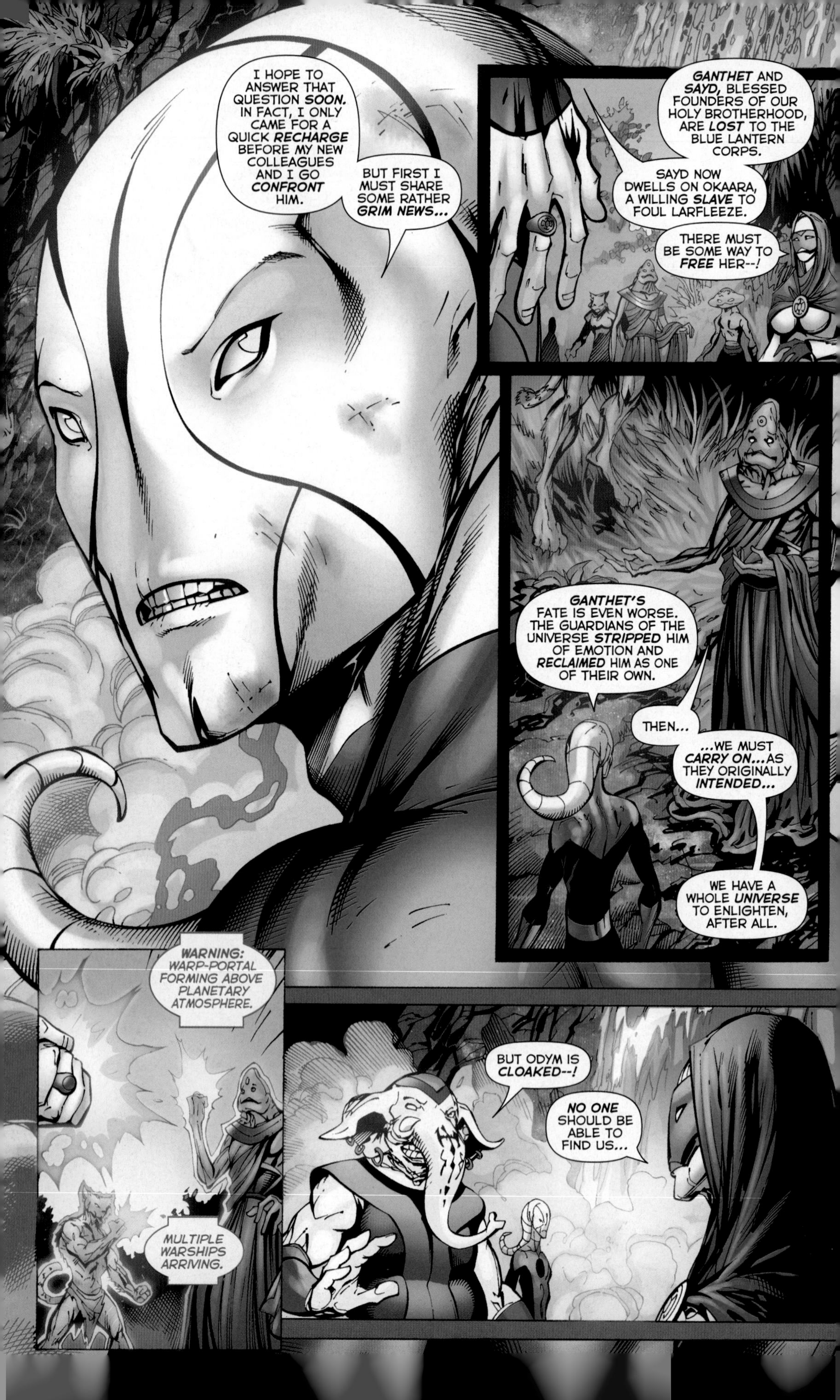
I HOPE TO ANSWER THAT QUESTION SOON. IN FACT, I ONLY CAME FOR A QUICK RECHARGE BEFORE MY NEW COLLEAGUES AND I GO CONFRONT HIM.
BUT FIRST I MUST SHARE SOME RATHER GRIM NEWS...
GANTHET AND SAYD, BLESSED FOUNDERS OF OUR HOLY BROTHERHOOD, ARE LOST TO THE BLUE LANTERN CORPS.
SAYD NOW DWELLS ON OKAARA, A WILLING SLAVE TO FOUL LARFLEEZE.
THERE MUST BE SOME WAY TO FREE HER--!
GANTHET'S FATE IS EVEN WORSE. THE GUARDIANS OF THE UNIVERSE STRIPPED HIM OF EMOTION AND RECLAIMED HIM AS ONE OF THEIR OWN.
THEN...
...WE MUST CARRY ON...AS THEY ORIGINALLY INTENDED...
WE HAVE A WHOLE UNIVERSE TO ENLIGHTEN, AFTER ALL.
WARNING: WARP-PORTAL FORMING ABOVE PLANETARY ATMOSPHERE.
MULTIPLE WARSHIPS ARRIVING.
BUT ODYM IS CLOAKED--!
NO ONE SHOULD BE ABLE TO FIND US...

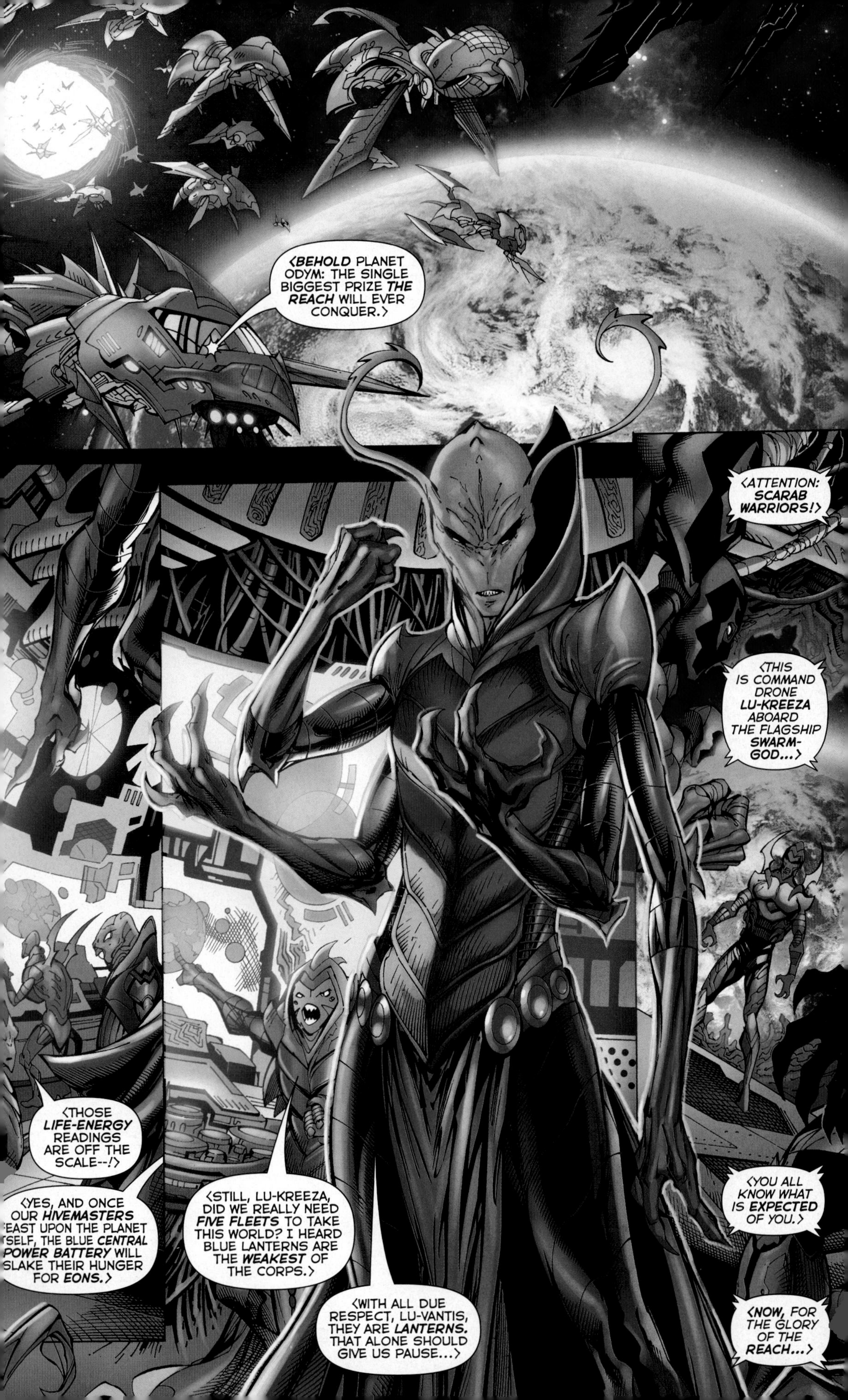
<BEHOLD PLANET ODYM: THE SINGLE BIGGEST PRIZE THE REACH WILL EVER CONQUER.>
<ATTENTION: SCARAB WARRIORS!>
<THIS IS COMMAND DRONE LU-KREEZA ABOARD THE FLAGSHIP SWARM-GOD...>
<THOSE LIFE-ENERGY READINGS ARE OFF THE SCALE--!>
<YES, AND ONCE OUR HIVEMASTERS FEAST UPON THE PLANET ITSELF, THE BLUE CENTRAL POWER BATTERY WILL SLAKE THEIR HUNGER FOR EONS.>
<STILL, LU-KREEZA, DID WE REALLY NEED FIVE FLEETS TO TAKE THIS WORLD? I HEARD BLUE LANTERNS ARE THE WEAKEST OF THE CORPS.>
<WITH ALL DUE RESPECT, LU-VANTIS, THEY ARE LANTERNS. THAT ALONE SHOULD GIVE US PAUSE...>
<YOU ALL KNOW WHAT IS EXPECTED OF YOU.>
<NOW, FOR THE GLORY OF THE REACH...>

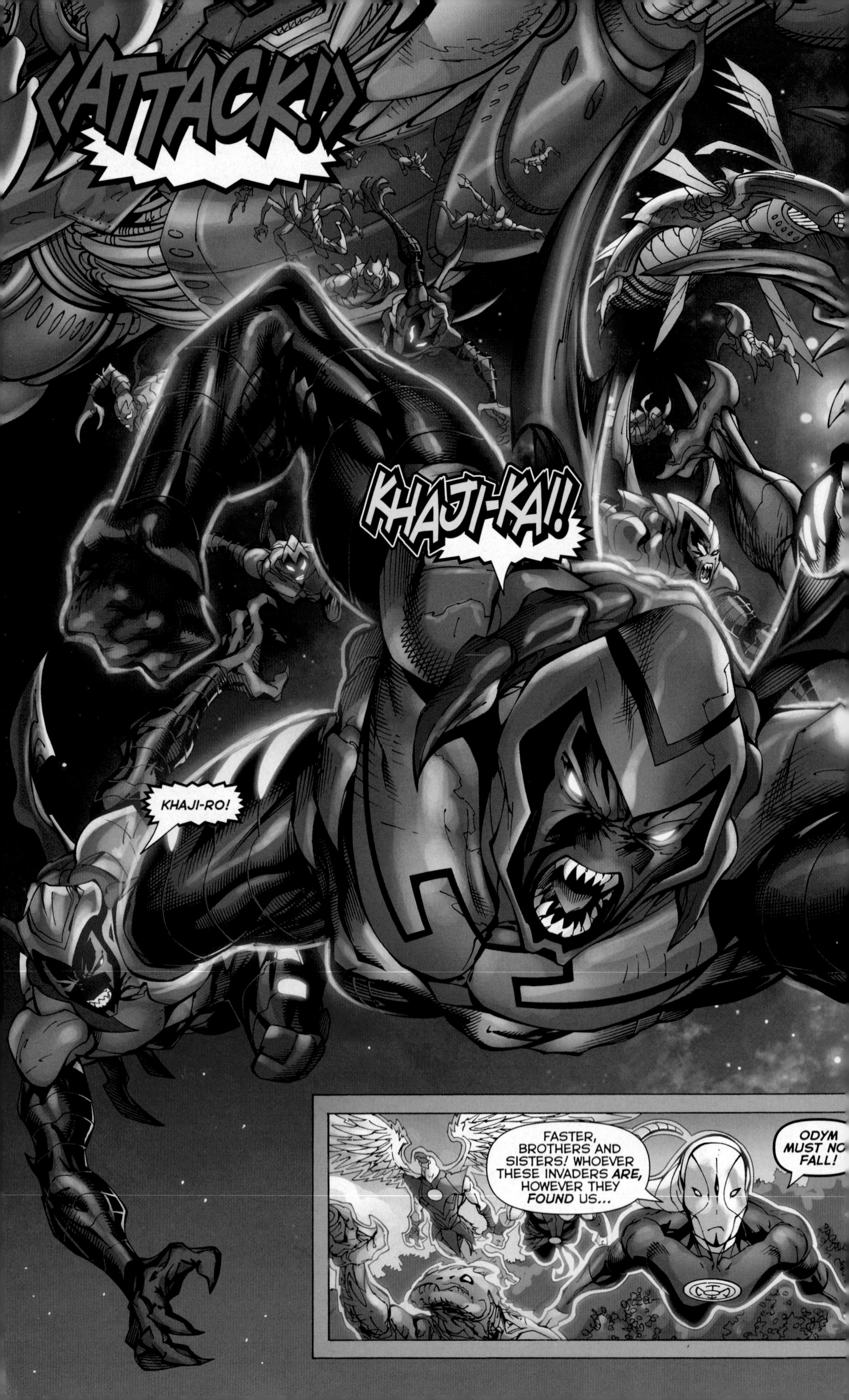

⟨ATTACK!⟩
KHAJI-KA!!
KHAJI-RO!
FASTER, BROTHERS AND SISTERS! WHOEVER THESE INVADERS *ARE*, HOWEVER THEY *FOUND* US...
ODYM MUST NO FALL!

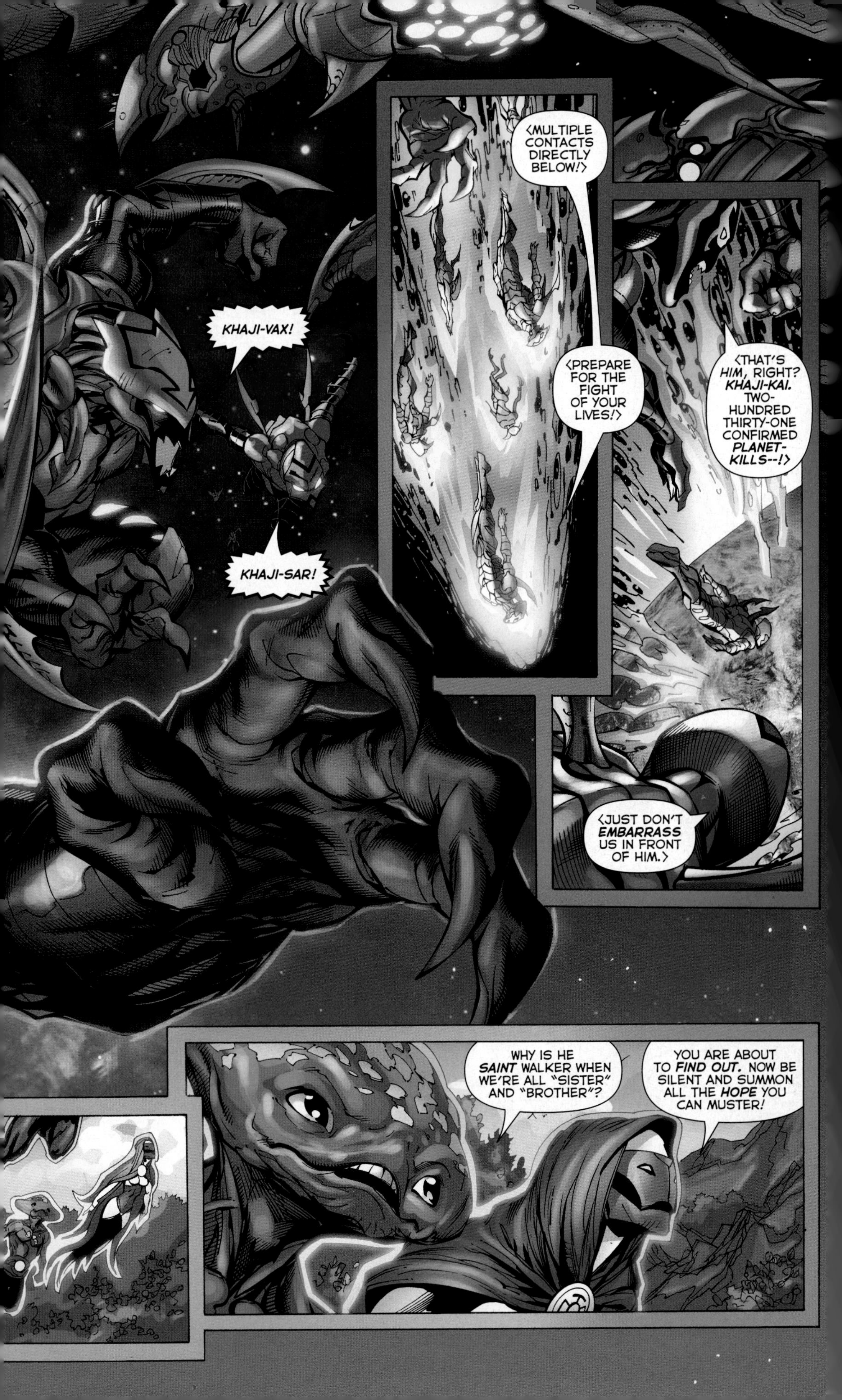

KHAJI-VAX!
KHAJI-SAR!
<MULTIPLE CONTACTS DIRECTLY BELOW!>
<PREPARE FOR THE FIGHT OF YOUR LIVES!>
<THAT'S HIM, RIGHT? KHAJI-KAI. TWO-HUNDRED THIRTY-ONE CONFIRMED PLANET-KILLS--!>
<JUST DON'T EMBARRASS US IN FRONT OF HIM.>
WHY IS HE SAINT WALKER WHEN WE'RE ALL "SISTER" AND "BROTHER"?
YOU ARE ABOUT TO FIND OUT. NOW BE SILENT AND SUMMON ALL THE HOPE YOU CAN MUSTER!

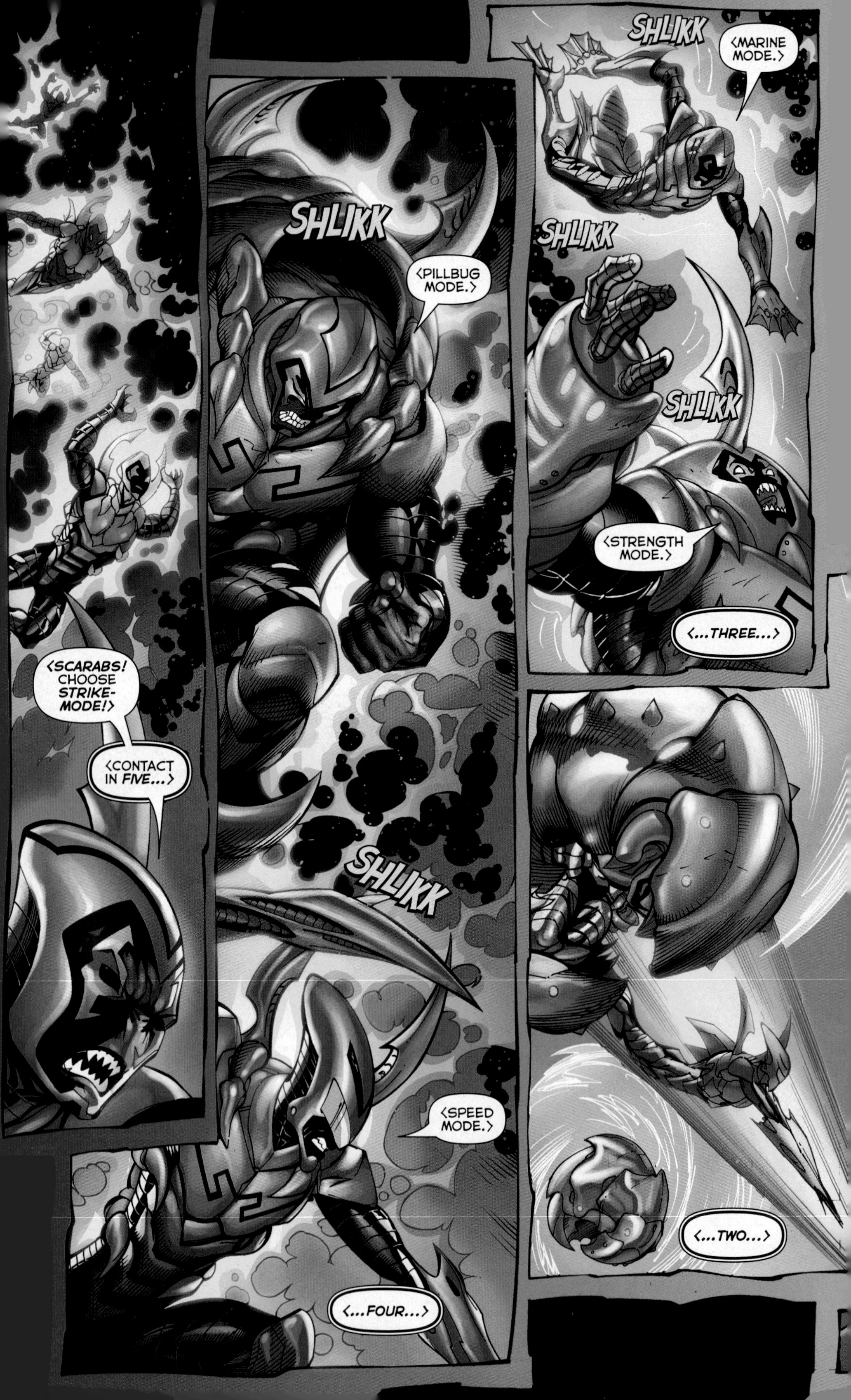

‹SCARABS! CHOOSE STRIKE-MODE!›
‹CONTACT IN FIVE...›
SHLIKK
‹PILLBUG MODE.›
SHLIKK
‹SPEED MODE.›
‹...FOUR...›
SHLIKK
‹MARINE MODE.›
SHLIKK
SHLIKK
‹STRENGTH MODE.›
‹...THREE...›
‹...TWO...›

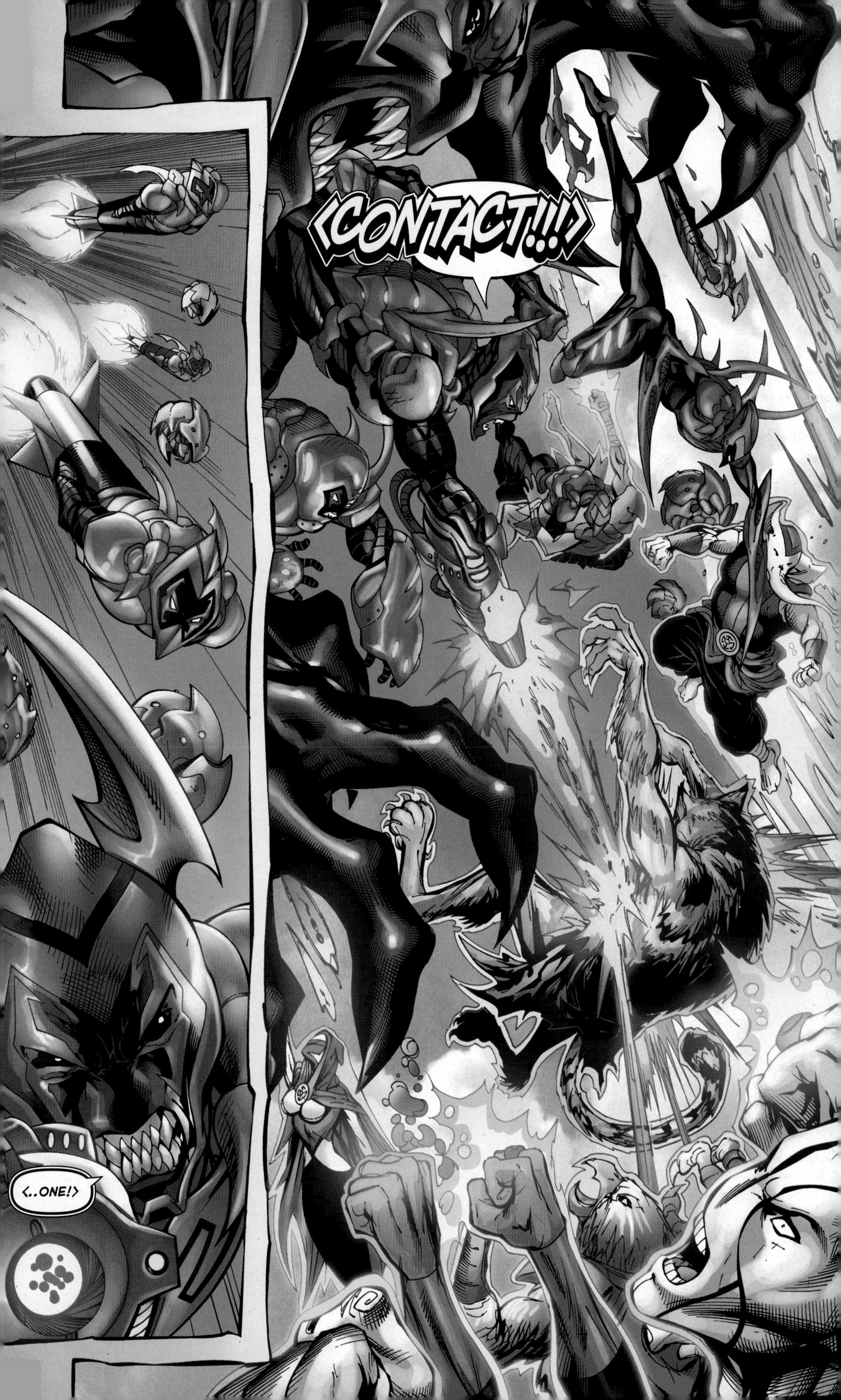
<CONTACT!!!>
<..ONE!>

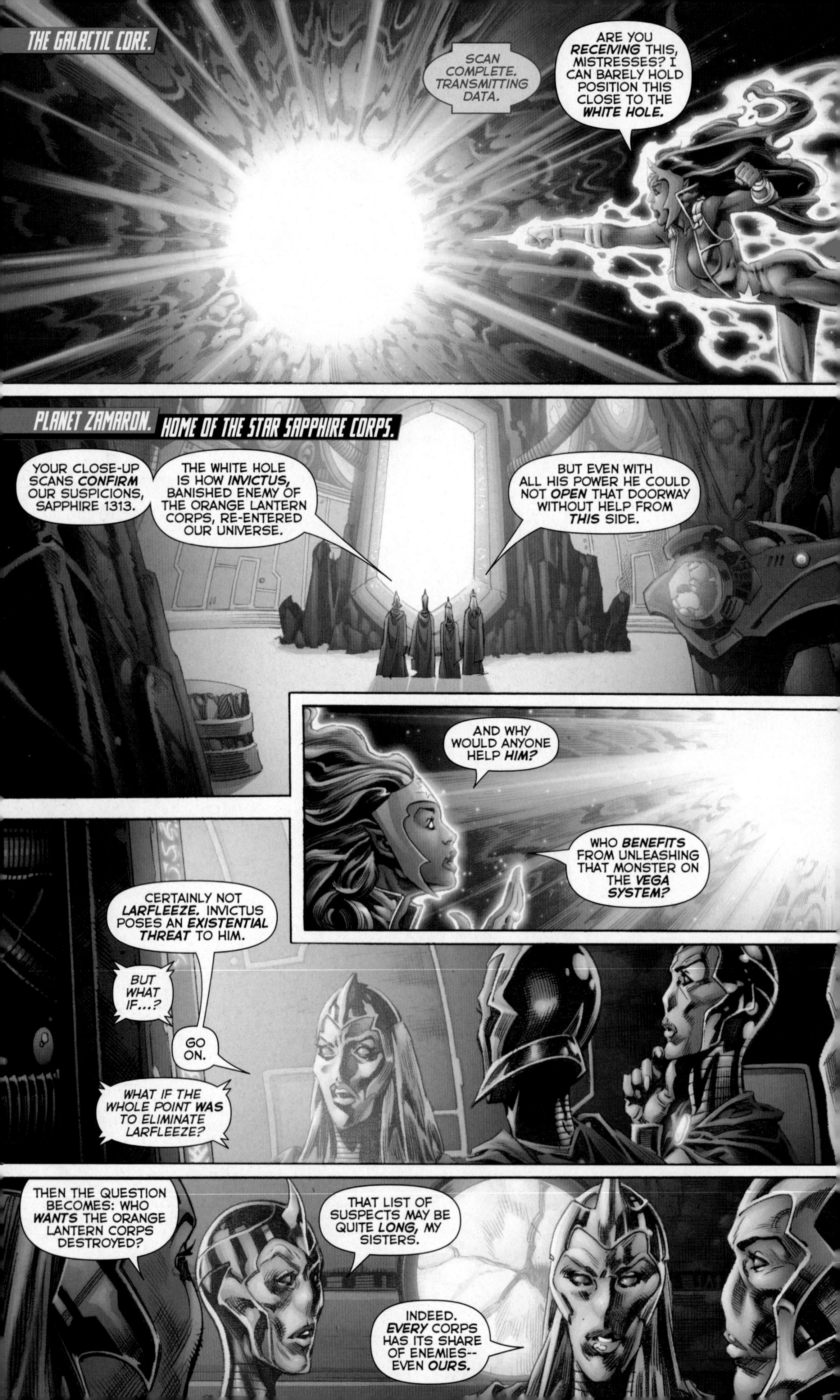
THE GALACTIC CORE.
SCAN COMPLETE. TRANSMITTING DATA.
ARE YOU RECEIVING THIS, MISTRESSES? I CAN BARELY HOLD POSITION THIS CLOSE TO THE WHITE HOLE.
PLANET ZAMARON. HOME OF THE STAR SAPPHIRE CORPS.
YOUR CLOSE-UP SCANS CONFIRM OUR SUSPICIONS, SAPPHIRE 1313.
THE WHITE HOLE IS HOW INVICTUS, BANISHED ENEMY OF THE ORANGE LANTERN CORPS, RE-ENTERED OUR UNIVERSE.
BUT EVEN WITH ALL HIS POWER HE COULD NOT OPEN THAT DOORWAY WITHOUT HELP FROM THIS SIDE.
AND WHY WOULD ANYONE HELP HIM?
WHO BENEFITS FROM UNLEASHING THAT MONSTER ON THE VEGA SYSTEM?
CERTAINLY NOT LARFLEEZE. INVICTUS POSES AN EXISTENTIAL THREAT TO HIM.
BUT WHAT IF...?
GO ON.
WHAT IF THE WHOLE POINT WAS TO ELIMINATE LARFLEEZE?
THEN THE QUESTION BECOMES: WHO WANTS THE ORANGE LANTERN CORPS DESTROYED?
THAT LIST OF SUSPECTS MAY BE QUITE LONG, MY SISTERS.
INDEED. EVERY CORPS HAS ITS SHARE OF ENEMIES-- EVEN OURS.

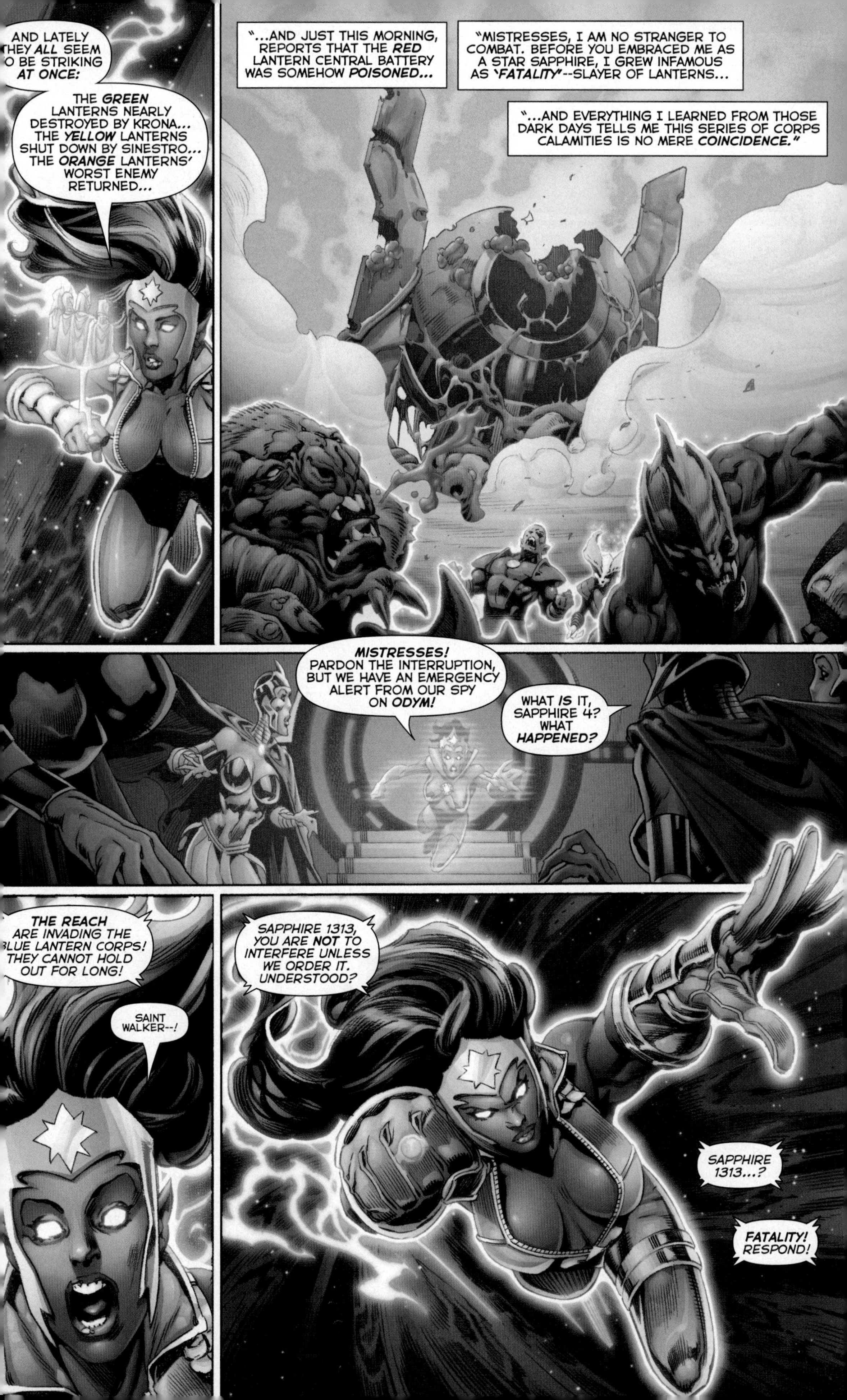

AND LATELY THEY *ALL* SEEM TO BE STRIKING *AT ONCE:*
THE *GREEN* LANTERNS NEARLY DESTROYED BY KRONA... THE *YELLOW* LANTERNS SHUT DOWN BY SINESTRO... THE *ORANGE* LANTERNS' WORST ENEMY RETURNED...
"...AND JUST THIS MORNING, REPORTS THAT THE *RED* LANTERN CENTRAL BATTERY WAS SOMEHOW *POISONED*...
"MISTRESSES, I AM NO STRANGER TO COMBAT. BEFORE YOU EMBRACED ME AS A STAR SAPPHIRE, I GREW INFAMOUS AS *'FATALITY'*--SLAYER OF LANTERNS...
"...AND EVERYTHING I LEARNED FROM THOSE DARK DAYS TELLS ME THIS SERIES OF CORPS CALAMITIES IS NO MERE *COINCIDENCE."*
MISTRESSES! PARDON THE INTERRUPTION, BUT WE HAVE AN EMERGENCY ALERT FROM OUR SPY ON *ODYM!*
WHAT *IS* IT, SAPPHIRE 4? WHAT *HAPPENED?*
THE REACH ARE INVADING THE BLUE LANTERN CORPS! THEY CANNOT HOLD OUT FOR LONG!
SAINT WALKER--!
SAPPHIRE 1313, YOU ARE *NOT* TO INTERFERE UNLESS WE ORDER IT. UNDERSTOOD?
SAPPHIRE 1313...?
FATALITY! RESPOND!

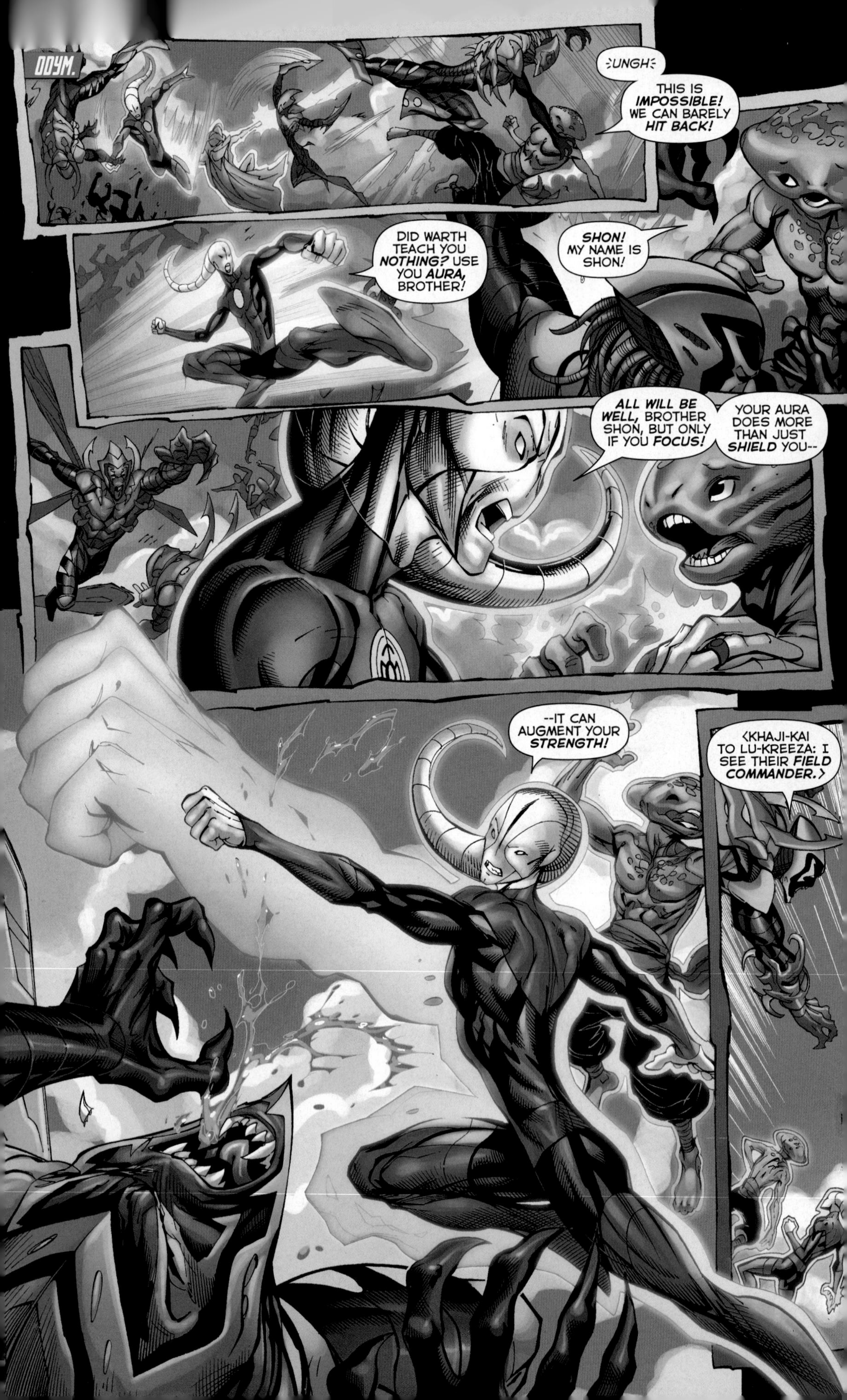
ODYM.
<UNGH>
THIS IS IMPOSSIBLE! WE CAN BARELY HIT BACK!
DID WARTH TEACH YOU NOTHING? USE YOU AURA, BROTHER!
SHON! MY NAME IS SHON!
ALL WILL BE WELL, BROTHER SHON, BUT ONLY IF YOU FOCUS!
YOUR AURA DOES MORE THAN JUST SHIELD YOU--
--IT CAN AUGMENT YOUR STRENGTH!
<KHAJI-KAI TO LU-KREEZA: I SEE THEIR FIELD COMMANDER.>

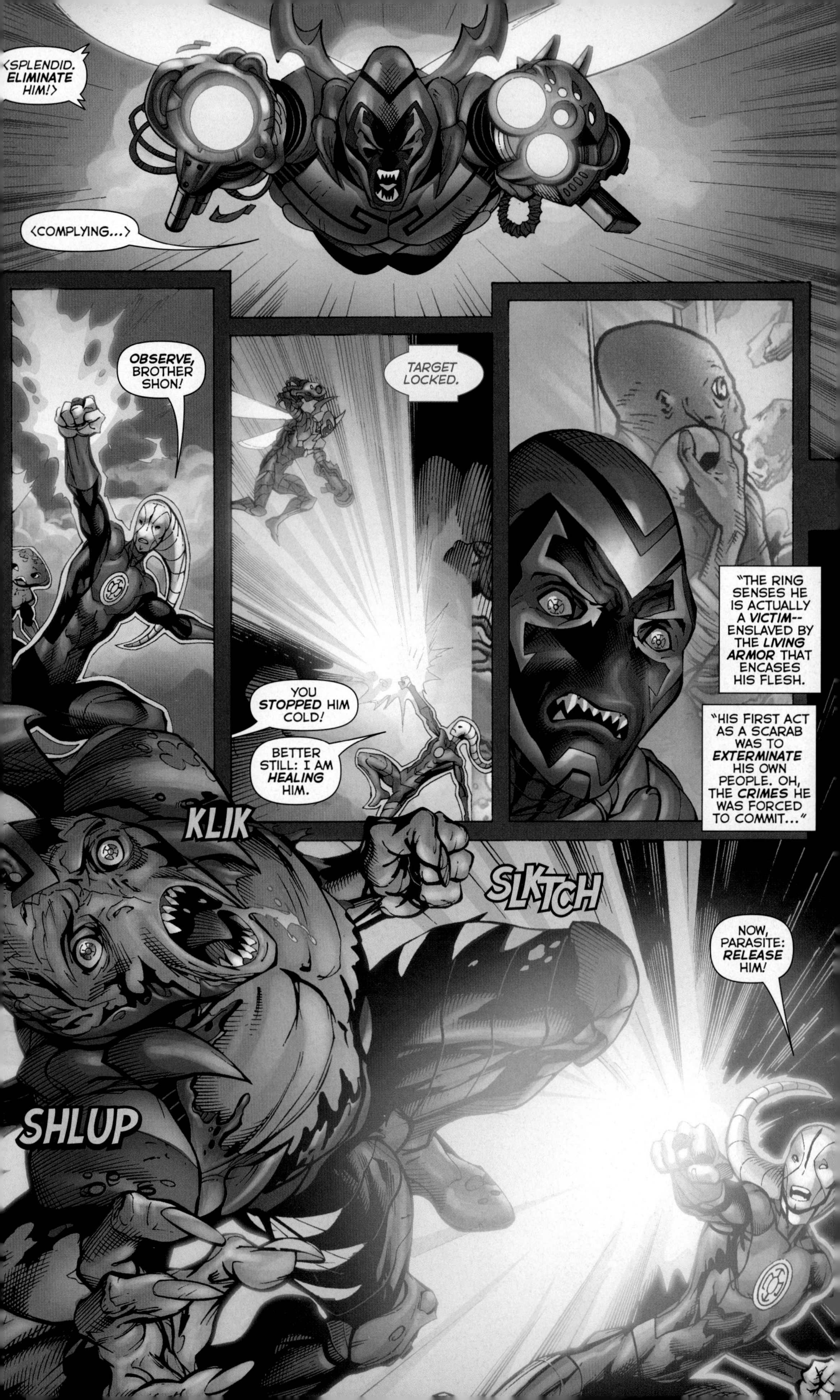

<SPLENDID. ELIMINATE HIM!>
<COMPLYING...>
OBSERVE, BROTHER SHON!
TARGET LOCKED.
YOU STOPPED HIM COLD!
BETTER STILL: I AM HEALING HIM.
"THE RING SENSES HE IS ACTUALLY A VICTIM--ENSLAVED BY THE LIVING ARMOR THAT ENCASES HIS FLESH.
"HIS FIRST ACT AS A SCARAB WAS TO EXTERMINATE HIS OWN PEOPLE. OH, THE CRIMES HE WAS FORCED TO COMMIT..."
KLIK
SLKTCH
NOW, PARASITE: RELEASE HIM!
SHLUP

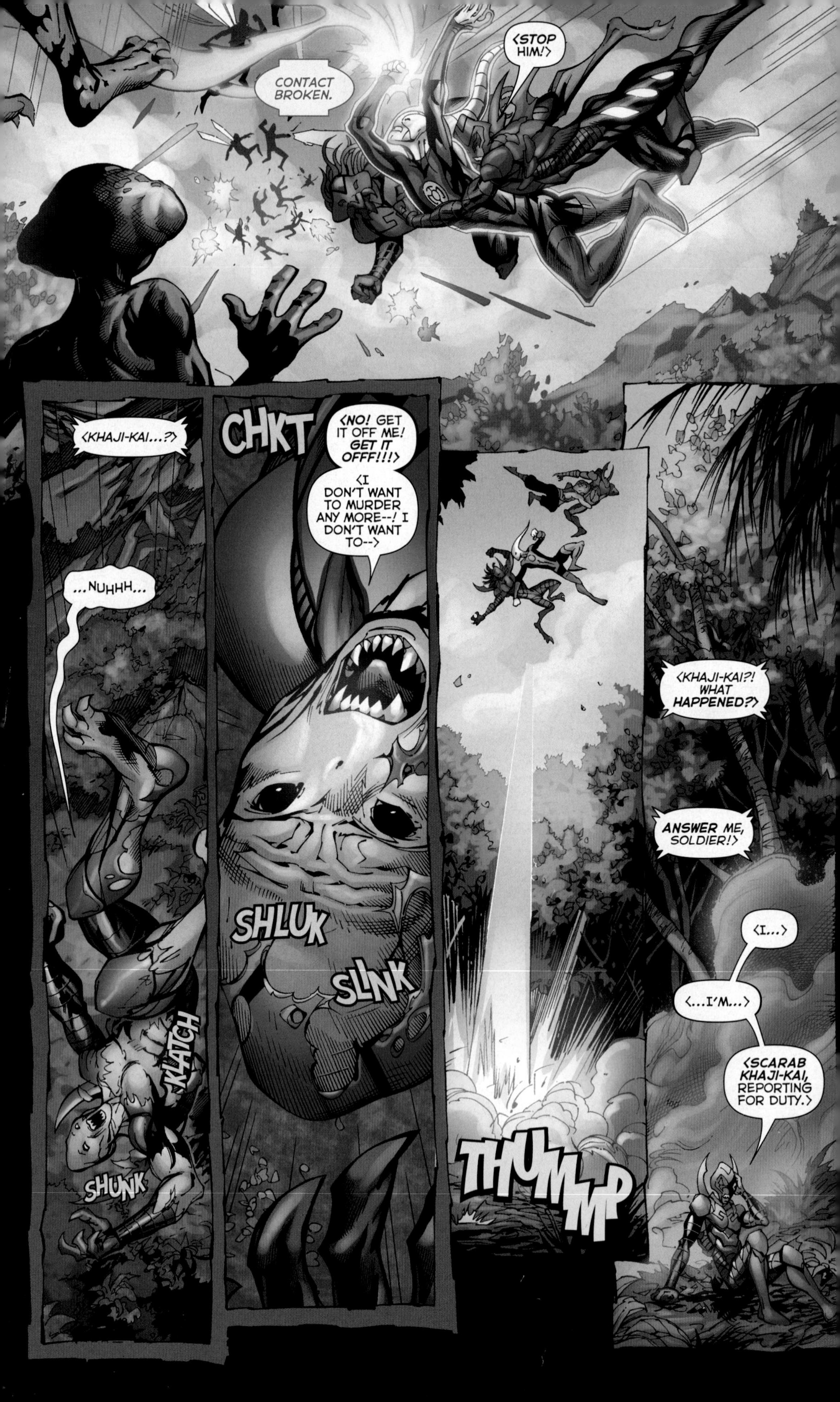
CONTACT BROKEN.
<STOP HIM!>
<KHAJI-KAI...?>
...NUHHH...
KLATCH
SHUNK
CHKT
<NO! GET IT OFF ME! GET IT OFFF!!!>
<I DON'T WANT TO MURDER ANY MORE--! I DON'T WANT TO-->
SHLUK
SLINK
THUMMMP
<KHAJI-KAI?! WHAT HAPPENED?>
<ANSWER ME, SOLDIER!>
<I...>
<...I'M...>
<SCARAB KHAJI-KAI, REPORTING FOR DUTY.>

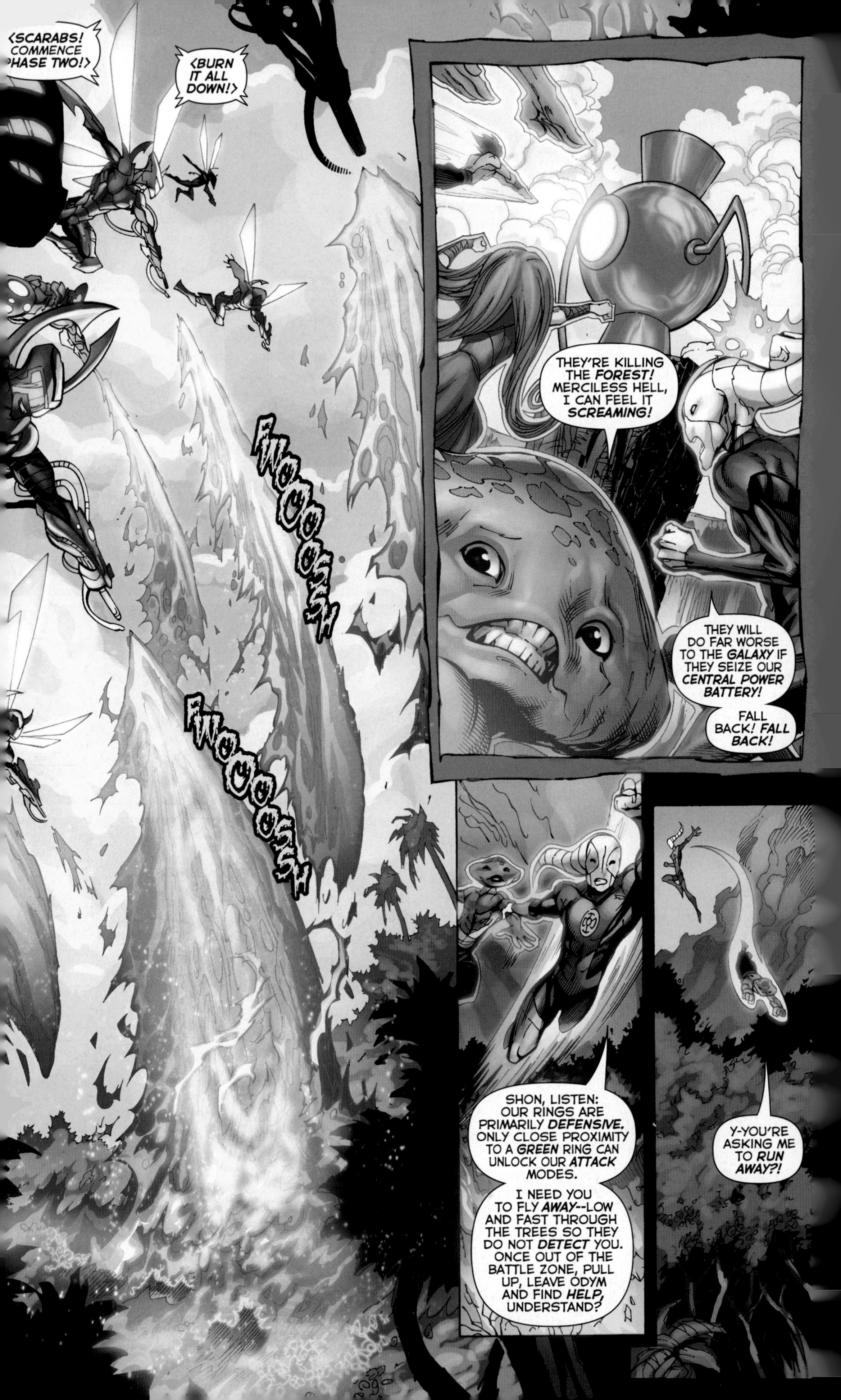

<SCARABS! COMMENCE PHASE TWO!>
<BURN IT ALL DOWN!>
FWOOOOSH
FWOOOOSH
THEY'RE KILLING THE FOREST! MERCILESS HELL, I CAN FEEL IT SCREAMING!
THEY WILL DO FAR WORSE TO THE GALAXY IF THEY SEIZE OUR CENTRAL POWER BATTERY!
FALL BACK! FALL BACK!
SHON, LISTEN: OUR RINGS ARE PRIMARILY DEFENSIVE. ONLY CLOSE PROXIMITY TO A GREEN RING CAN UNLOCK OUR ATTACK MODES.
I NEED YOU TO FLY AWAY--LOW AND FAST THROUGH THE TREES SO THEY DO NOT DETECT YOU. ONCE OUT OF THE BATTLE ZONE, PULL UP, LEAVE ODYM AND FIND HELP, UNDERSTAND?
Y-YOU'RE ASKING ME TO RUN AWAY?!

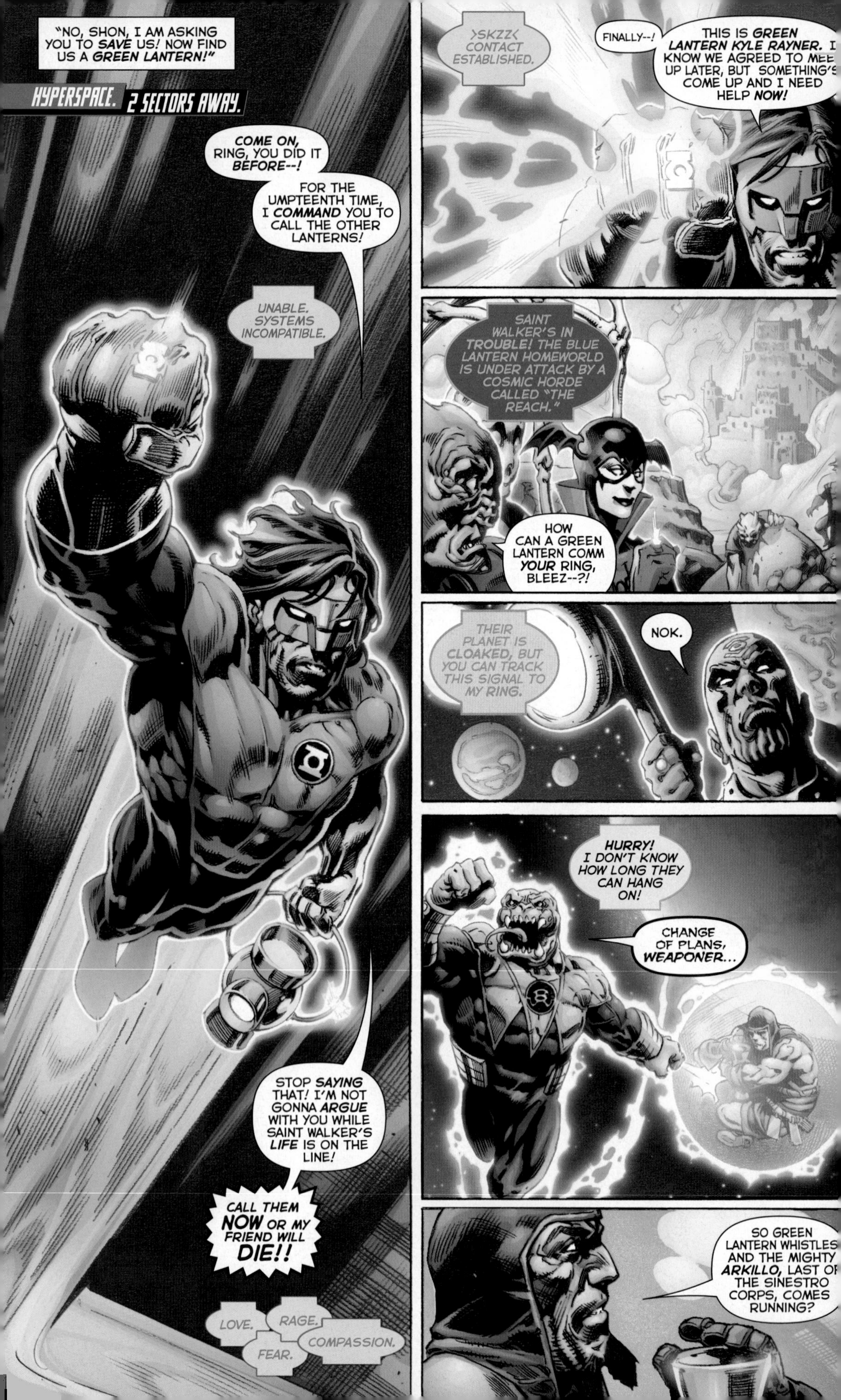

"NO, SHON, I AM ASKING YOU TO SAVE US! NOW FIND US A GREEN LANTERN!"
HYPERSPACE. 2 SECTORS AWAY.
COME ON, RING, YOU DID IT BEFORE--!
FOR THE UMPTEENTH TIME, I COMMAND YOU TO CALL THE OTHER LANTERNS!
UNABLE. SYSTEMS INCOMPATIBLE.
STOP SAYING THAT! I'M NOT GONNA ARGUE WITH YOU WHILE SAINT WALKER'S LIFE IS ON THE LINE!
CALL THEM NOW OR MY FRIEND WILL DIE!!
LOVE.
RAGE.
FEAR.
COMPASSION.
>SKZZ< CONTACT ESTABLISHED.
FINALLY--!
THIS IS GREEN LANTERN KYLE RAYNER. I KNOW WE AGREED TO MEET UP LATER, BUT SOMETHING'S COME UP AND I NEED HELP NOW!
SAINT WALKER'S IN TROUBLE! THE BLUE LANTERN HOMEWORLD IS UNDER ATTACK BY A COSMIC HORDE CALLED "THE REACH."
HOW CAN A GREEN LANTERN COMM YOUR RING, BLEEZ--?!
THEIR PLANET IS CLOAKED, BUT YOU CAN TRACK THIS SIGNAL TO MY RING.
NOK.
HURRY! I DON'T KNOW HOW LONG THEY CAN HANG ON!
CHANGE OF PLANS, WEAPONER...
SO GREEN LANTERN WHISTLES AND THE MIGHTY ARKILLO, LAST OF THE SINESTRO CORPS, COMES RUNNING?

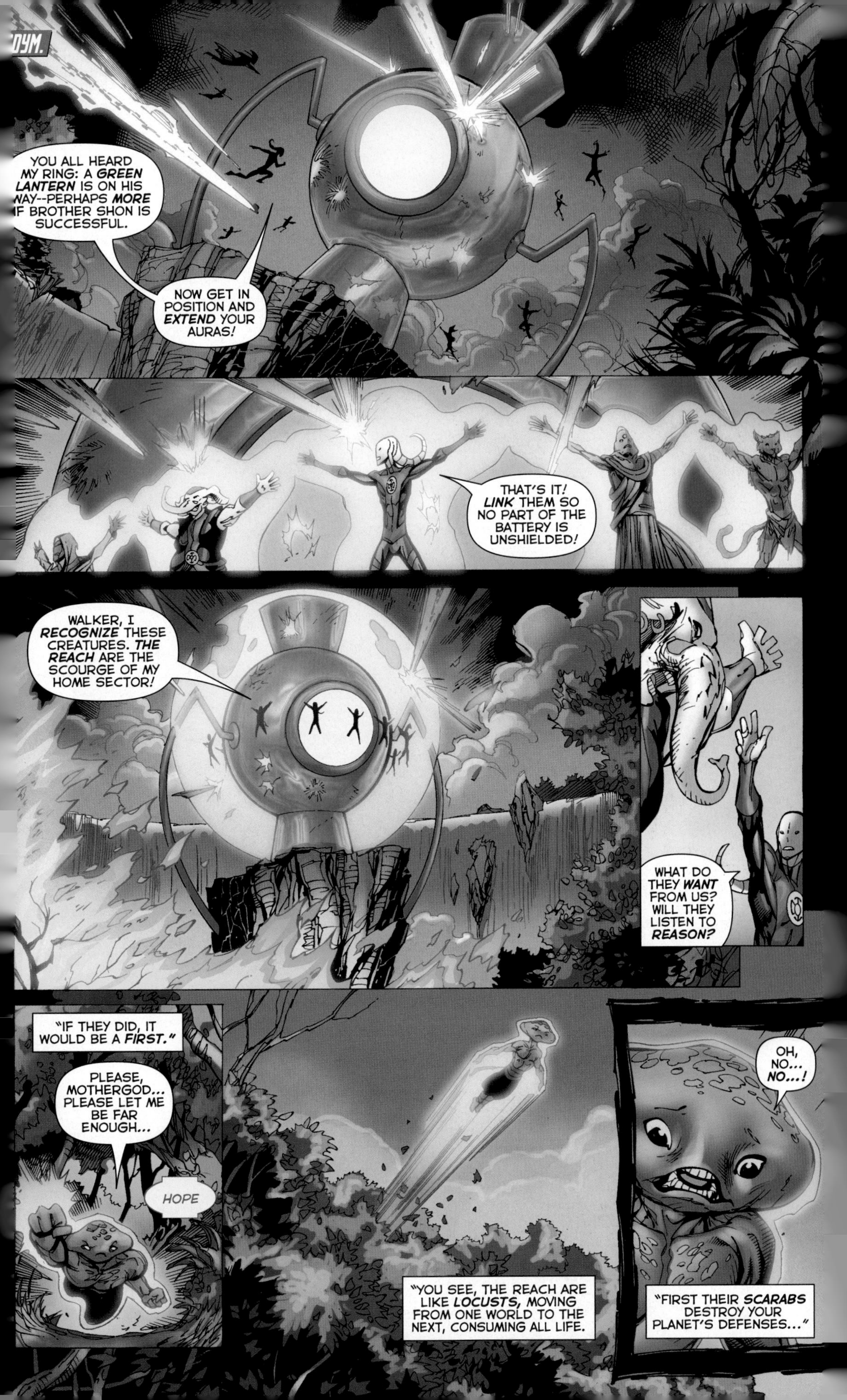
YOU ALL HEARD MY RING: A GREEN LANTERN IS ON HIS WAY--PERHAPS MORE IF BROTHER SHON IS SUCCESSFUL.
NOW GET IN POSITION AND EXTEND YOUR AURAS!
THAT'S IT! LINK THEM SO NO PART OF THE BATTERY IS UNSHIELDED!
WALKER, I RECOGNIZE THESE CREATURES. THE REACH ARE THE SCOURGE OF MY HOME SECTOR!
WHAT DO THEY WANT FROM US? WILL THEY LISTEN TO REASON?
"IF THEY DID, IT WOULD BE A FIRST."
PLEASE, MOTHERGOD... PLEASE LET ME BE FAR ENOUGH...
HOPE
"YOU SEE, THE REACH ARE LIKE LOCUSTS, MOVING FROM ONE WORLD TO THE NEXT, CONSUMING ALL LIFE.
OH, NO... NO...!
"FIRST THEIR SCARABS DESTROY YOUR PLANET'S DEFENSES..."

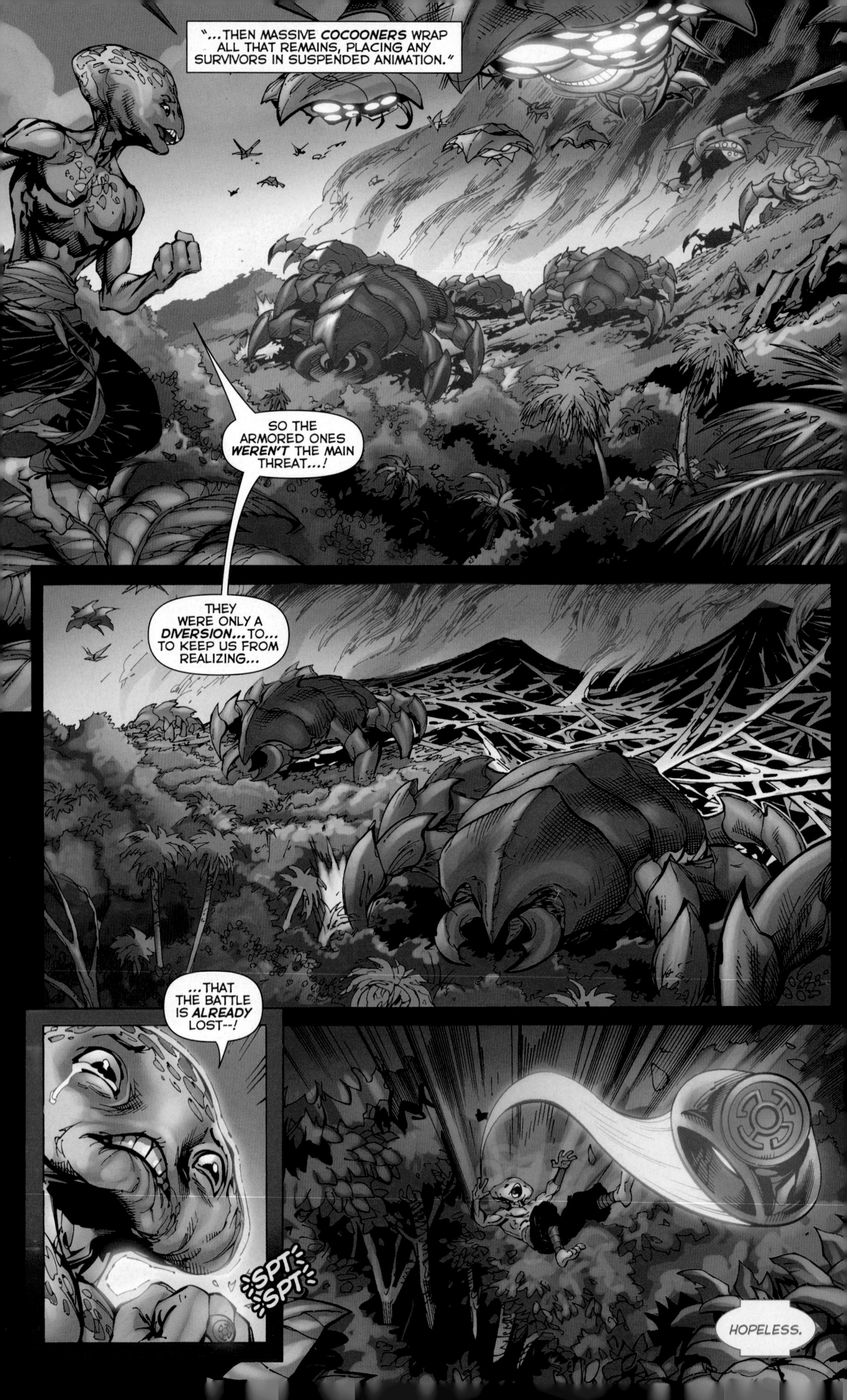
"...THEN MASSIVE COCOONERS WRAP ALL THAT REMAINS, PLACING ANY SURVIVORS IN SUSPENDED ANIMATION."
SO THE ARMORED ONES WEREN'T THE MAIN THREAT...!
THEY WERE ONLY A DIVERSION...TO... TO KEEP US FROM REALIZING...
...THAT THE BATTLE IS ALREADY LOST--!
SPT SPT
HOPELESS.

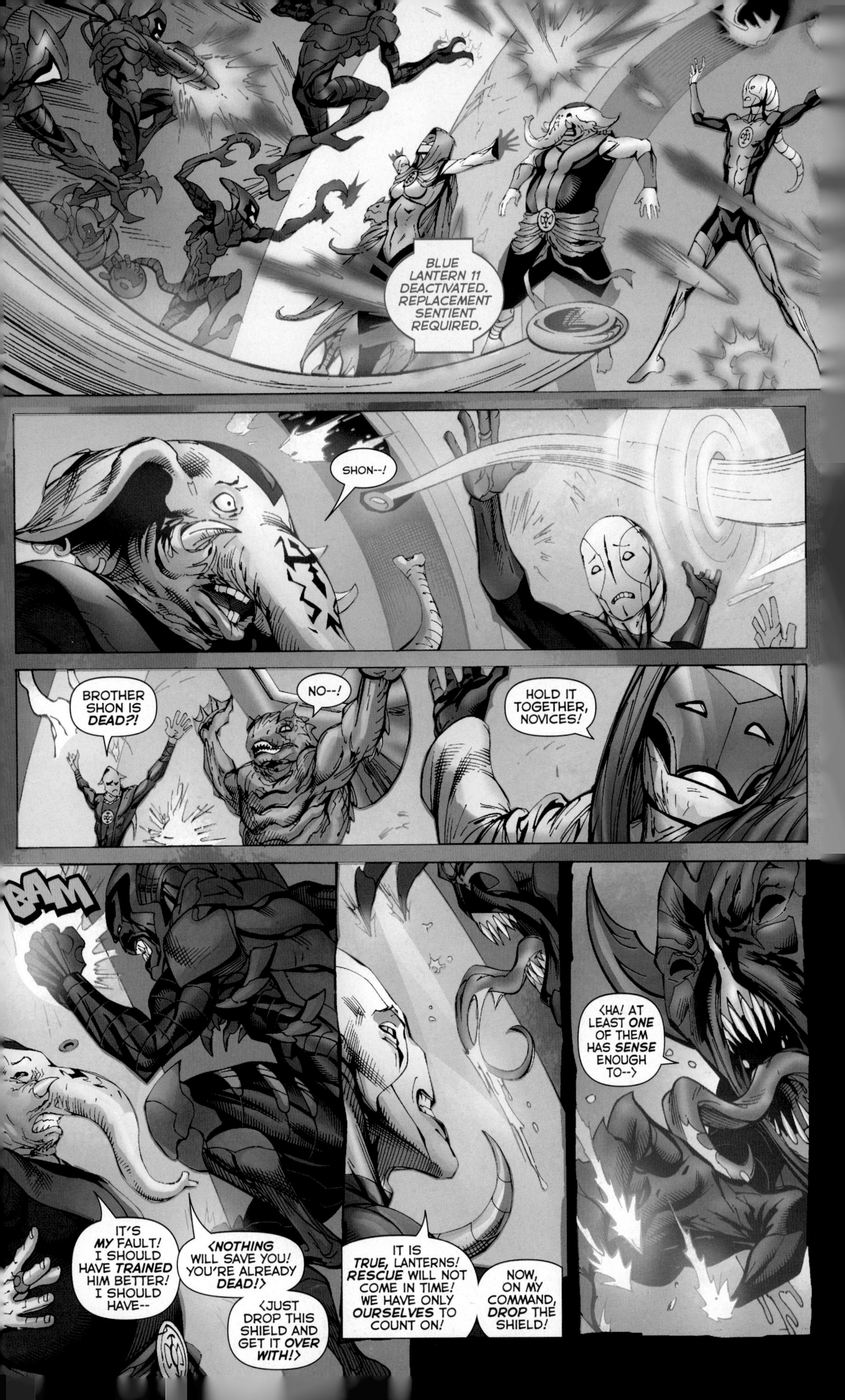
BLUE LANTERN 11 DEACTIVATED. REPLACEMENT SENTIENT REQUIRED.
SHON--!
BROTHER SHON IS DEAD?!
NO--!
HOLD IT TOGETHER, NOVICES!
BAM
IT'S MY FAULT! I SHOULD HAVE TRAINED HIM BETTER! I SHOULD HAVE--
<NOTHING WILL SAVE YOU! YOU'RE ALREADY DEAD!>
<JUST DROP THIS SHIELD AND GET IT OVER WITH!>
IT IS TRUE, LANTERNS! RESCUE WILL NOT COME IN TIME! WE HAVE ONLY OURSELVES TO COUNT ON!
NOW, ON MY COMMAND, DROP THE SHIELD!
<HA! AT LEAST ONE OF THEM HAS SENSE ENOUGH TO-->

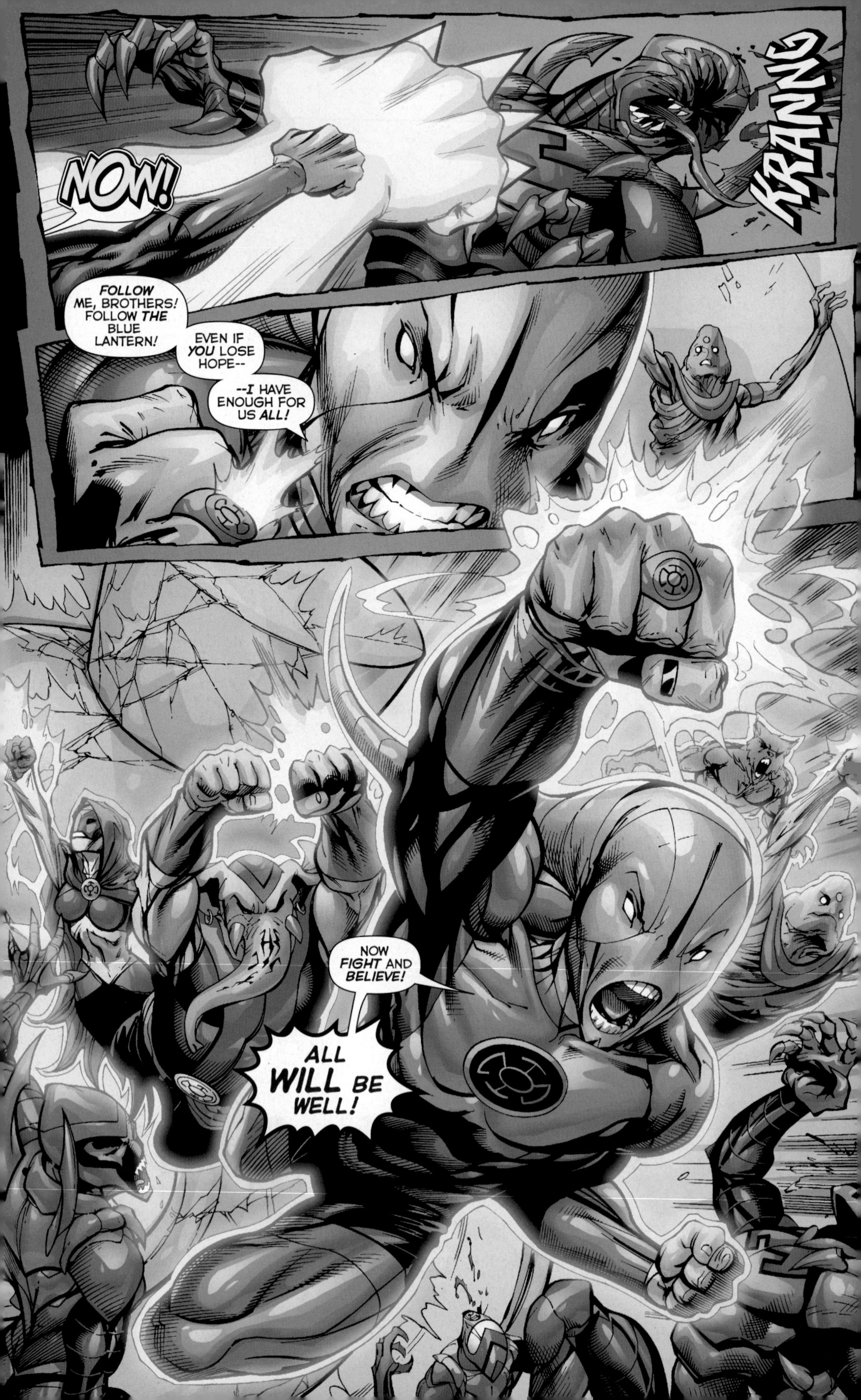
NOW!
KRANNG
FOLLOW ME, BROTHERS! FOLLOW THE BLUE LANTERN!
EVEN IF YOU LOSE HOPE--
--I HAVE ENOUGH FOR US ALL!
NOW FIGHT AND BELIEVE!
ALL WILL BE WELL!

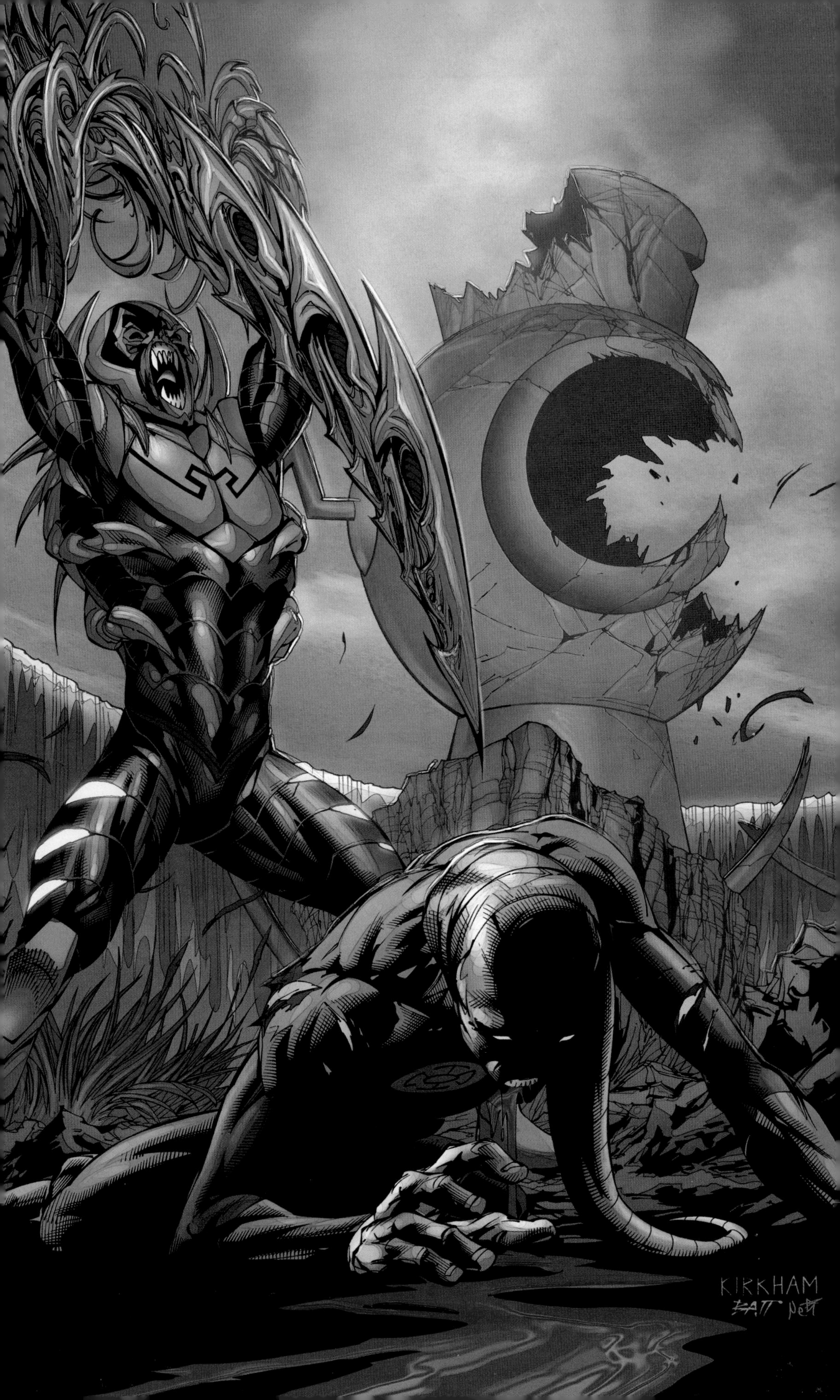
KIRKHAM

BEYOND HOPE: CONCLUSION

TONY BEDARD writer **TOMAS GIORELLO** penciller cover by **TYLER KIRKHAM, BATT & NEI RUFFINO**

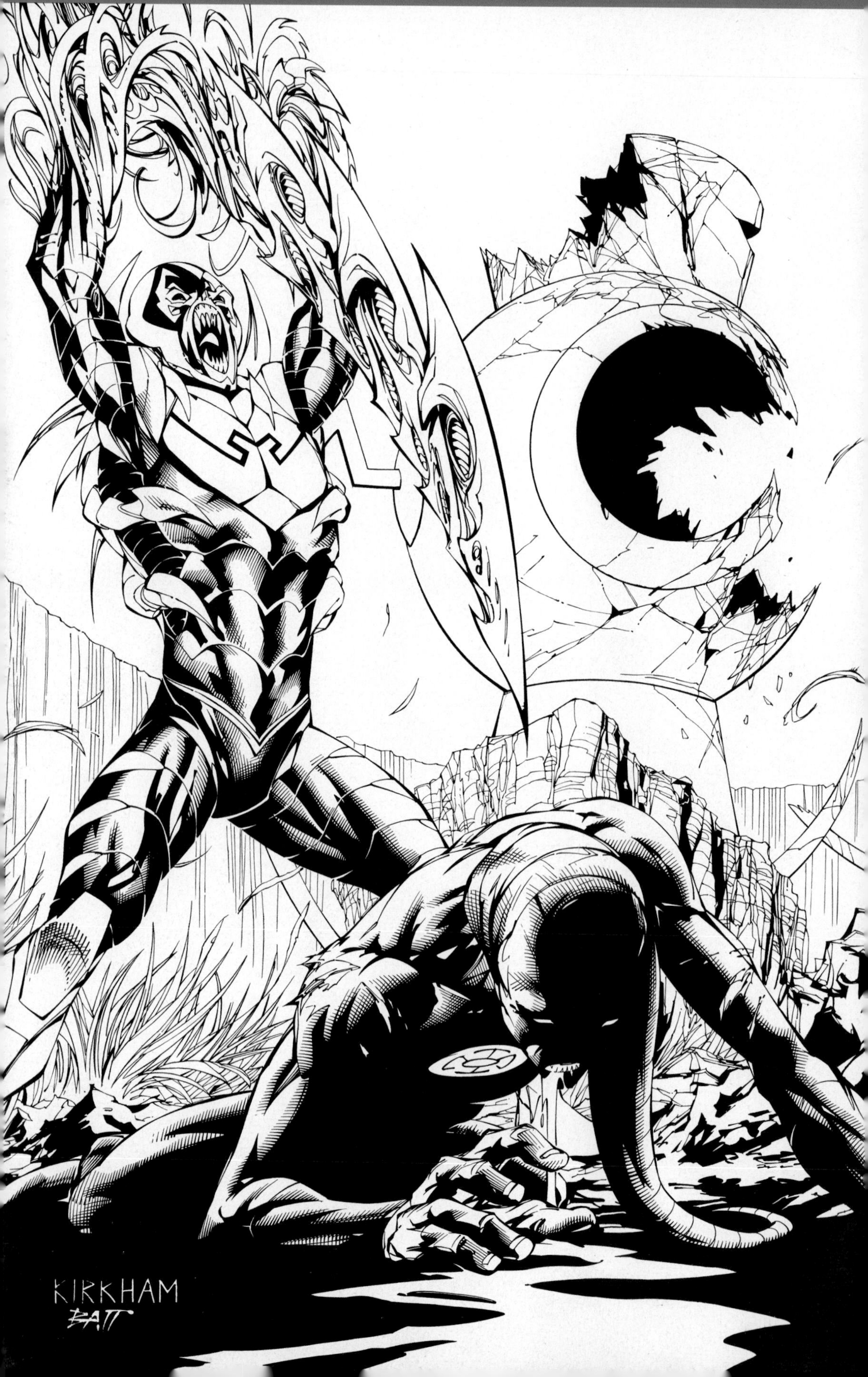
KIRKHAM
BATT

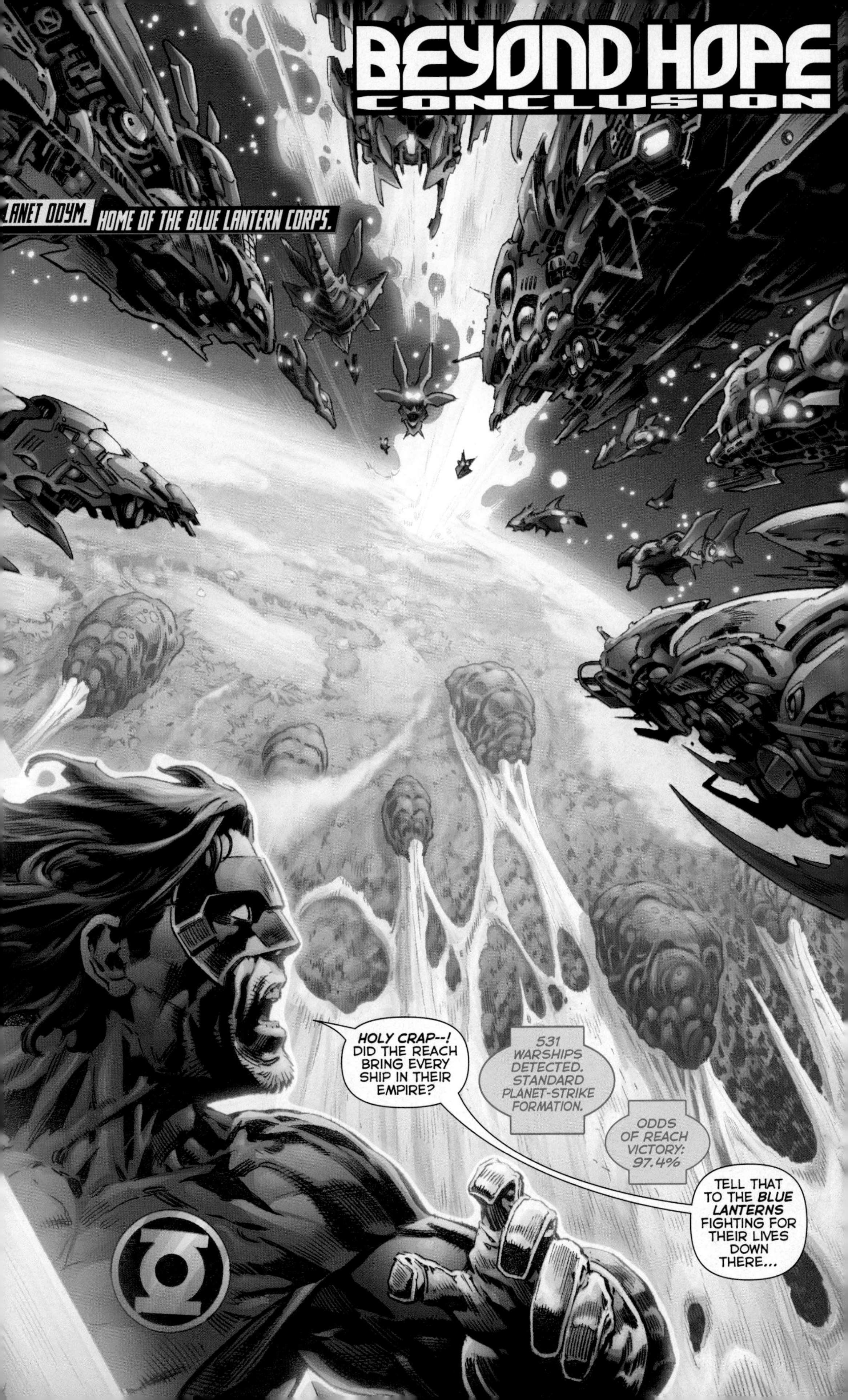
BEYOND HOPE
CONCLUSION
LANET ODYM.
HOME OF THE BLUE LANTERN CORPS.
HOLY CRAP--! DID THE REACH BRING EVERY SHIP IN THEIR EMPIRE?
531 WARSHIPS DETECTED. STANDARD PLANET-STRIKE FORMATION.
ODDS OF REACH VICTORY: 97.4%
TELL THAT TO THE BLUE LANTERNS FIGHTING FOR THEIR LIVES DOWN THERE...

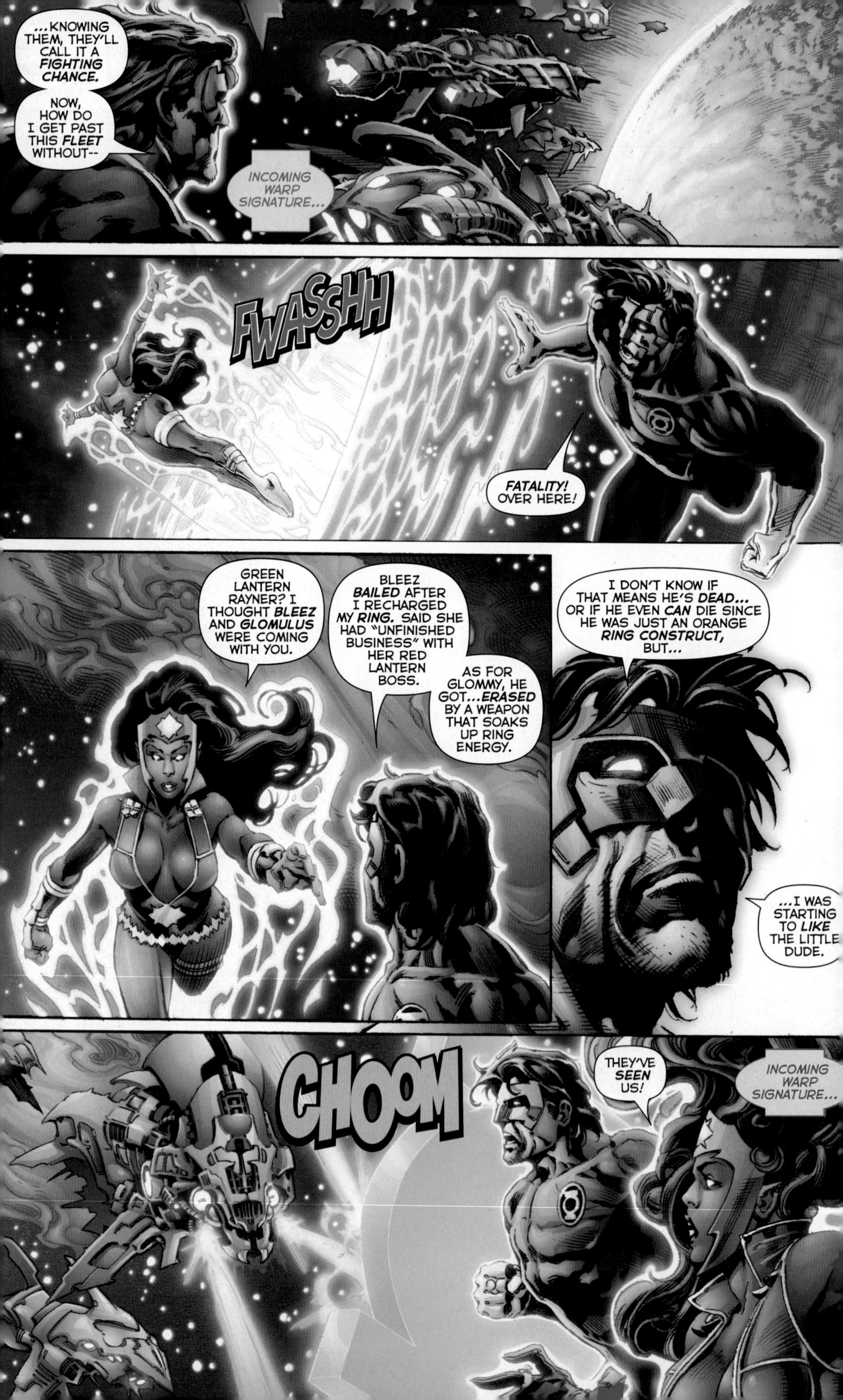
...KNOWING THEM, THEY'LL CALL IT A FIGHTING CHANCE.
NOW, HOW DO I GET PAST THIS FLEET WITHOUT--
INCOMING WARP SIGNATURE...
FWASSHH
FATALITY! OVER HERE!
GREEN LANTERN RAYNER? I THOUGHT BLEEZ AND GLOMULUS WERE COMING WITH YOU.
BLEEZ BAILED AFTER I RECHARGED MY RING. SAID SHE HAD "UNFINISHED BUSINESS" WITH HER RED LANTERN BOSS.
AS FOR GLOMMY, HE GOT...ERASED BY A WEAPON THAT SOAKS UP RING ENERGY.
I DON'T KNOW IF THAT MEANS HE'S DEAD... OR IF HE EVEN CAN DIE SINCE HE WAS JUST AN ORANGE RING CONSTRUCT, BUT...
...I WAS STARTING TO LIKE THE LITTLE DUDE.
CHOOM
THEY'VE SEEN US!
INCOMING WARP SIGNATURE...

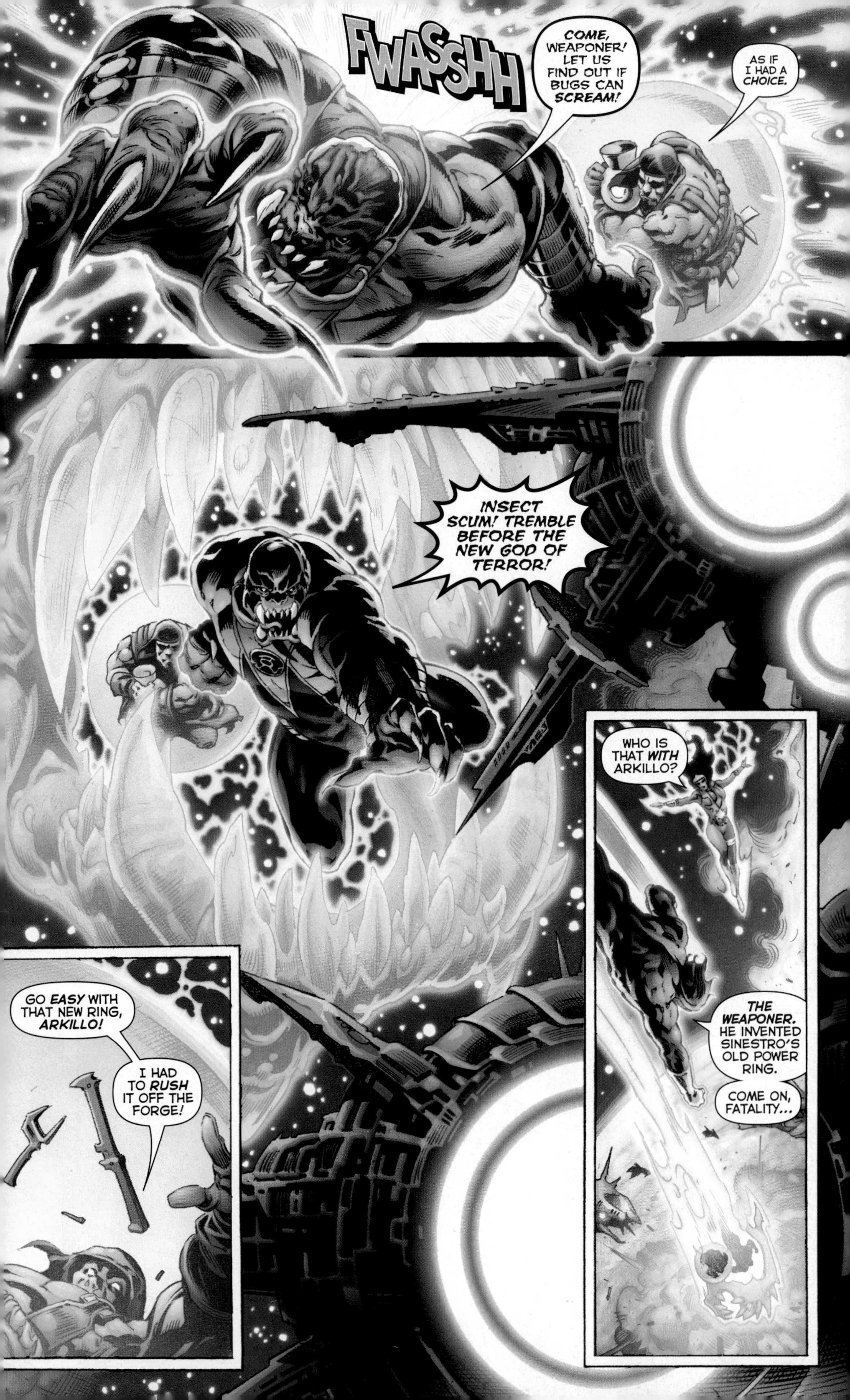
FWASSHH
COME, WEAPONER! LET US FIND OUT IF BUGS CAN SCREAM!
AS IF I HAD A CHOICE.
INSECT SCUM! TREMBLE BEFORE THE NEW GOD OF TERROR!
WHO IS THAT WITH ARKILLO?
THE WEAPONER. HE INVENTED SINESTRO'S OLD POWER RING.
COME ON, FATALITY...
GO EASY WITH THAT NEW RING, ARKILLO!
I HAD TO RUSH IT OFF THE FORGE!

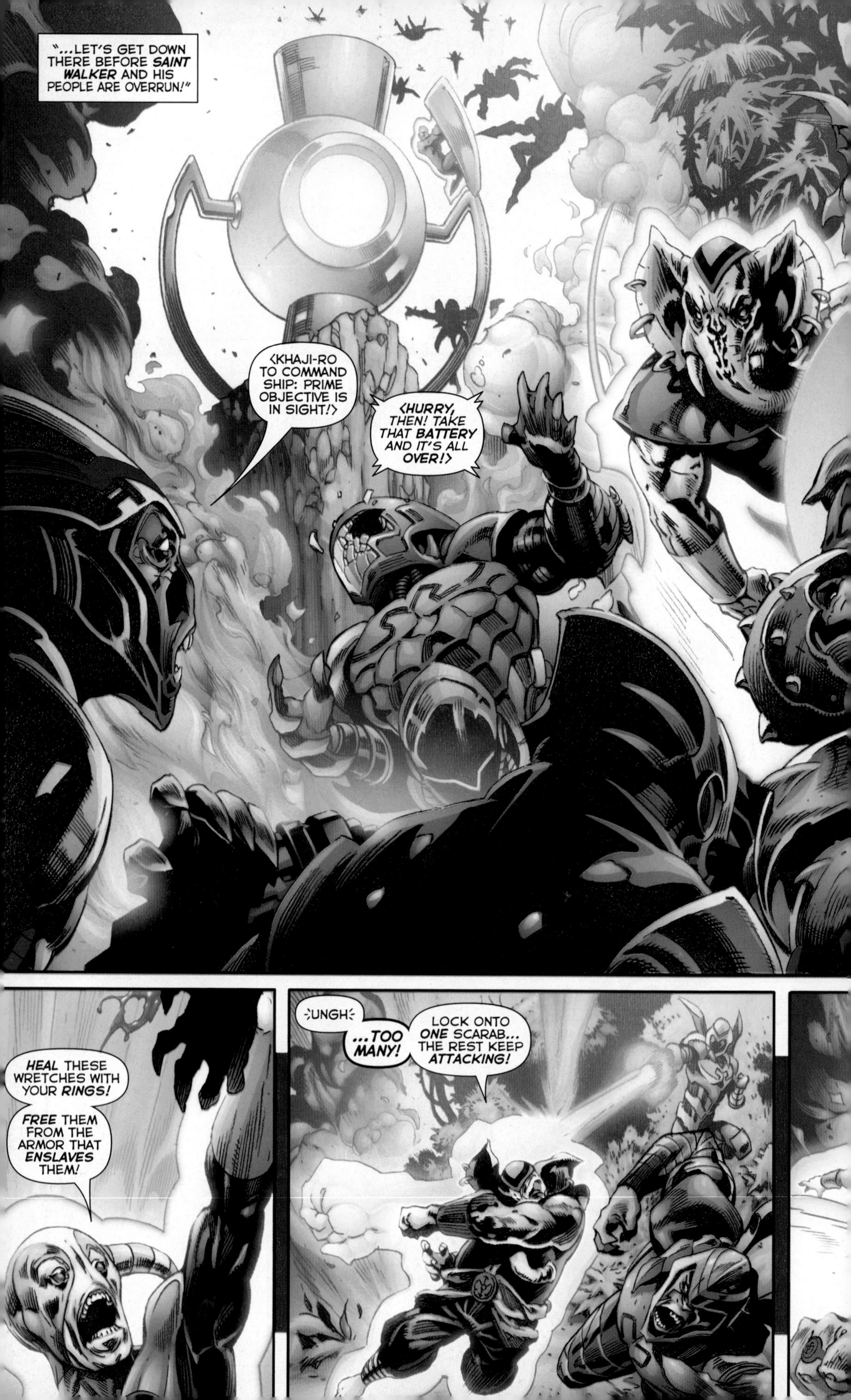
"...LET'S GET DOWN THERE BEFORE SAINT WALKER AND HIS PEOPLE ARE OVERRUN!"
<KHAJI-RO TO COMMAND SHIP: PRIME OBJECTIVE IS IN SIGHT!>
<HURRY, THEN! TAKE THAT BATTERY AND IT'S ALL OVER!>
HEAL THESE WRETCHES WITH YOUR RINGS!
FREE THEM FROM THE ARMOR THAT ENSLAVES THEM!
UNGH
...TOO MANY!
LOCK ONTO ONE SCARAB... THE REST KEEP ATTACKING!

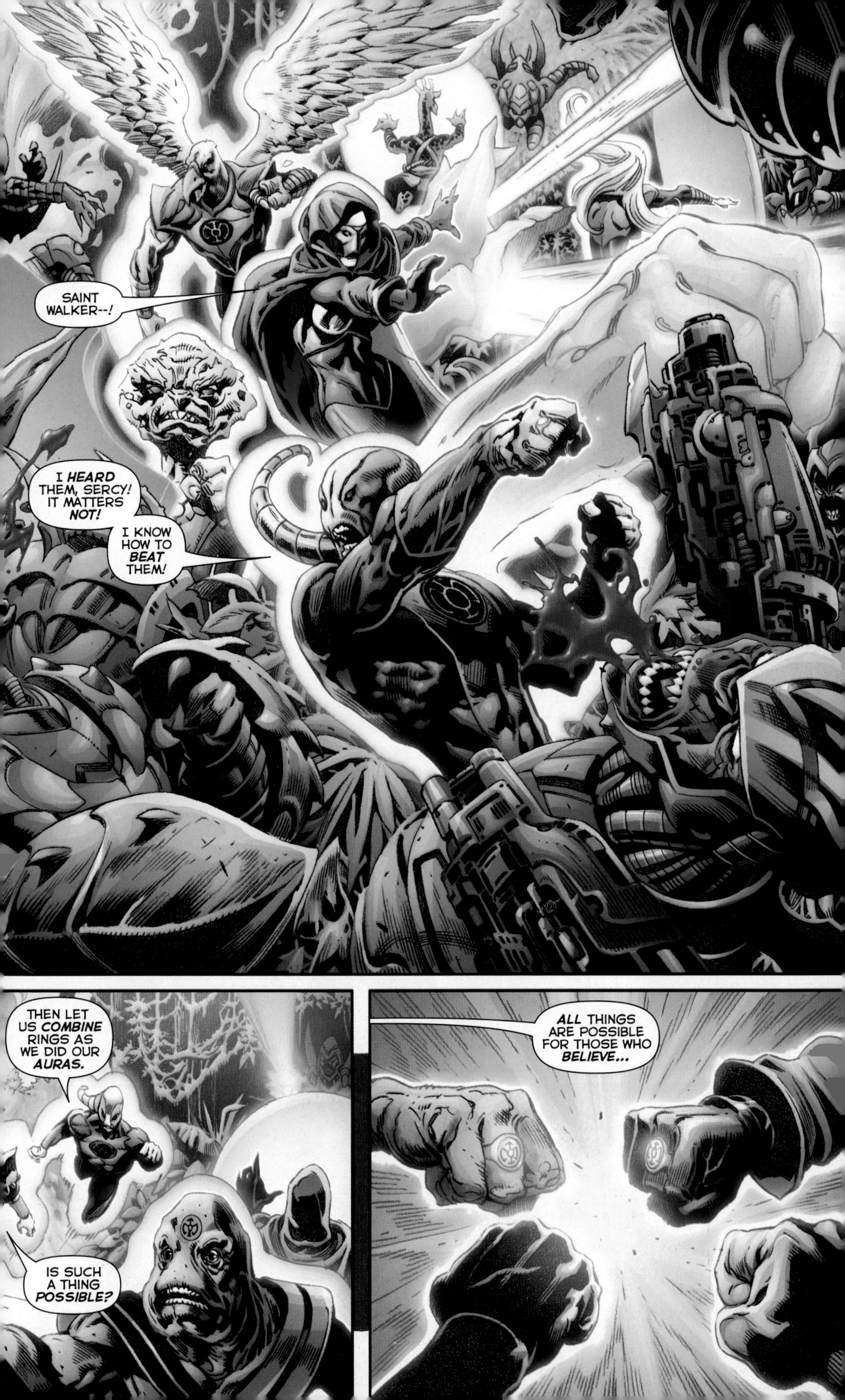
SAINT WALKER--!
I HEARD THEM, SERCY! IT MATTERS NOT!
I KNOW HOW TO BEAT THEM!
THEN LET US COMBINE RINGS AS WE DID OUR AURAS.
IS SUCH A THING POSSIBLE?
ALL THINGS ARE POSSIBLE FOR THOSE WHO BELIEVE...

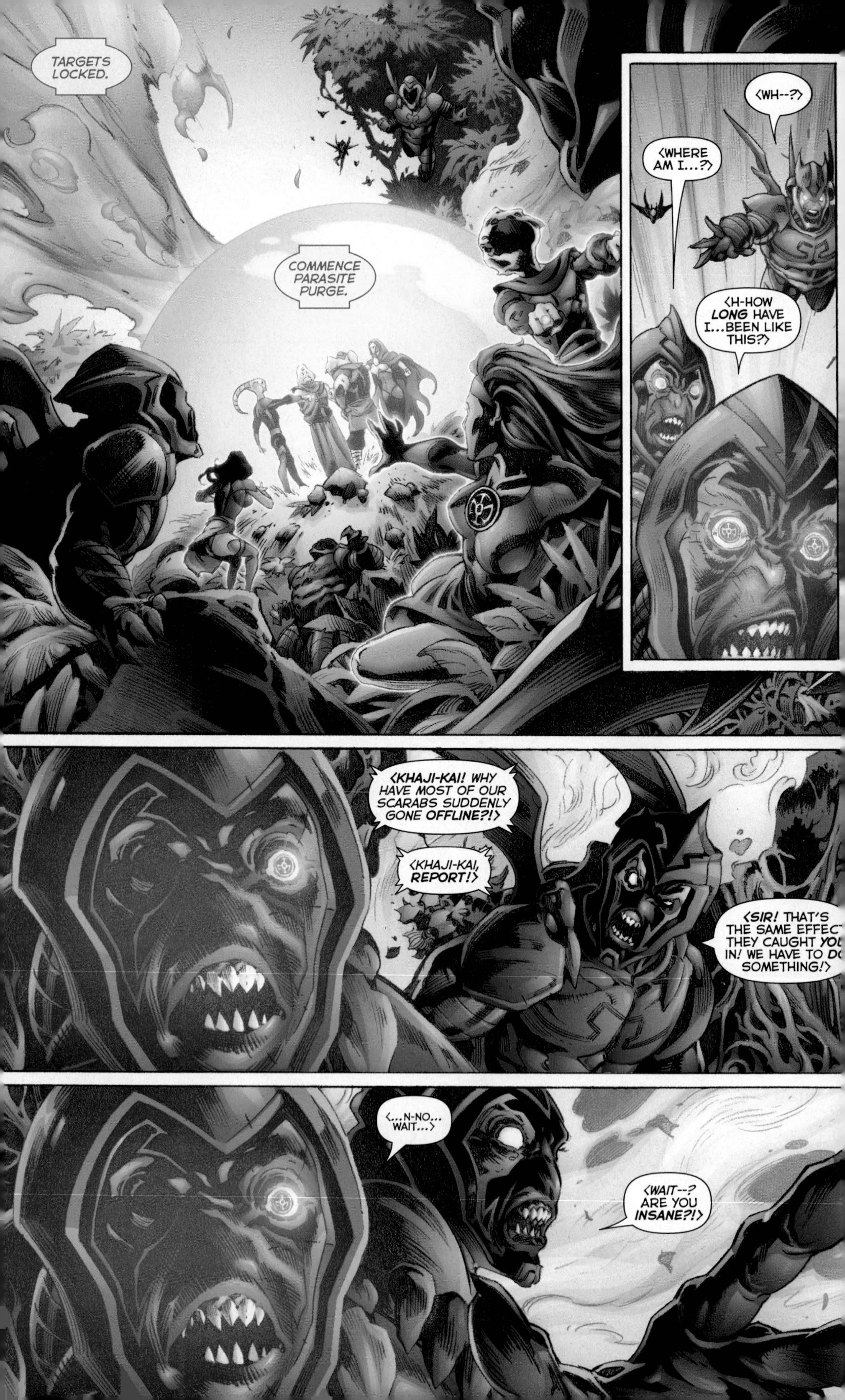
TARGETS LOCKED.
COMMENCE PARASITE PURGE.
<WH--?>
<WHERE AM I...?>
<H-HOW LONG HAVE I...BEEN LIKE THIS?>
<KHAJI-KAI! WHY HAVE MOST OF OUR SCARABS SUDDENLY GONE OFFLINE?!>
<KHAJI-KAI, REPORT!>
<SIR! THAT'S THE SAME EFFECT THEY CAUGHT YOU IN! WE HAVE TO DO SOMETHING!>
<...N-NO... WAIT...>
<WAIT--? ARE YOU INSANE?!>

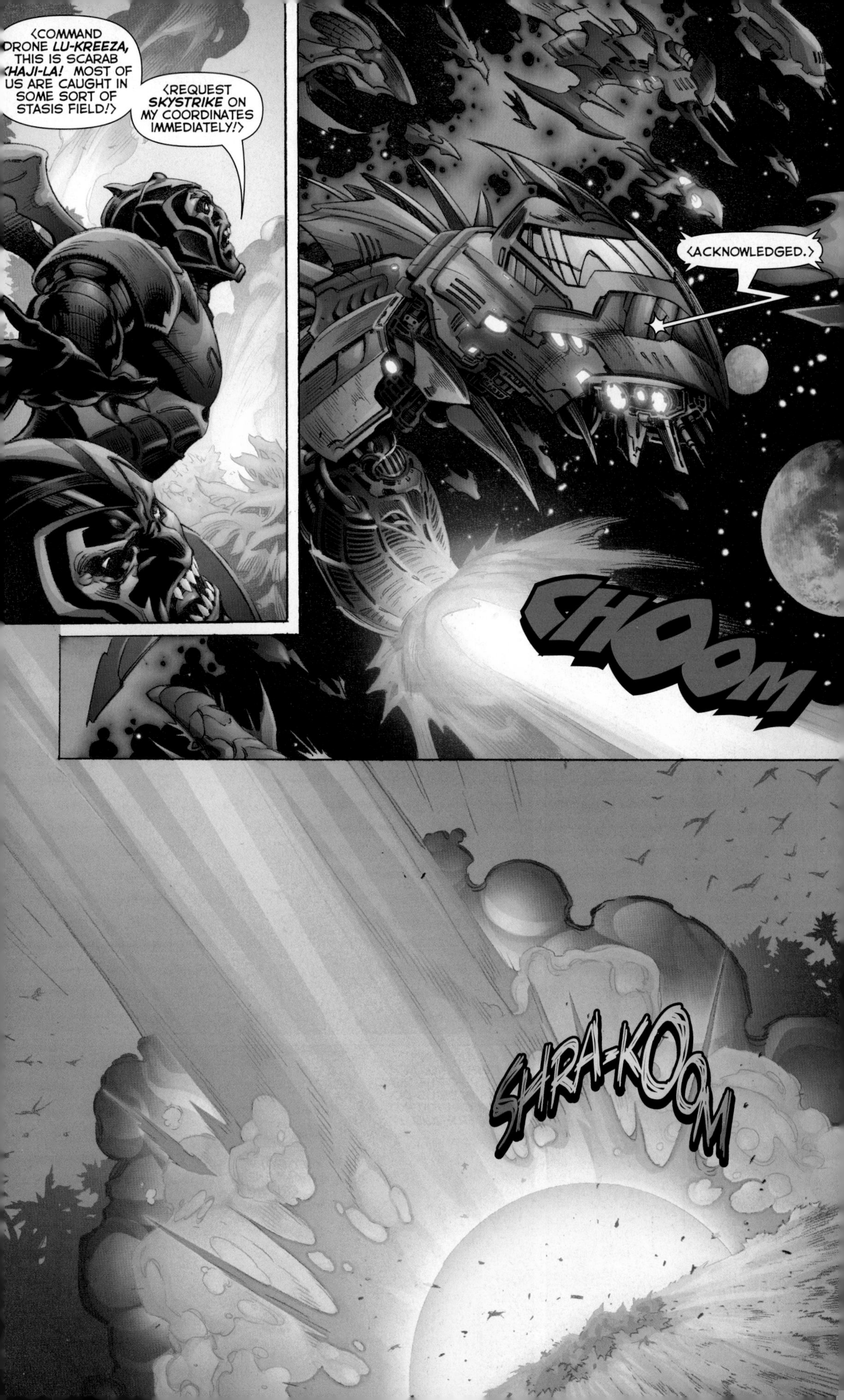
<COMMAND DRONE LU-KREEZA, THIS IS SCARAB KHAJI-LA! MOST OF US ARE CAUGHT IN SOME SORT OF STASIS FIELD!>
<REQUEST SKYSTRIKE ON MY COORDINATES IMMEDIATELY!>
<ACKNOWLEDGED.>
CHOOM
SHRA-KOOM

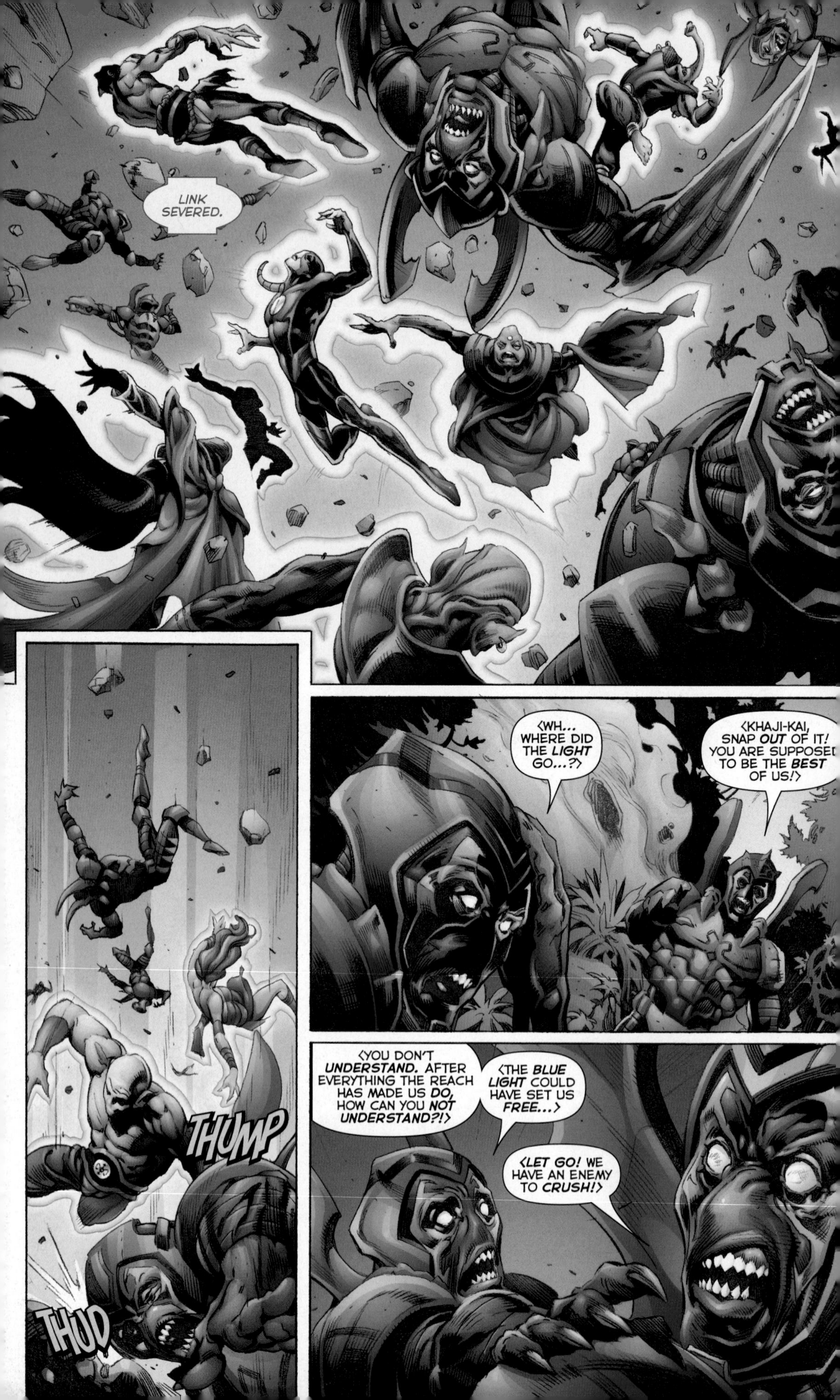
LINK SEVERED.
THUMP
THUD
<WH... WHERE DID THE LIGHT GO...?>
<KHAJI-KAI, SNAP OUT OF IT! YOU ARE SUPPOSED TO BE THE BEST OF US!>
<YOU DON'T UNDERSTAND. AFTER EVERYTHING THE REACH HAS MADE US DO, HOW CAN YOU NOT UNDERSTAND?!>
<THE BLUE LIGHT COULD HAVE SET US FREE...>
<LET GO! WE HAVE AN ENEMY TO CRUSH!>

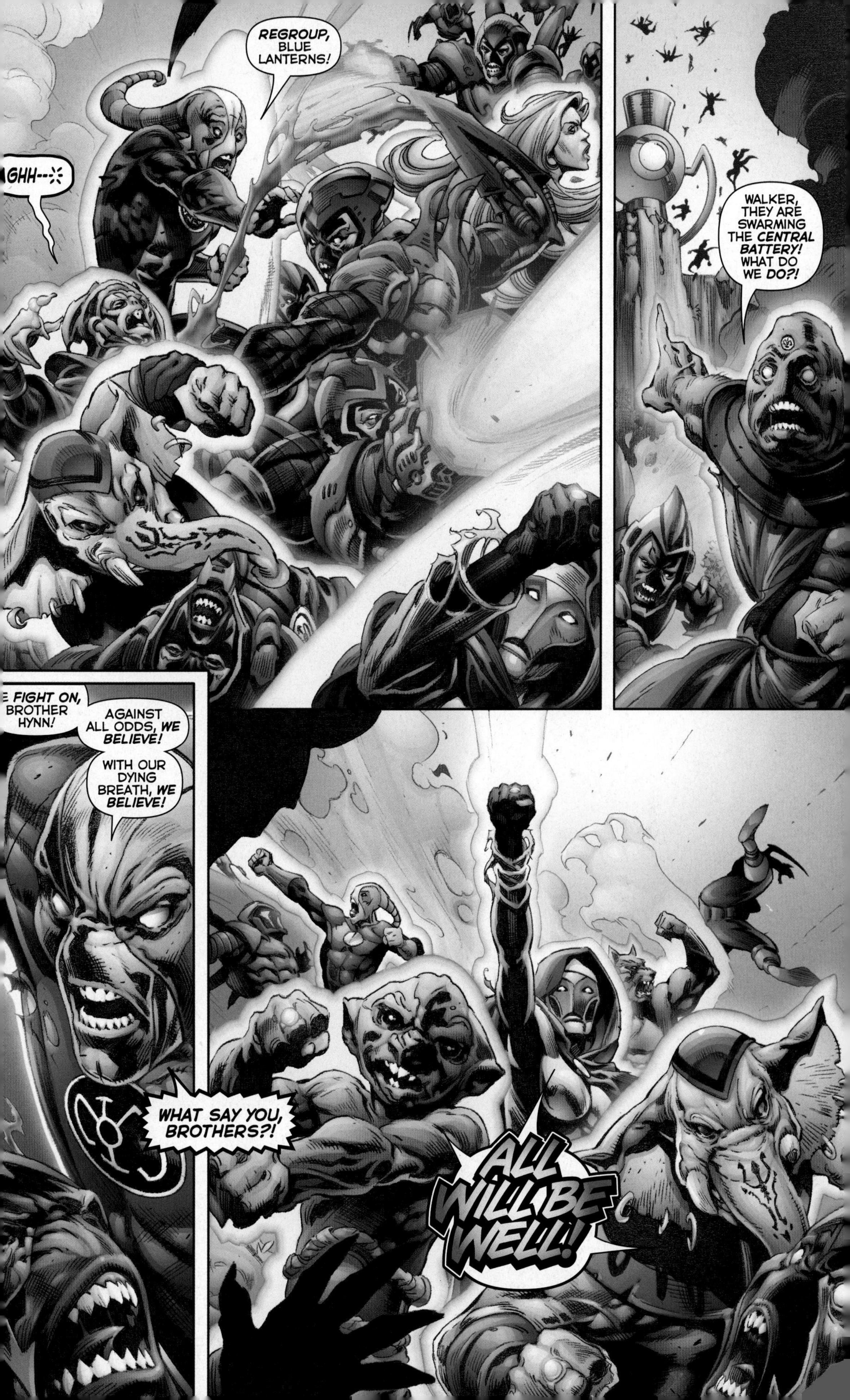

AGHH--!
REGROUP, BLUE LANTERNS!
WALKER, THEY ARE SWARMING THE CENTRAL BATTERY! WHAT DO WE DO?!
E FIGHT ON, BROTHER HYNN!
AGAINST ALL ODDS, WE BELIEVE!
WITH OUR DYING BREATH, WE BELIEVE!
WHAT SAY YOU, BROTHERS?!
ALL WILL BE WELL!

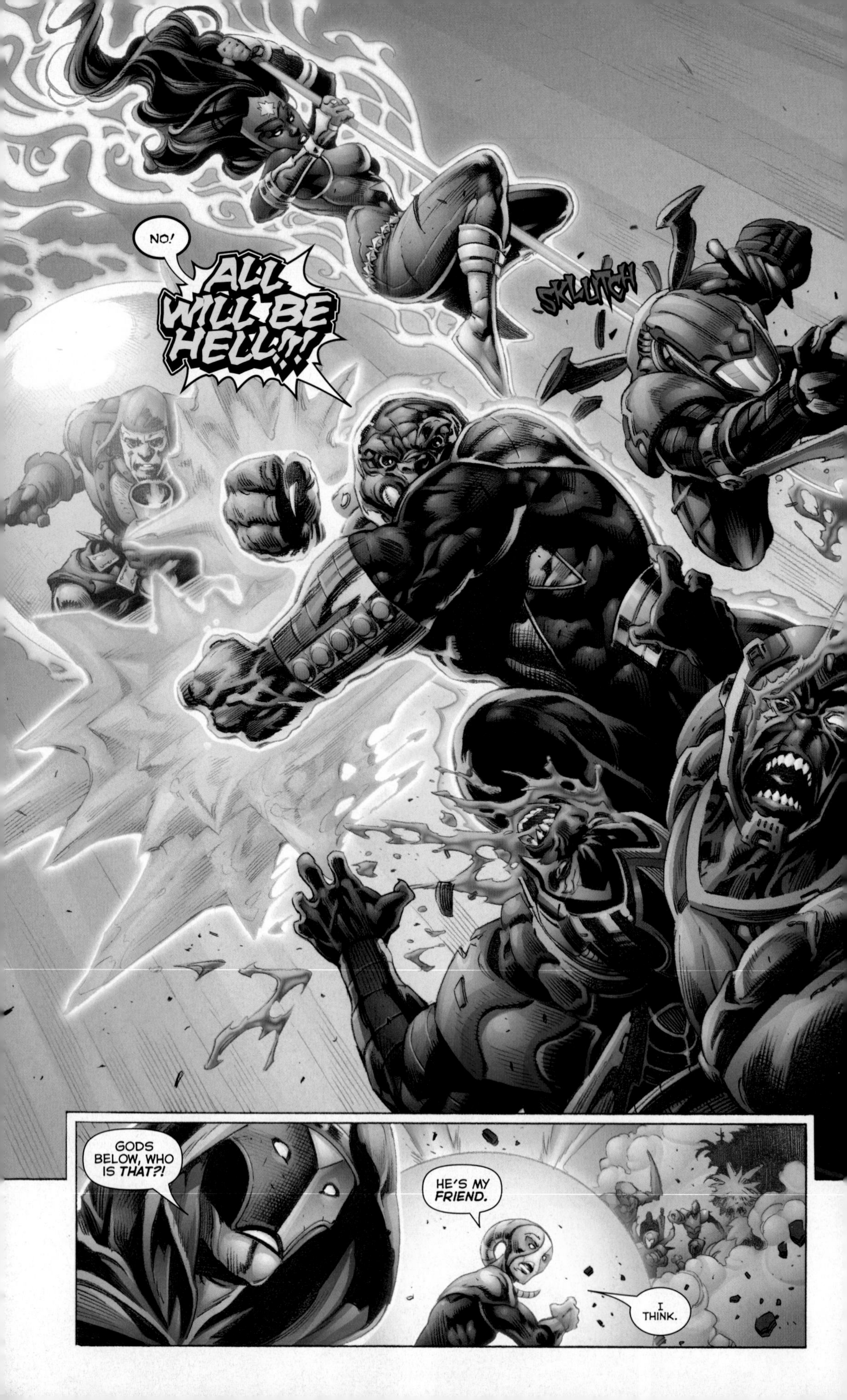
NO!
ALL WILL BE HELL!!!
SKLUTCH
GODS BELOW, WHO IS THAT?!
HE'S MY FRIEND.
I THINK.

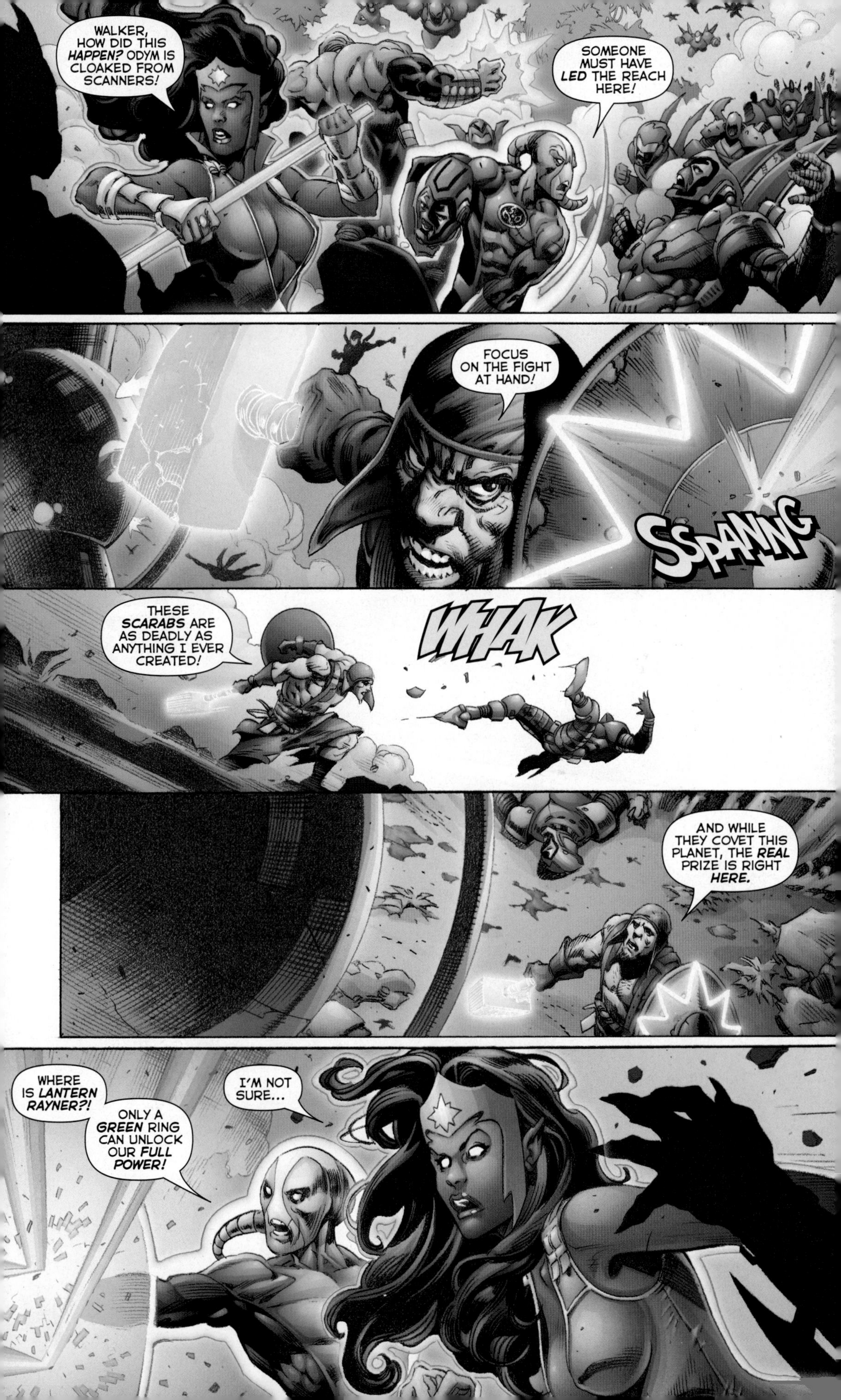
WALKER, HOW DID THIS HAPPEN? ODYM IS CLOAKED FROM SCANNERS!
SOMEONE MUST HAVE LED THE REACH HERE!
FOCUS ON THE FIGHT AT HAND!
SSPANNG
THESE SCARABS ARE AS DEADLY AS ANYTHING I EVER CREATED!
WHAK
AND WHILE THEY COVET THIS PLANET, THE REAL PRIZE IS RIGHT HERE.
WHERE IS LANTERN RAYNER?!
ONLY A GREEN RING CAN UNLOCK OUR FULL POWER!
I'M NOT SURE...

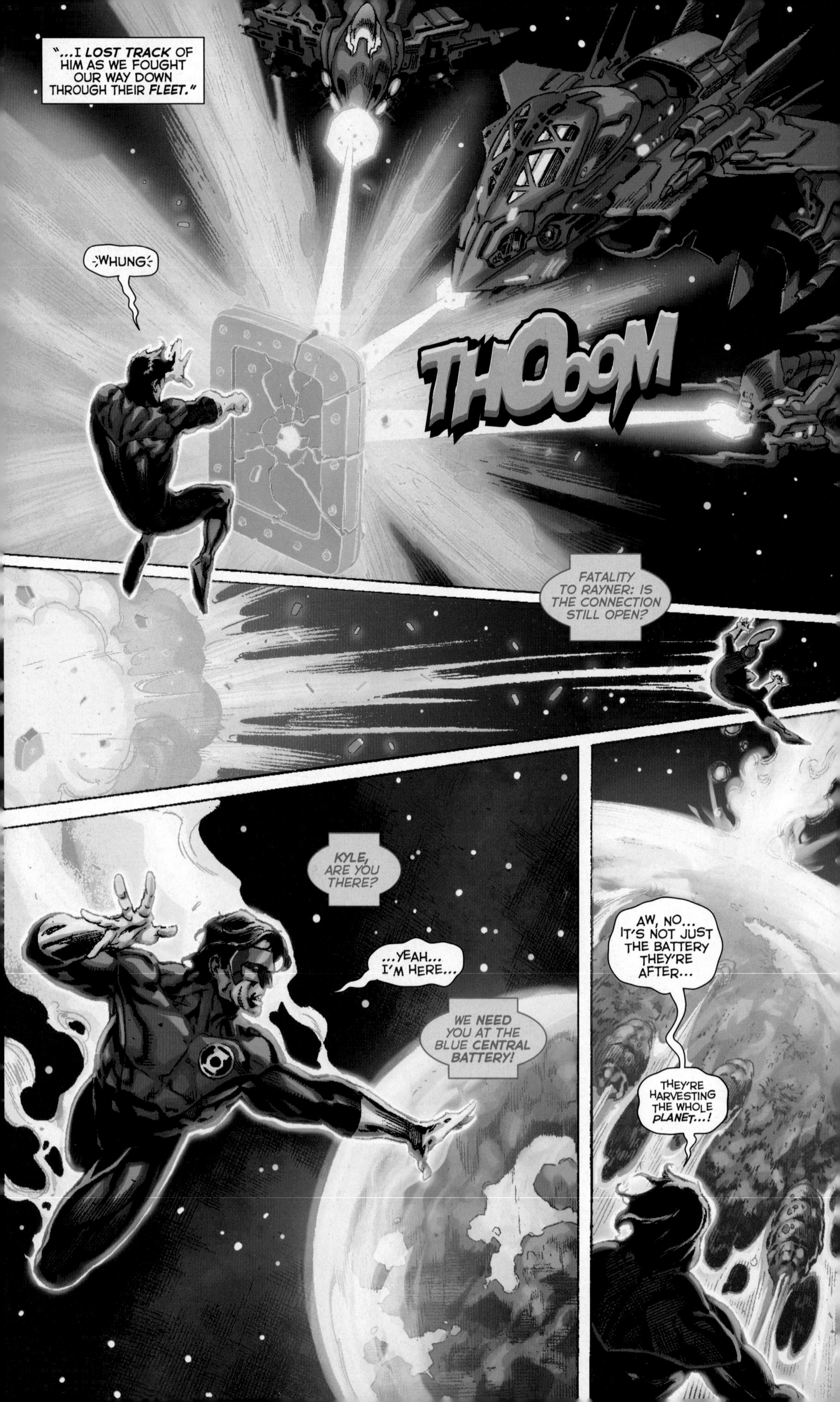
"...I LOST TRACK OF HIM AS WE FOUGHT OUR WAY DOWN THROUGH THEIR FLEET."
WHUNG
THOOOM
FATALITY TO RAYNER: IS THE CONNECTION STILL OPEN?
KYLE, ARE YOU THERE?
...YEAH... I'M HERE...
WE NEED YOU AT THE BLUE CENTRAL BATTERY!
AW, NO... IT'S NOT JUST THE BATTERY THEY'RE AFTER...
THEY'RE HARVESTING THE WHOLE PLANET...!

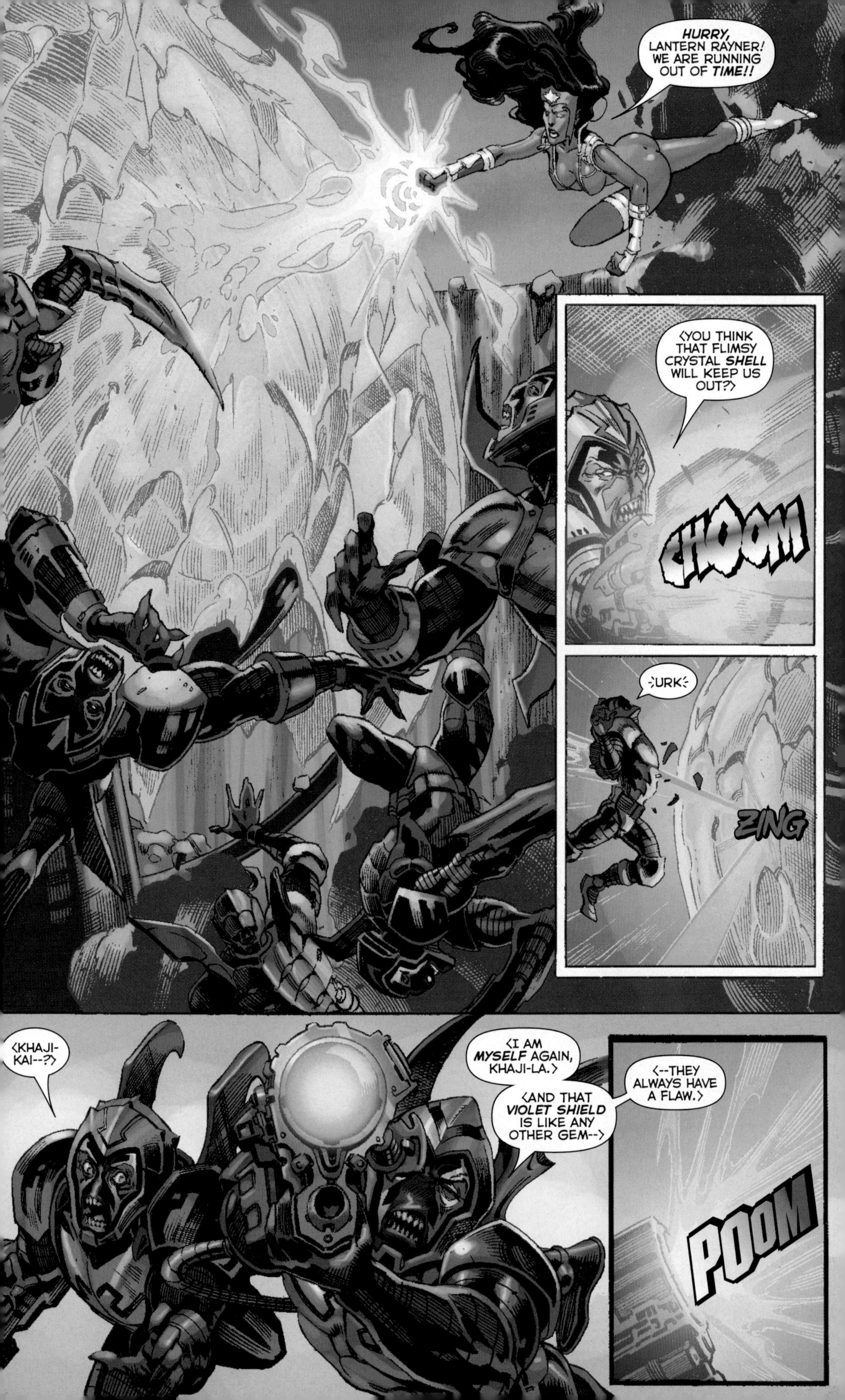
HURRY, LANTERN RAYNER! WE ARE RUNNING OUT OF TIME!!
<YOU THINK THAT FLIMSY CRYSTAL SHELL WILL KEEP US OUT?>
CHOOM
URK
ZING
<KHAJI-KAI--?>
<I AM MYSELF AGAIN, KHAJI-LA.>
<AND THAT VIOLET SHIELD IS LIKE ANY OTHER GEM-->
<--THEY ALWAYS HAVE A FLAW.>
POOM

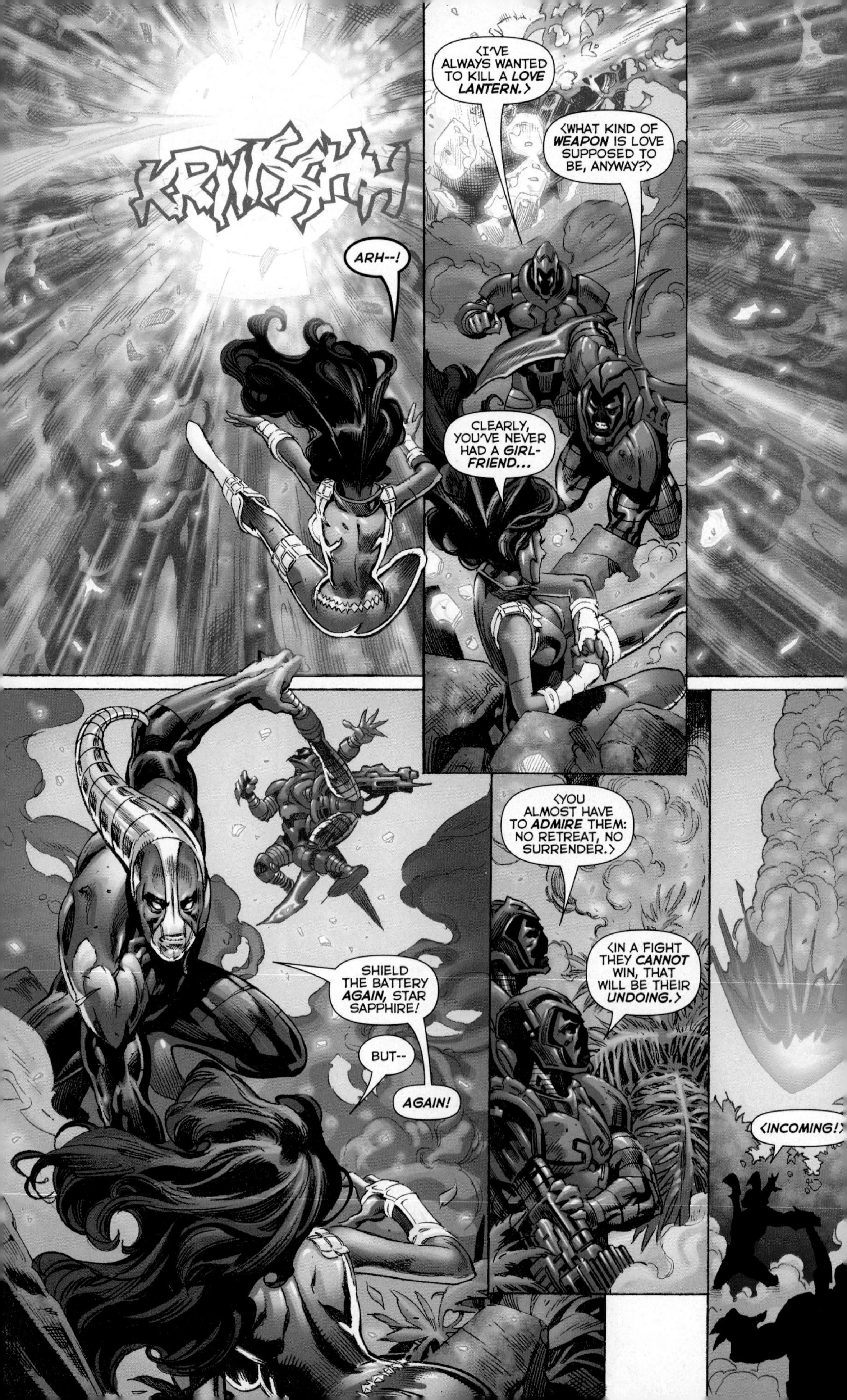
KRITCKH
ARH--!
<I'VE ALWAYS WANTED TO KILL A LOVE LANTERN.>
<WHAT KIND OF WEAPON IS LOVE SUPPOSED TO BE, ANYWAY?>
CLEARLY, YOU'VE NEVER HAD A GIRL-FRIEND...
SHIELD THE BATTERY AGAIN, STAR SAPPHIRE!
BUT--
AGAIN!
<YOU ALMOST HAVE TO ADMIRE THEM: NO RETREAT, NO SURRENDER.>
<IN A FIGHT THEY CANNOT WIN, THAT WILL BE THEIR UNDOING.>
<INCOMING!>

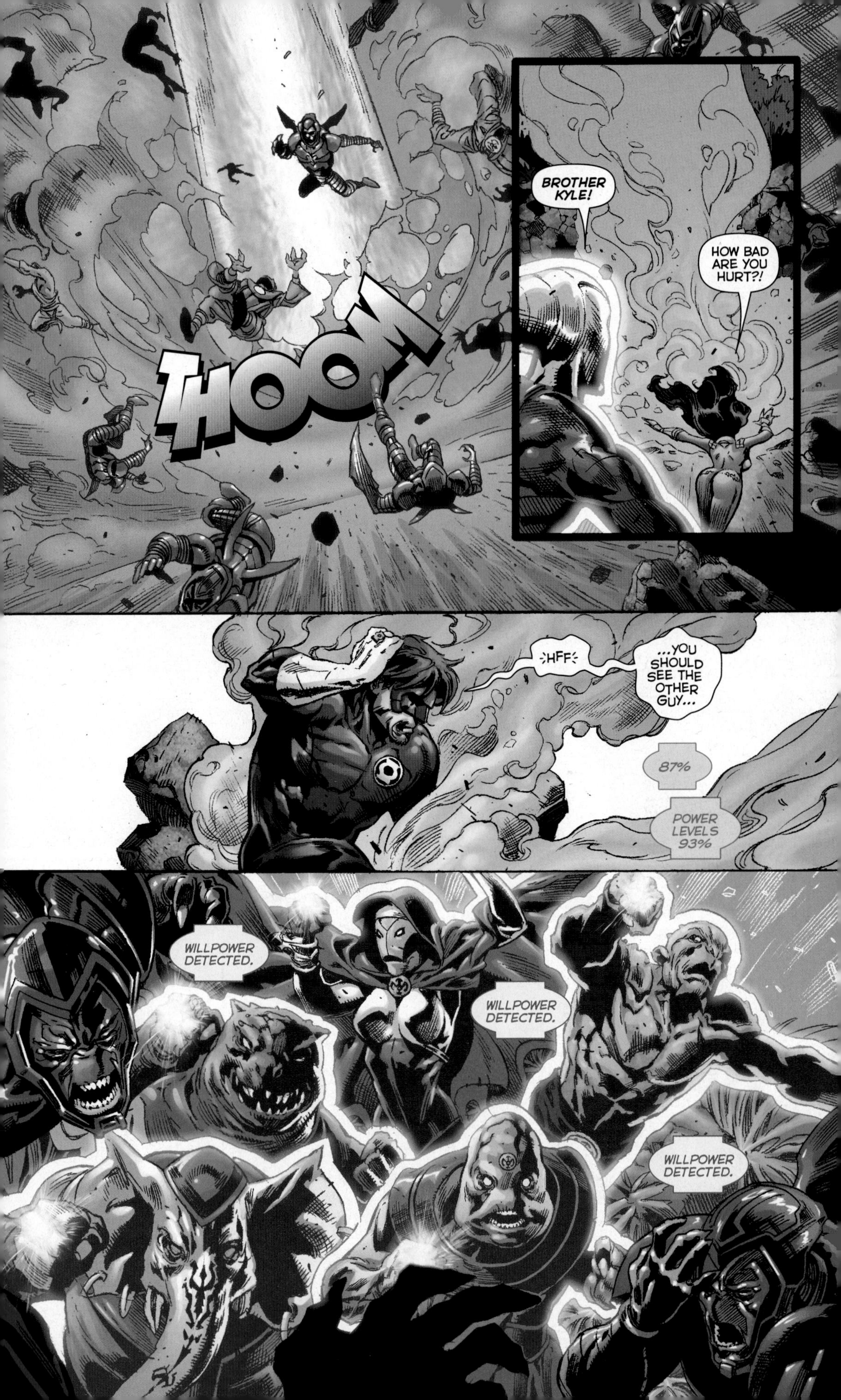
THOOM
BROTHER KYLE!
HOW BAD ARE YOU HURT?!
HFF
...YOU SHOULD SEE THE OTHER GUY...
87%
POWER LEVELS 93%
WILLPOWER DETECTED.
WILLPOWER DETECTED.
WILLPOWER DETECTED.

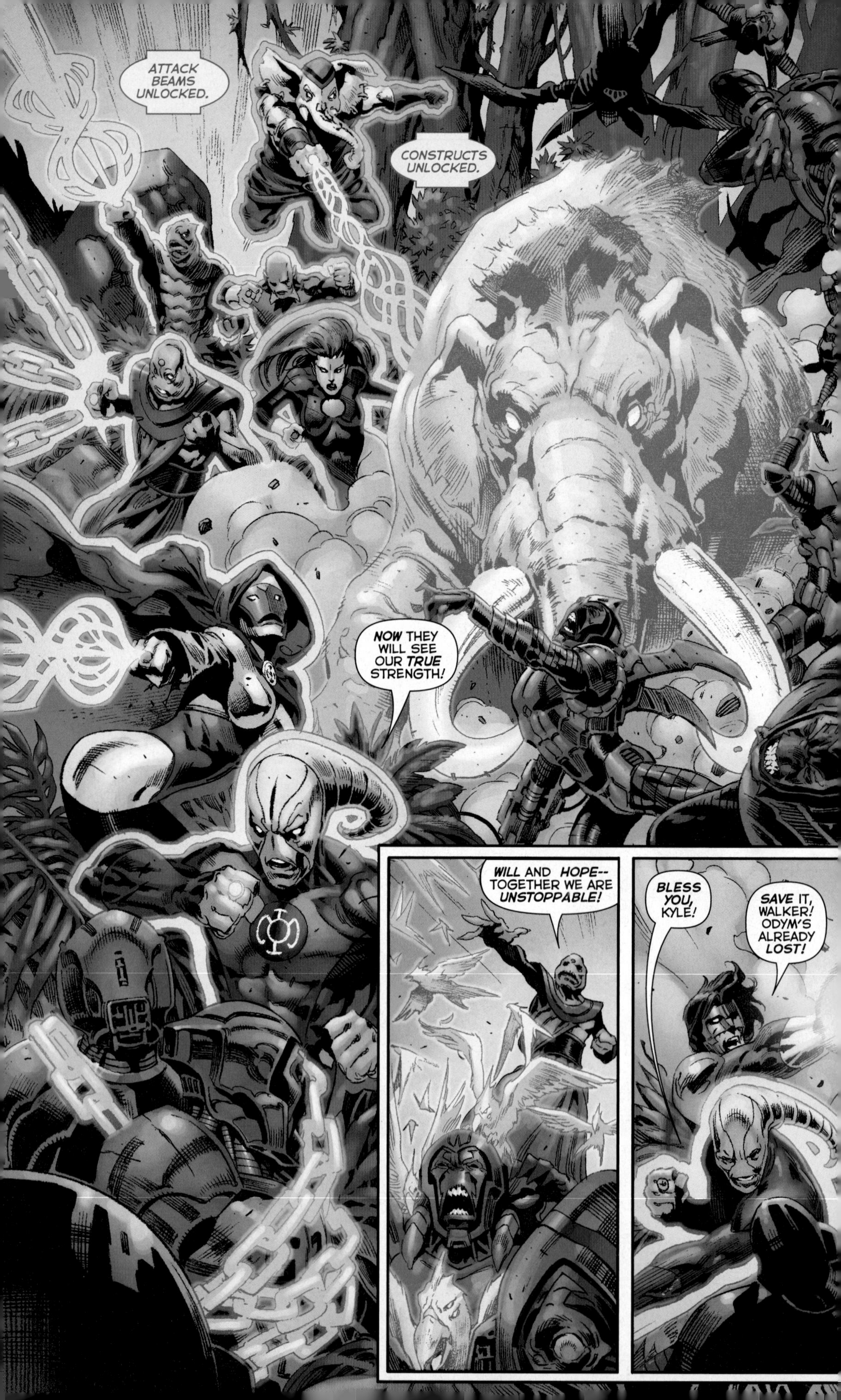
ATTACK BEAMS UNLOCKED.
CONSTRUCTS UNLOCKED.
NOW THEY WILL SEE OUR TRUE STRENGTH!
WILL AND HOPE-- TOGETHER WE ARE UNSTOPPABLE!
BLESS YOU, KYLE!
SAVE IT, WALKER! ODYM'S ALREADY LOST!

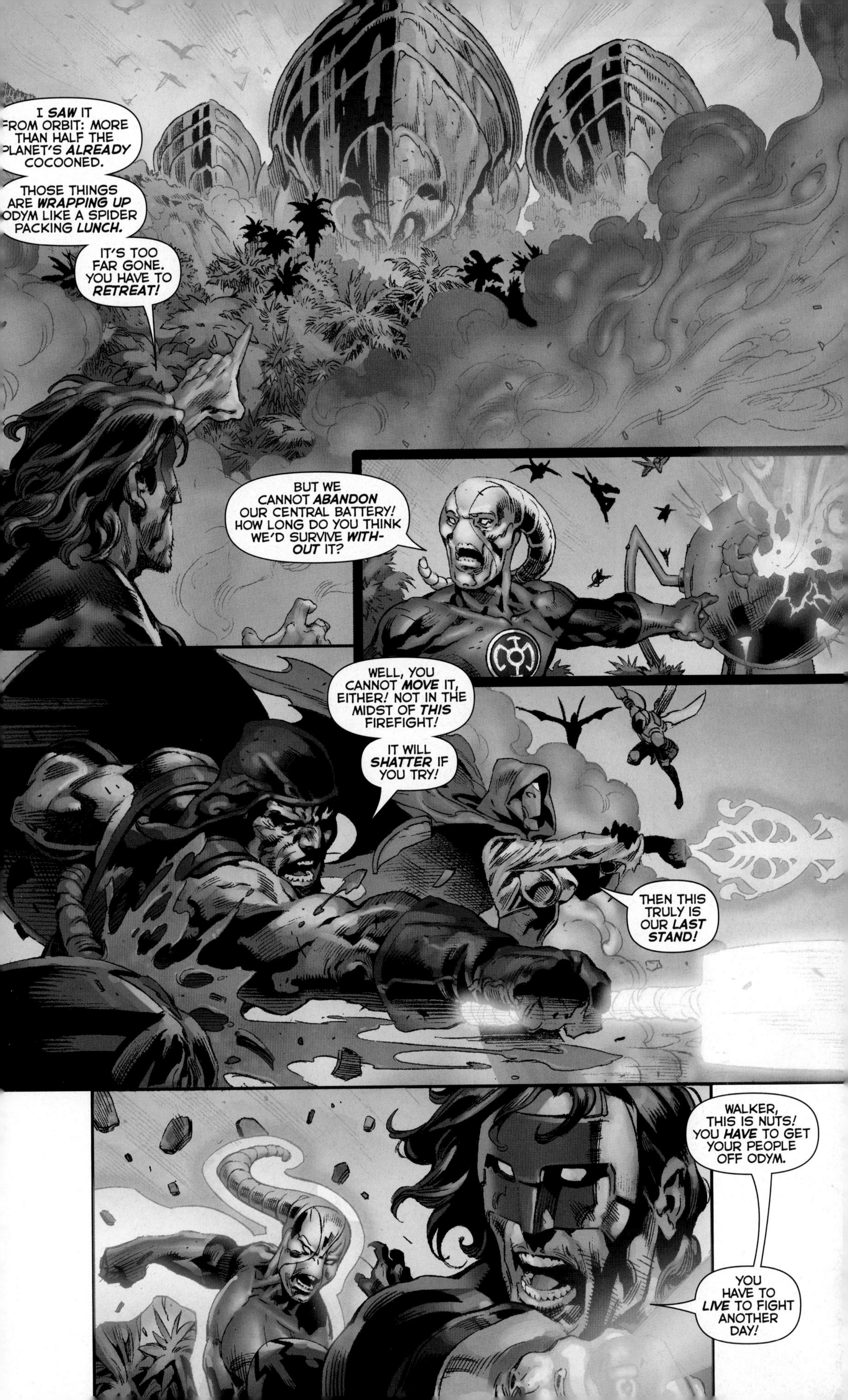
I SAW IT FROM ORBIT: MORE THAN HALF THE PLANET'S ALREADY COCOONED.
THOSE THINGS ARE WRAPPING UP ODYM LIKE A SPIDER PACKING LUNCH.
IT'S TOO FAR GONE. YOU HAVE TO RETREAT!
BUT WE CANNOT ABANDON OUR CENTRAL BATTERY! HOW LONG DO YOU THINK WE'D SURVIVE WITH-OUT IT?
WELL, YOU CANNOT MOVE IT, EITHER! NOT IN THE MIDST OF THIS FIREFIGHT!
IT WILL SHATTER IF YOU TRY!
THEN THIS TRULY IS OUR LAST STAND!
WALKER, THIS IS NUTS! YOU HAVE TO GET YOUR PEOPLE OFF ODYM.
YOU HAVE TO LIVE TO FIGHT ANOTHER DAY!

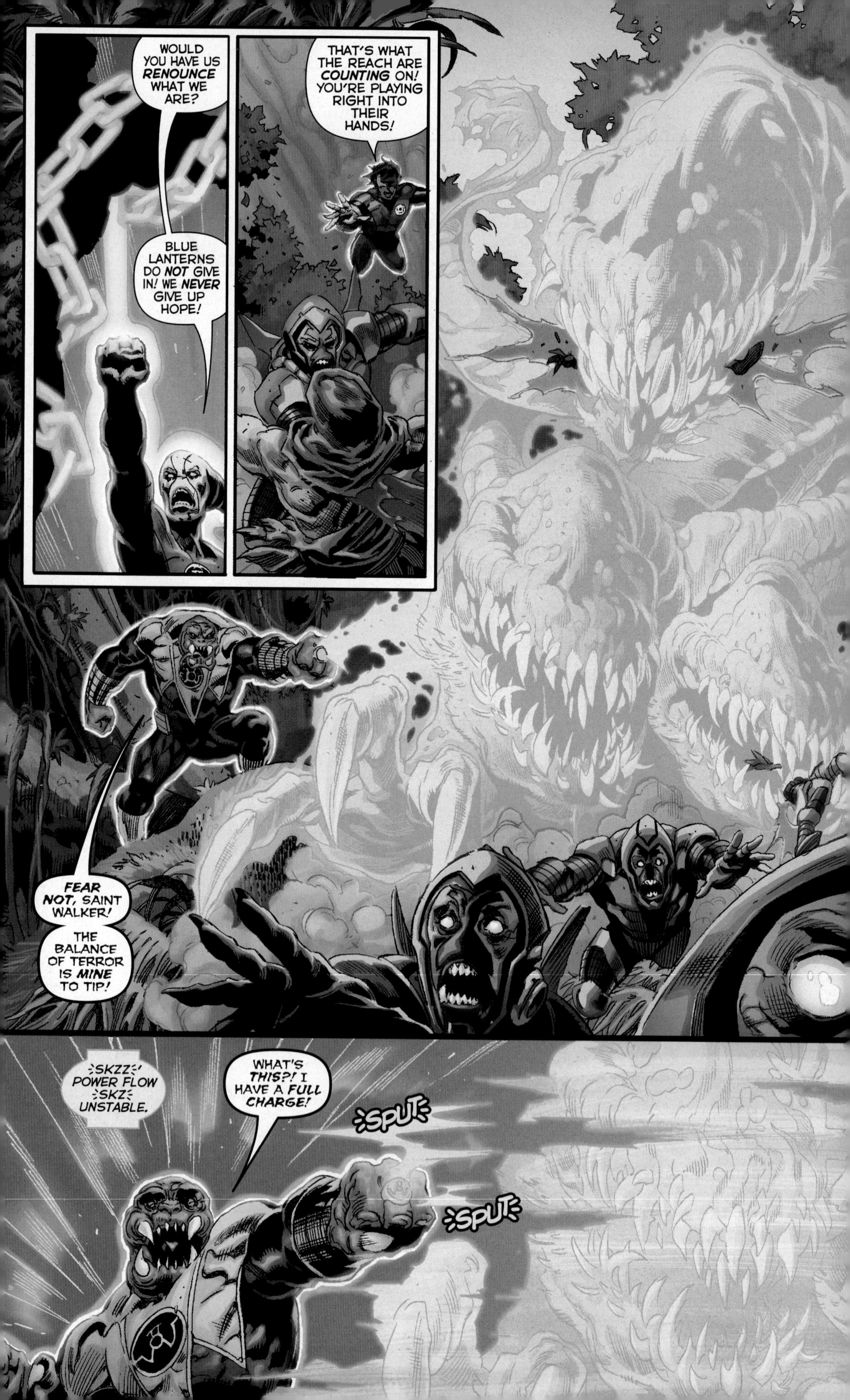
WOULD YOU HAVE US RENOUNCE WHAT WE ARE?
BLUE LANTERNS DO NOT GIVE IN! WE NEVER GIVE UP HOPE!
THAT'S WHAT THE REACH ARE COUNTING ON! YOU'RE PLAYING RIGHT INTO THEIR HANDS!
FEAR NOT, SAINT WALKER!
THE BALANCE OF TERROR IS MINE TO TIP!
SKZZ POWER FLOW SKZ UNSTABLE.
WHAT'S THIS?! I HAVE A FULL CHARGE!
SPUT
SPUT

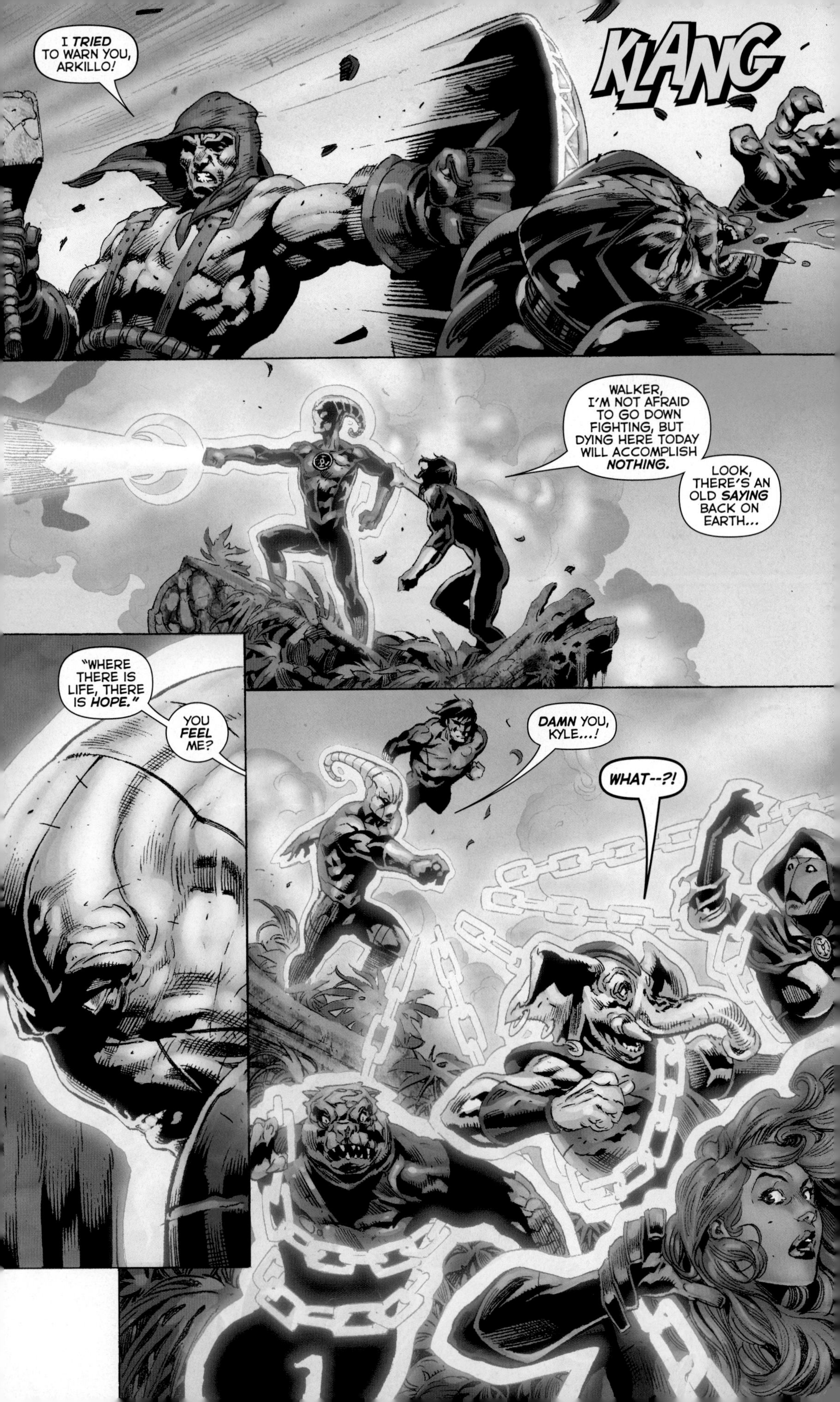
I TRIED TO WARN YOU, ARKILLO!
KLANG
WALKER, I'M NOT AFRAID TO GO DOWN FIGHTING, BUT DYING HERE TODAY WILL ACCOMPLISH NOTHING.
LOOK, THERE'S AN OLD SAYING BACK ON EARTH...
"WHERE THERE IS LIFE, THERE IS HOPE."
YOU FEEL ME?
DAMN YOU, KYLE...!
WHAT--?!

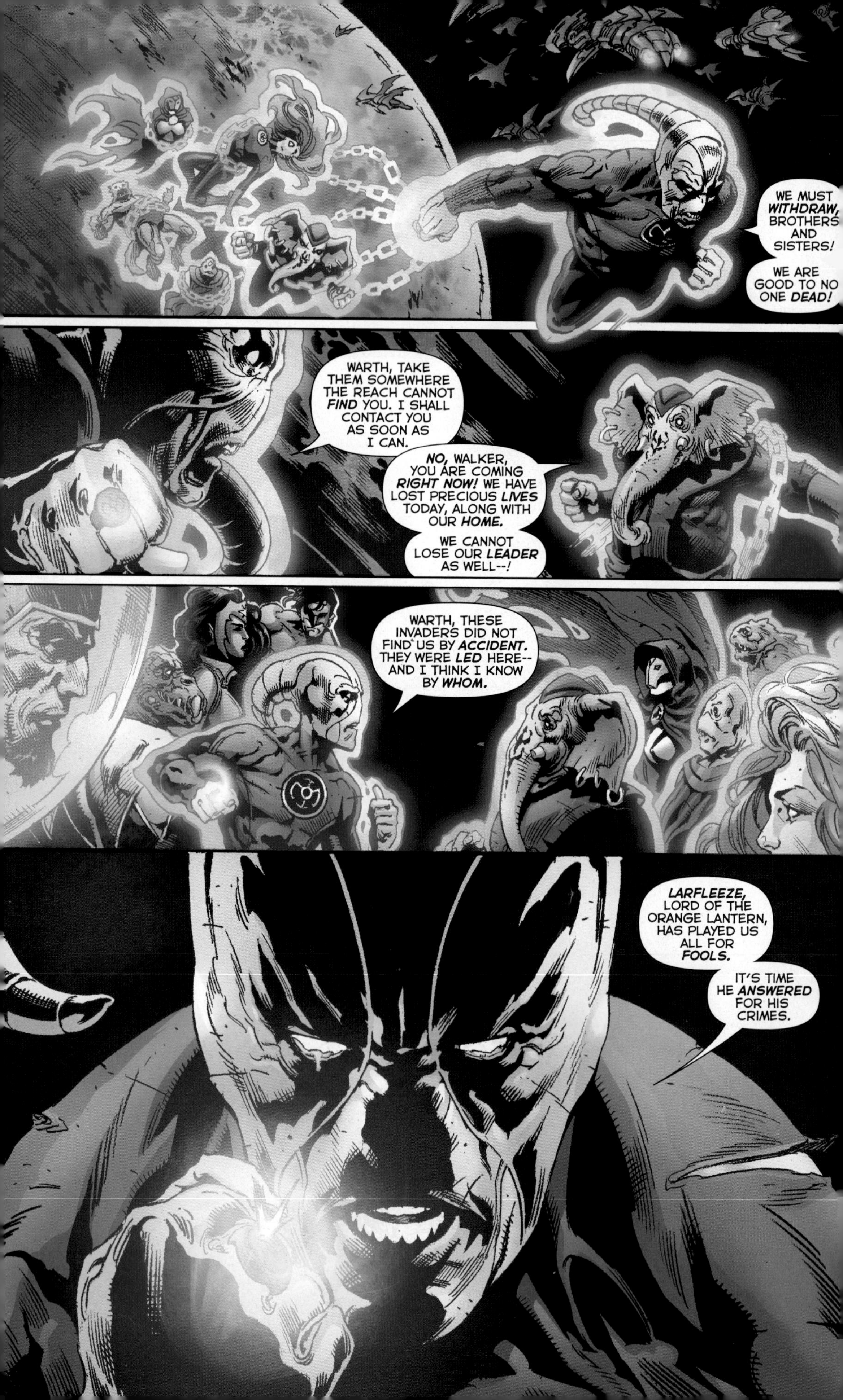
WE MUST WITHDRAW, BROTHERS AND SISTERS!
WE ARE GOOD TO NO ONE DEAD!
WARTH, TAKE THEM SOMEWHERE THE REACH CANNOT FIND YOU. I SHALL CONTACT YOU AS SOON AS I CAN.
NO, WALKER, YOU ARE COMING RIGHT NOW! WE HAVE LOST PRECIOUS LIVES TODAY, ALONG WITH OUR HOME.
WE CANNOT LOSE OUR LEADER AS WELL--!
WARTH, THESE INVADERS DID NOT FIND US BY ACCIDENT. THEY WERE LED HERE-- AND I THINK I KNOW BY WHOM.
LARFLEEZE, LORD OF THE ORANGE LANTERN, HAS PLAYED US ALL FOR FOOLS.
IT'S TIME HE ANSWERED FOR HIS CRIMES.

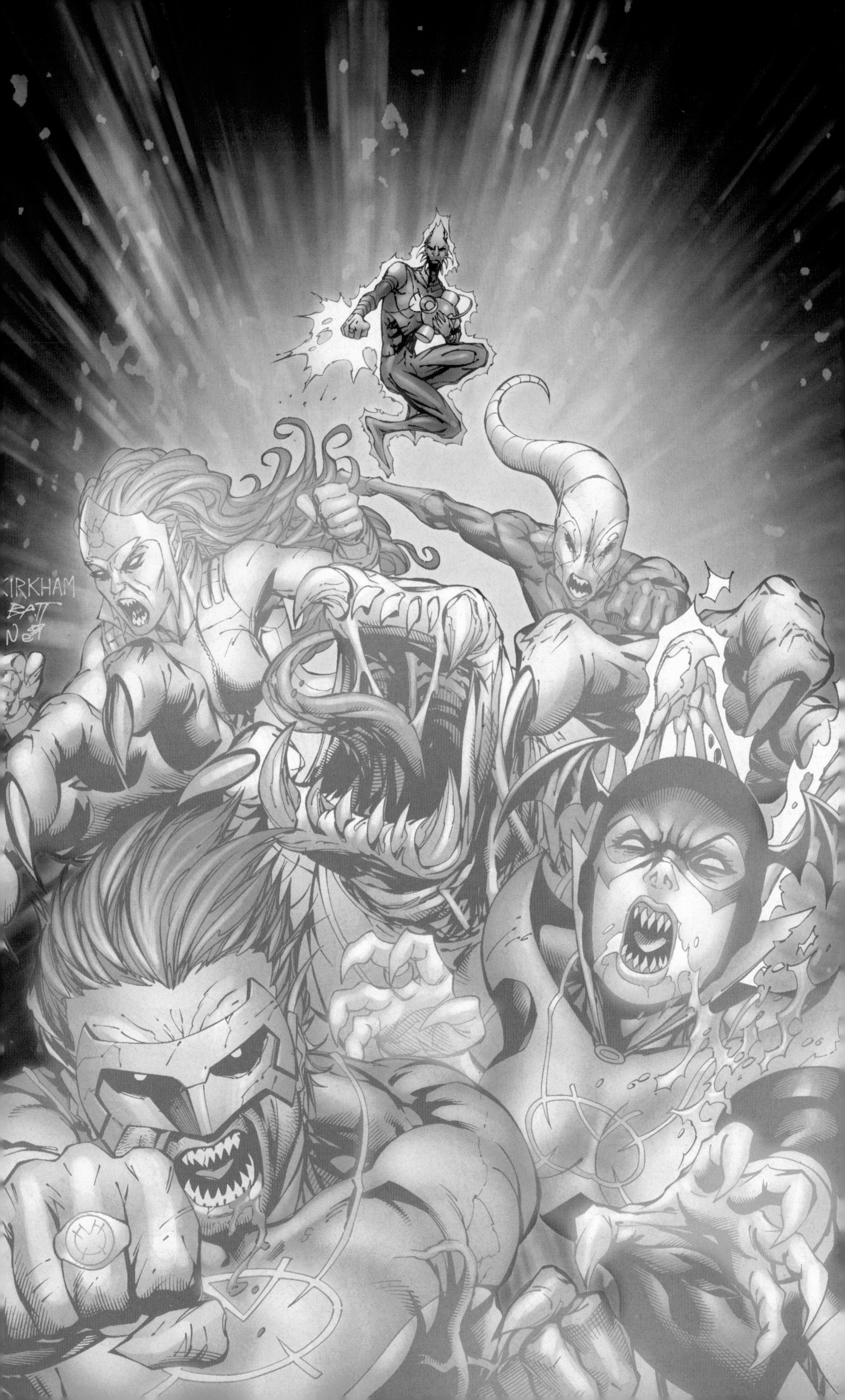

OPERATION: AGENT ORANGE

TONY BEDARD writer **TYLER KIRKHAM** penciller **BATT** inker cover by **TYLER KIRKHAM, BATT & NEI RUFFINO**

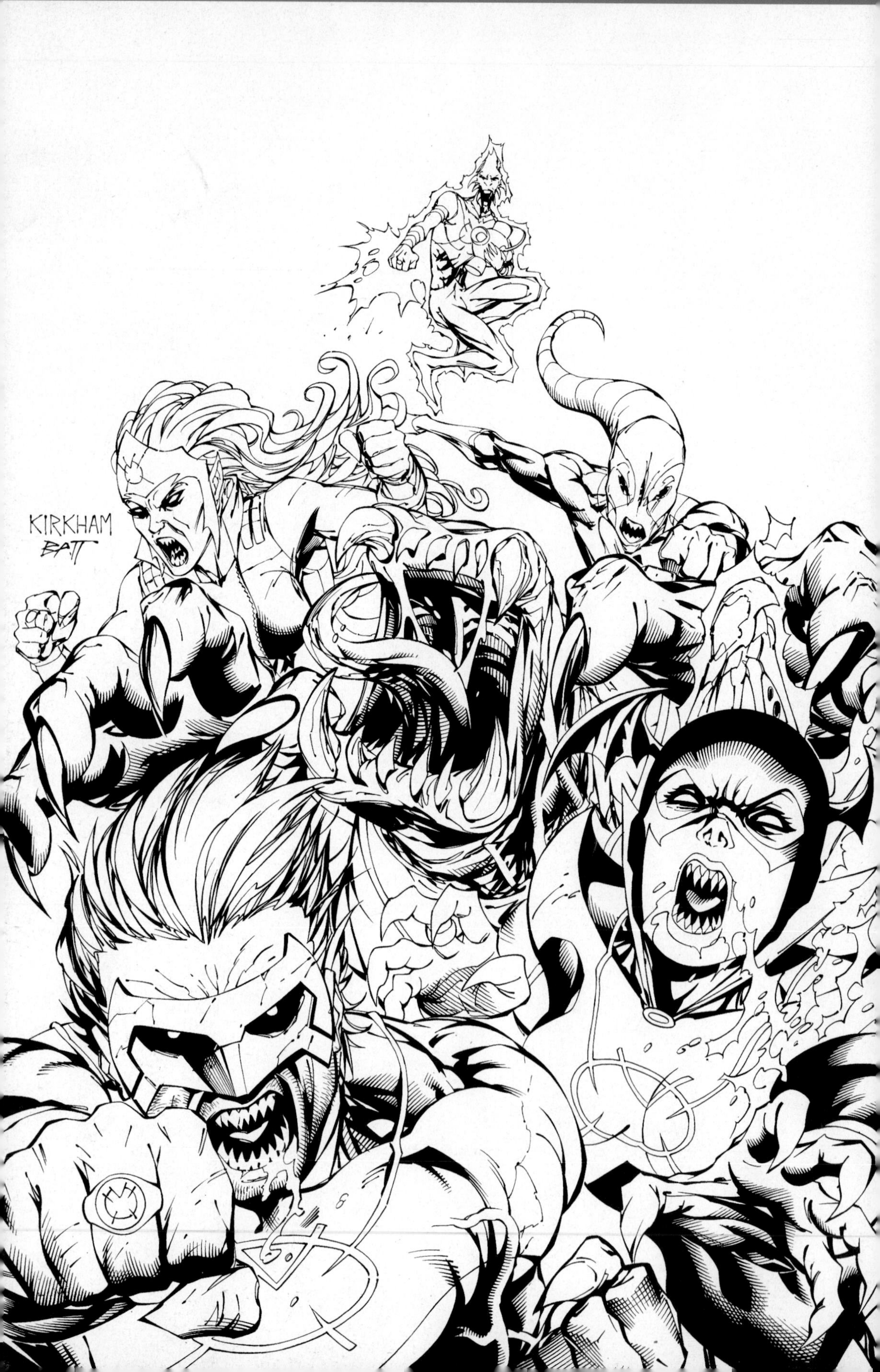
KIRKHAM
BATT

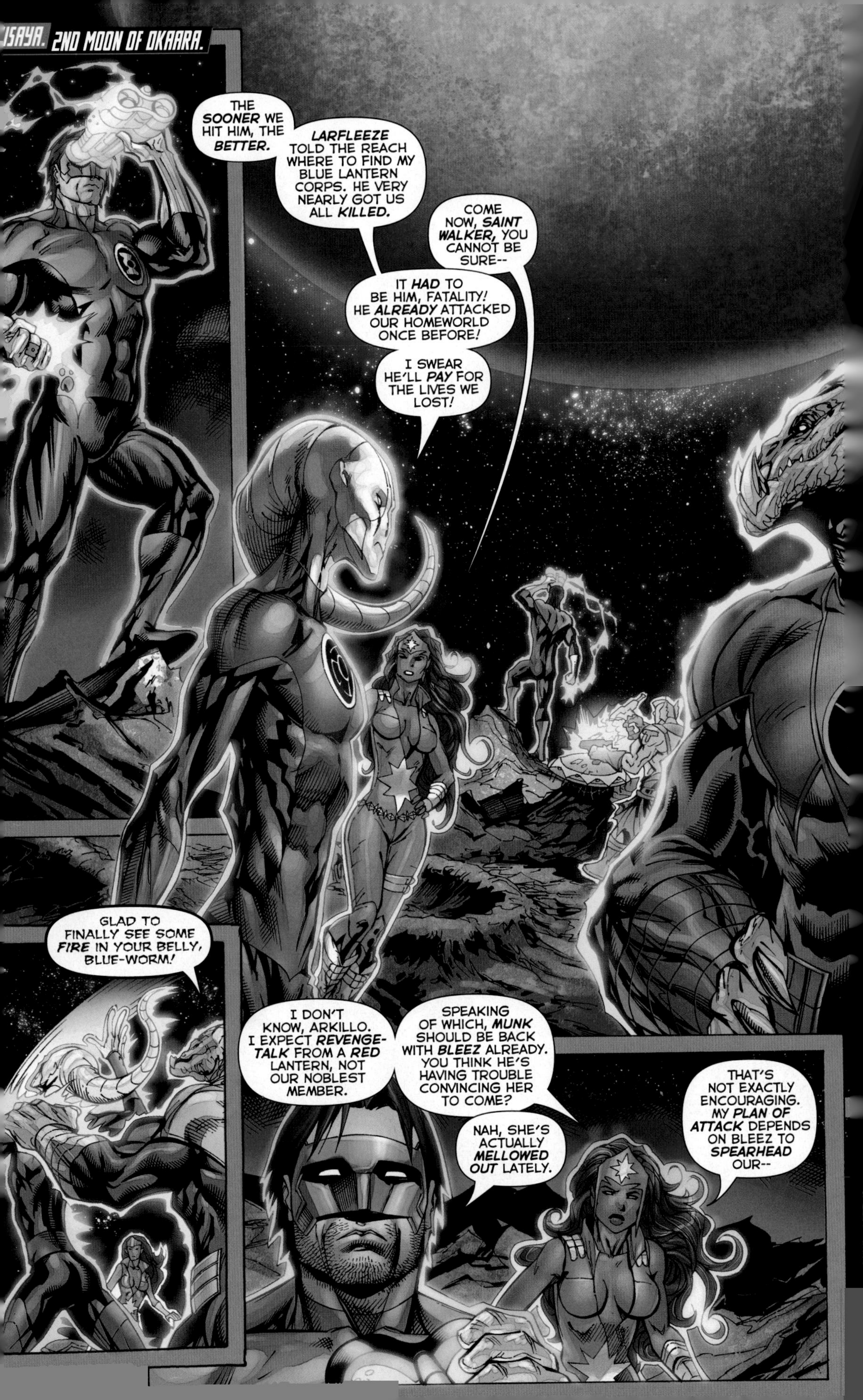

SAYA. 2ND MOON OF OKAARA.
THE SOONER WE HIT HIM, THE BETTER.
LARFLEEZE TOLD THE REACH WHERE TO FIND MY BLUE LANTERN CORPS. HE VERY NEARLY GOT US ALL KILLED.
COME NOW, SAINT WALKER, YOU CANNOT BE SURE--
IT HAD TO BE HIM, FATALITY! HE ALREADY ATTACKED OUR HOMEWORLD ONCE BEFORE!
I SWEAR HE'LL PAY FOR THE LIVES WE LOST!
GLAD TO FINALLY SEE SOME FIRE IN YOUR BELLY, BLUE-WORM!
I DON'T KNOW, ARKILLO. I EXPECT REVENGE-TALK FROM A RED LANTERN, NOT OUR NOBLEST MEMBER.
SPEAKING OF WHICH, MUNK SHOULD BE BACK WITH BLEEZ ALREADY. YOU THINK HE'S HAVING TROUBLE CONVINCING HER TO COME?
NAH, SHE'S ACTUALLY MELLOWED OUT LATELY.
THAT'S NOT EXACTLY ENCOURAGING. MY PLAN OF ATTACK DEPENDS ON BLEEZ TO SPEARHEAD OUR--

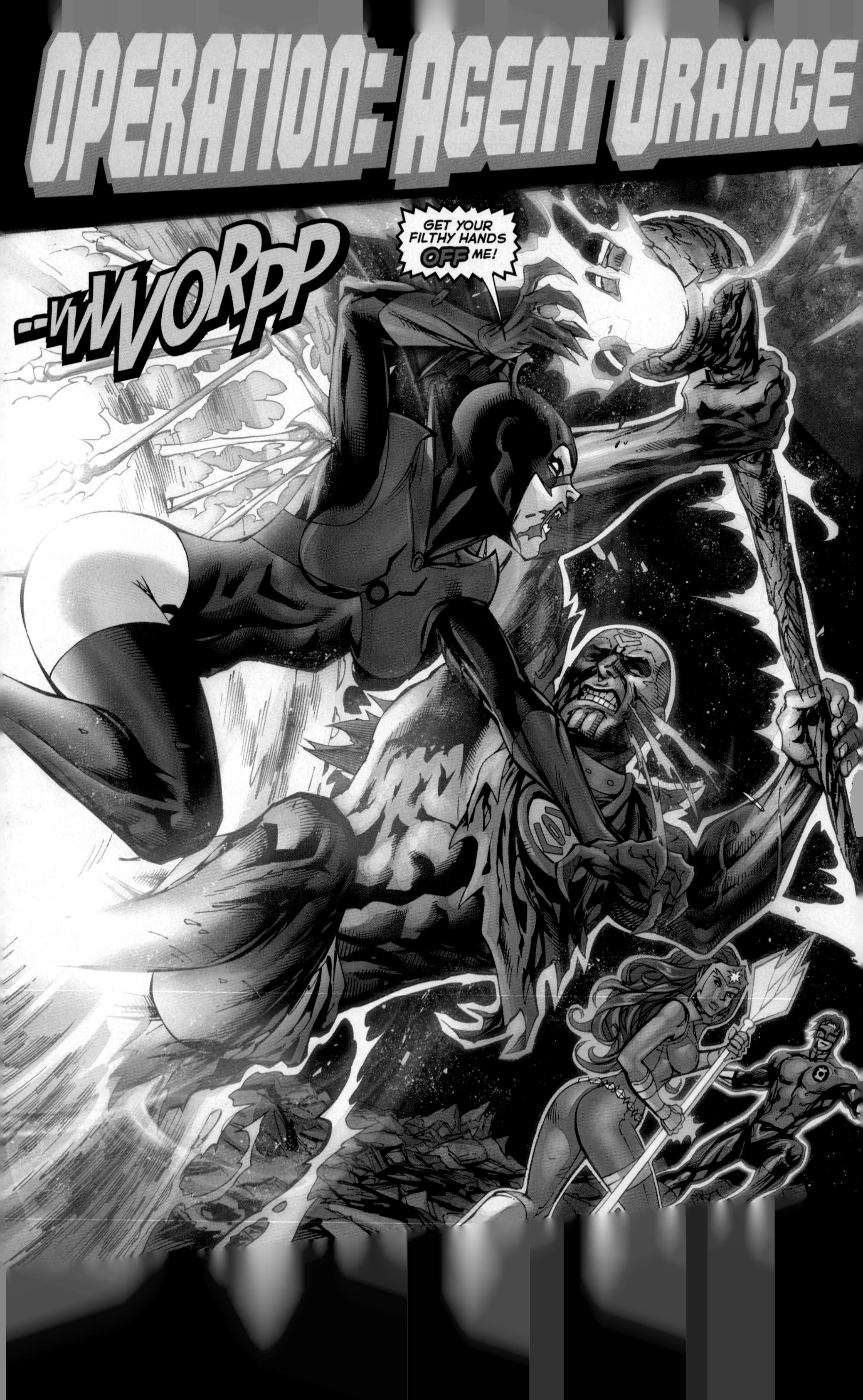
OPERATION: AGENT ORANGE
--VVWORPP
GET YOUR FILTHY HANDS OFF ME!

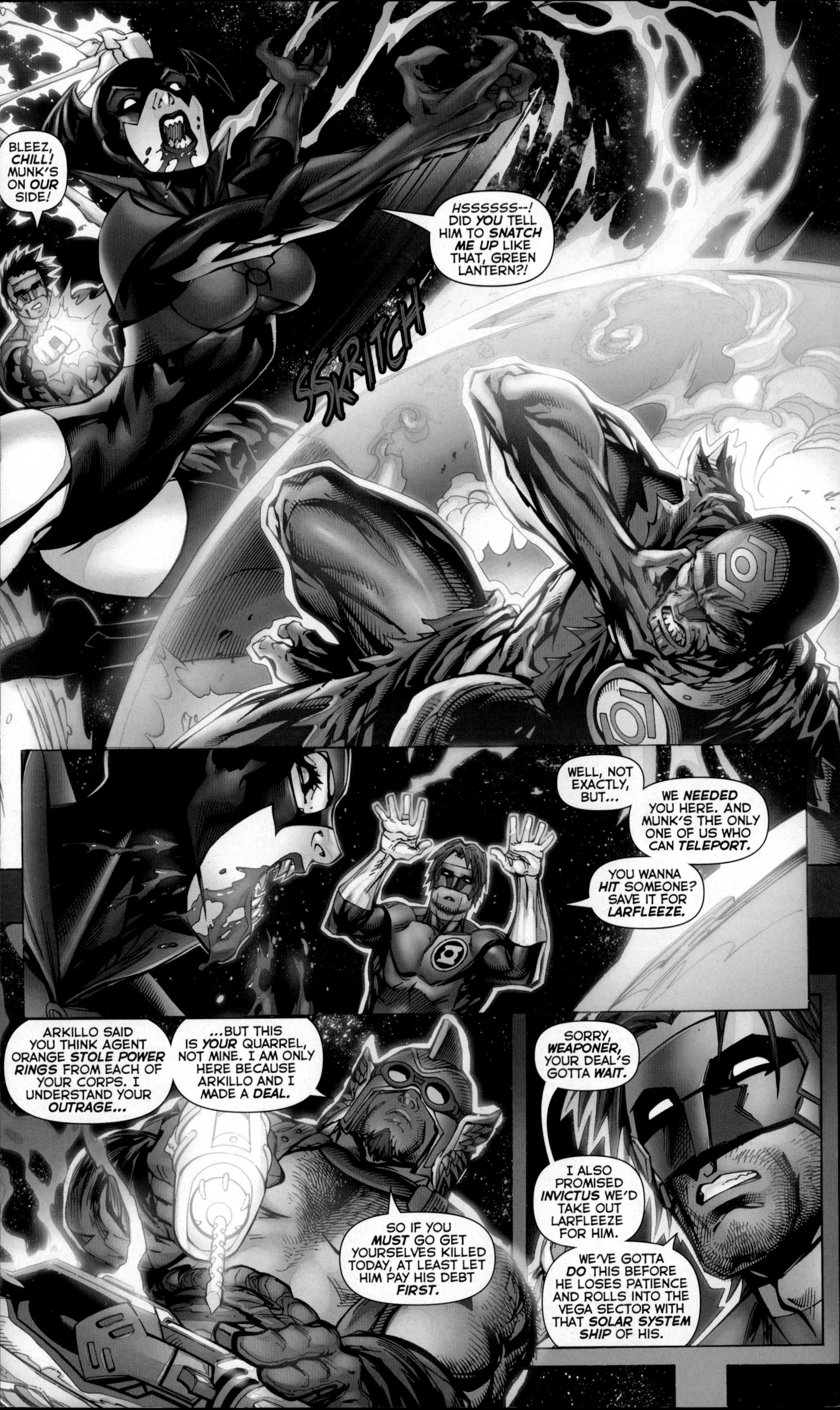
BLEEZ, CHILL! MUNK'S ON OUR SIDE!
HSSSSSS--! DID YOU TELL HIM TO SNATCH ME UP LIKE THAT, GREEN LANTERN?!
SSKRITCH
WELL, NOT EXACTLY, BUT...
WE NEEDED YOU HERE. AND MUNK'S THE ONLY ONE OF US WHO CAN TELEPORT.
YOU WANNA HIT SOMEONE? SAVE IT FOR LARFLEEZE.
ARKILLO SAID YOU THINK AGENT ORANGE STOLE POWER RINGS FROM EACH OF YOUR CORPS. I UNDERSTAND YOUR OUTRAGE...
...BUT THIS IS YOUR QUARREL, NOT MINE. I AM ONLY HERE BECAUSE ARKILLO AND I MADE A DEAL.
SO IF YOU MUST GO GET YOURSELVES KILLED TODAY, AT LEAST LET HIM PAY HIS DEBT FIRST.
SORRY, WEAPONER, YOUR DEAL'S GOTTA WAIT.
I ALSO PROMISED INVICTUS WE'D TAKE OUT LARFLEEZE FOR HIM.
WE'VE GOTTA DO THIS BEFORE HE LOSES PATIENCE AND ROLLS INTO THE VEGA SECTOR WITH THAT SOLAR SYSTEM SHIP OF HIS.

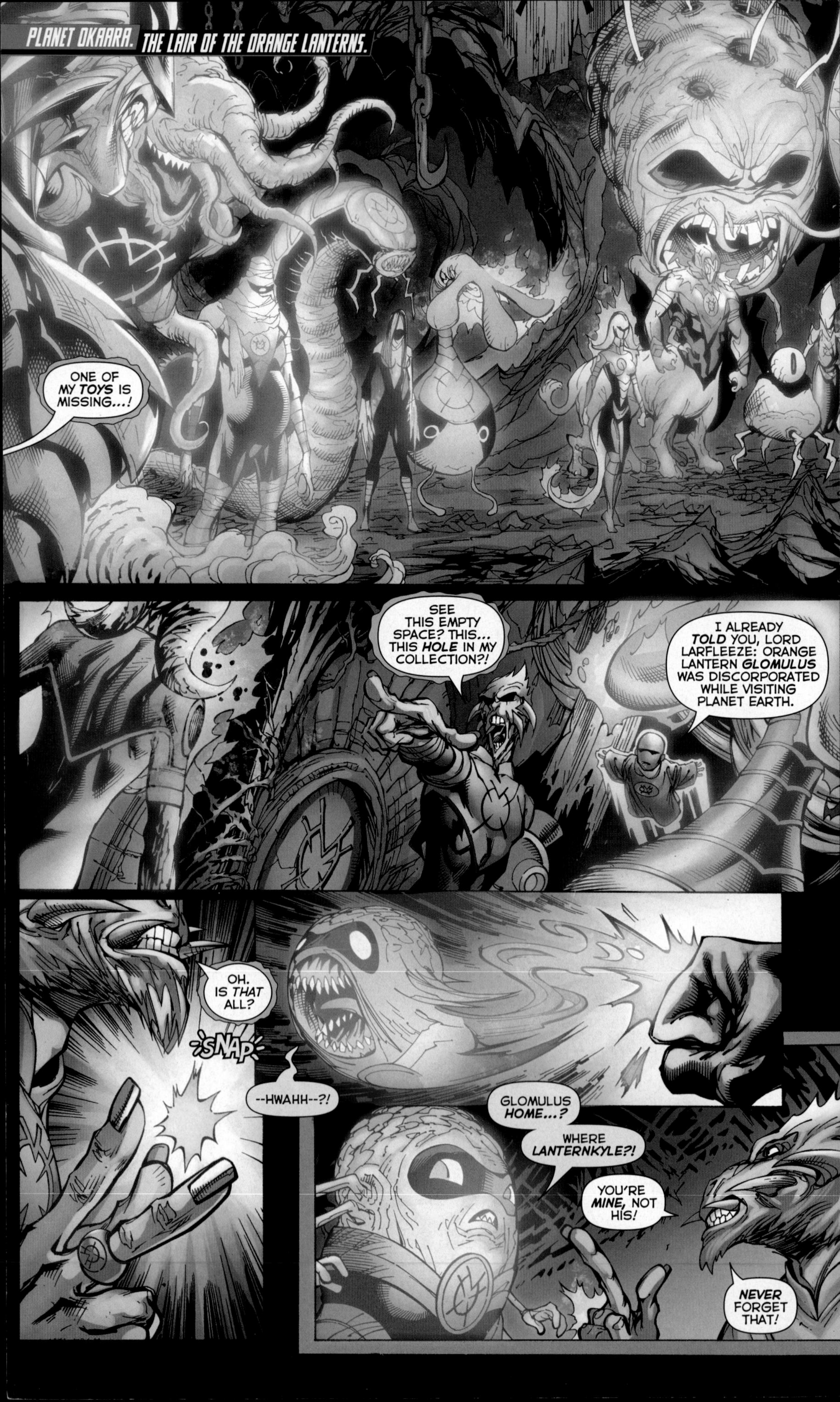
PLANET OKAARA. THE LAIR OF THE ORANGE LANTERNS.
ONE OF MY TOYS IS MISSING...!
SEE THIS EMPTY SPACE? THIS... THIS HOLE IN MY COLLECTION?!
I ALREADY TOLD YOU, LORD LARFLEEZE: ORANGE LANTERN GLOMULUS WAS DISCORPORATED WHILE VISITING PLANET EARTH.
OH. IS THAT ALL?
SNAP
--HWAHH--?!
GLOMULUS HOME...?
WHERE LANTERNKYLE?!
YOU'RE MINE, NOT HIS!
NEVER FORGET THAT!

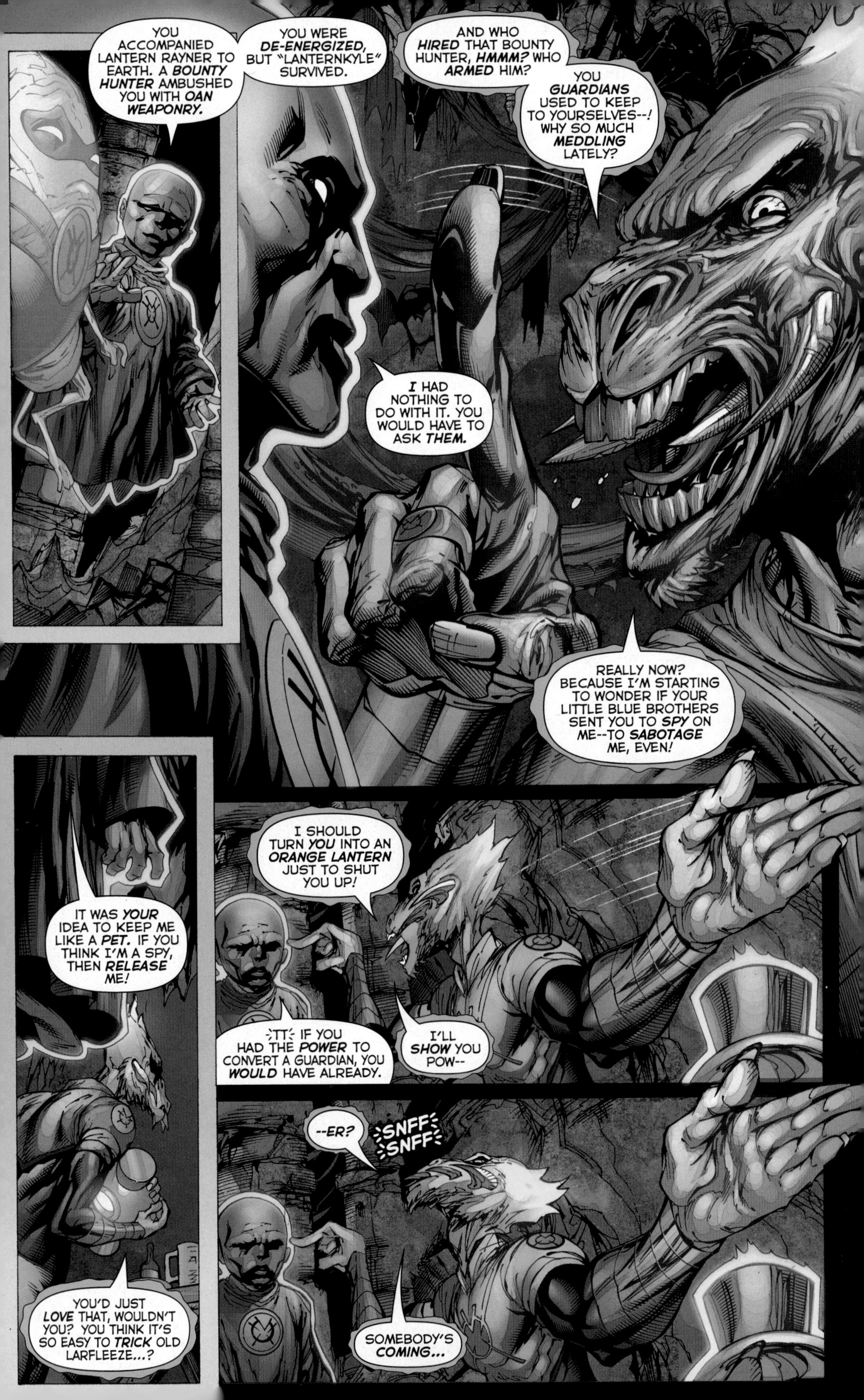
YOU ACCOMPANIED LANTERN RAYNER TO EARTH. A BOUNTY HUNTER AMBUSHED YOU WITH OAN WEAPONRY.
YOU WERE DE-ENERGIZED, BUT "LANTERNKYLE" SURVIVED.
AND WHO HIRED THAT BOUNTY HUNTER, HMMM? WHO ARMED HIM?
YOU GUARDIANS USED TO KEEP TO YOURSELVES--! WHY SO MUCH MEDDLING LATELY?
I HAD NOTHING TO DO WITH IT. YOU WOULD HAVE TO ASK THEM.
REALLY NOW? BECAUSE I'M STARTING TO WONDER IF YOUR LITTLE BLUE BROTHERS SENT YOU TO SPY ON ME--TO SABOTAGE ME, EVEN!
IT WAS YOUR IDEA TO KEEP ME LIKE A PET. IF YOU THINK I'M A SPY, THEN RELEASE ME!
I SHOULD TURN YOU INTO AN ORANGE LANTERN JUST TO SHUT YOU UP!
TT IF YOU HAD THE POWER TO CONVERT A GUARDIAN, YOU WOULD HAVE ALREADY.
I'LL SHOW YOU POW--
--ER?
SNFF SNFF
YOU'D JUST LOVE THAT, WOULDN'T YOU? YOU THINK IT'S SO EASY TO TRICK OLD LARFLEEZE...?
SOMEBODY'S COMING...

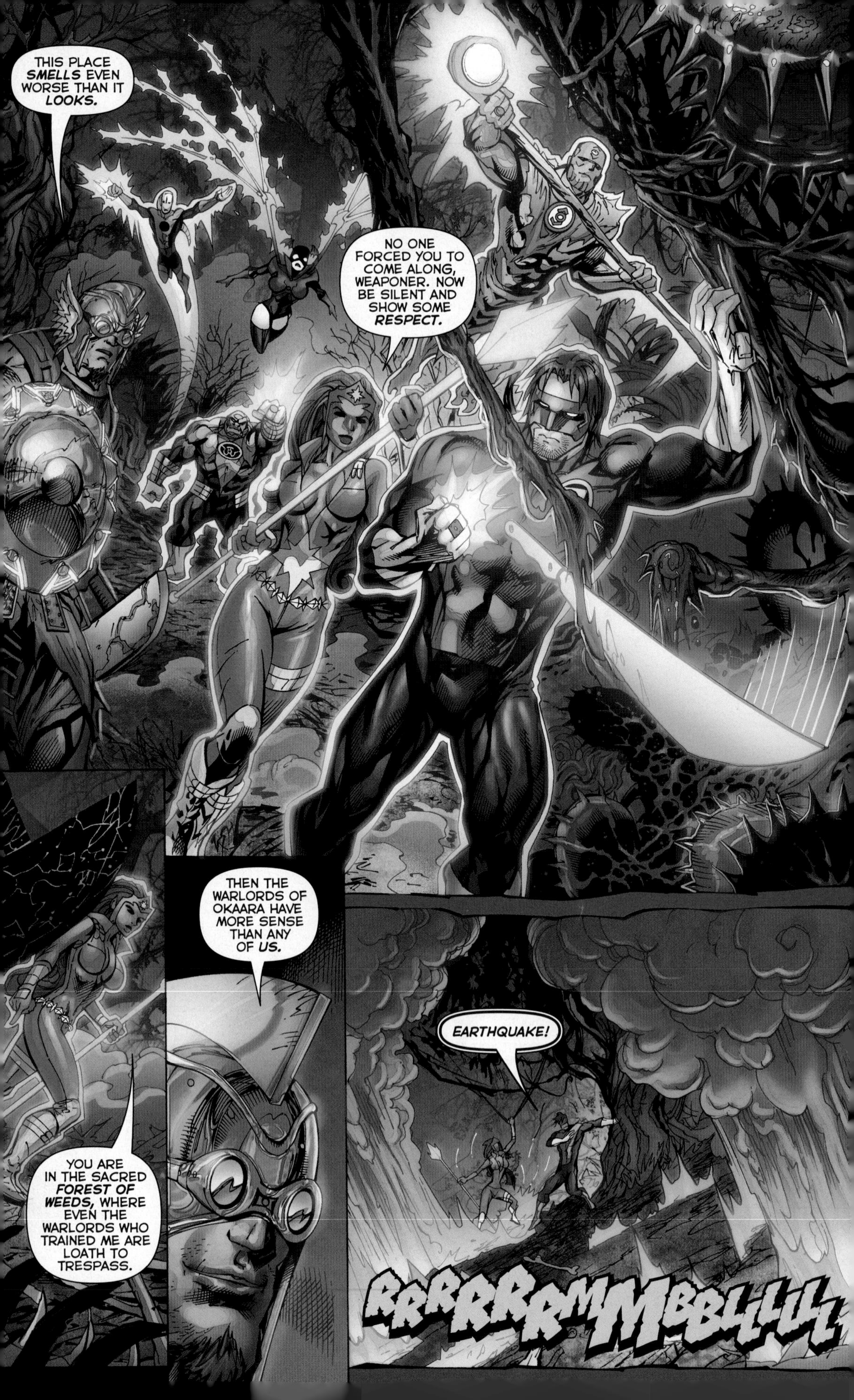
THIS PLACE SMELLS EVEN WORSE THAN IT LOOKS.
NO ONE FORCED YOU TO COME ALONG, WEAPONER. NOW BE SILENT AND SHOW SOME RESPECT.
YOU ARE IN THE SACRED FOREST OF WEEDS, WHERE EVEN THE WARLORDS WHO TRAINED ME ARE LOATH TO TRESPASS.
THEN THE WARLORDS OF OKAARA HAVE MORE SENSE THAN ANY OF US.
EARTHQUAKE!
RRRRRRMMBBLLLL

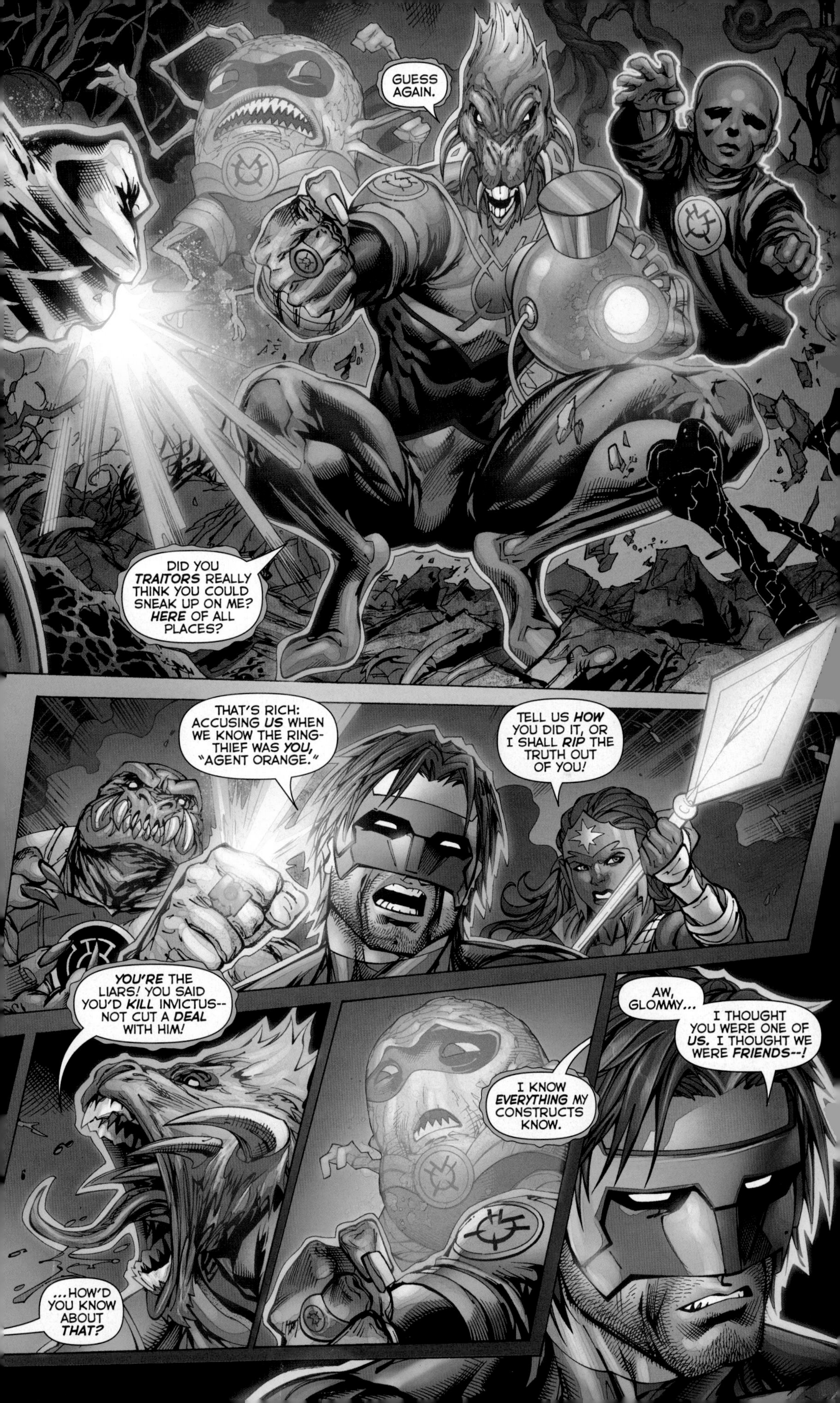
GUESS AGAIN.
DID YOU TRAITORS REALLY THINK YOU COULD SNEAK UP ON ME? HERE OF ALL PLACES?
THAT'S RICH: ACCUSING US WHEN WE KNOW THE RING-THIEF WAS YOU, "AGENT ORANGE."
TELL US HOW YOU DID IT, OR I SHALL RIP THE TRUTH OUT OF YOU!
YOU'RE THE LIARS! YOU SAID YOU'D KILL INVICTUS--NOT CUT A DEAL WITH HIM!
...HOW'D YOU KNOW ABOUT THAT?
I KNOW EVERYTHING MY CONSTRUCTS KNOW.
AW, GLOMMY...
I THOUGHT YOU WERE ONE OF US. I THOUGHT WE WERE FRIENDS--!

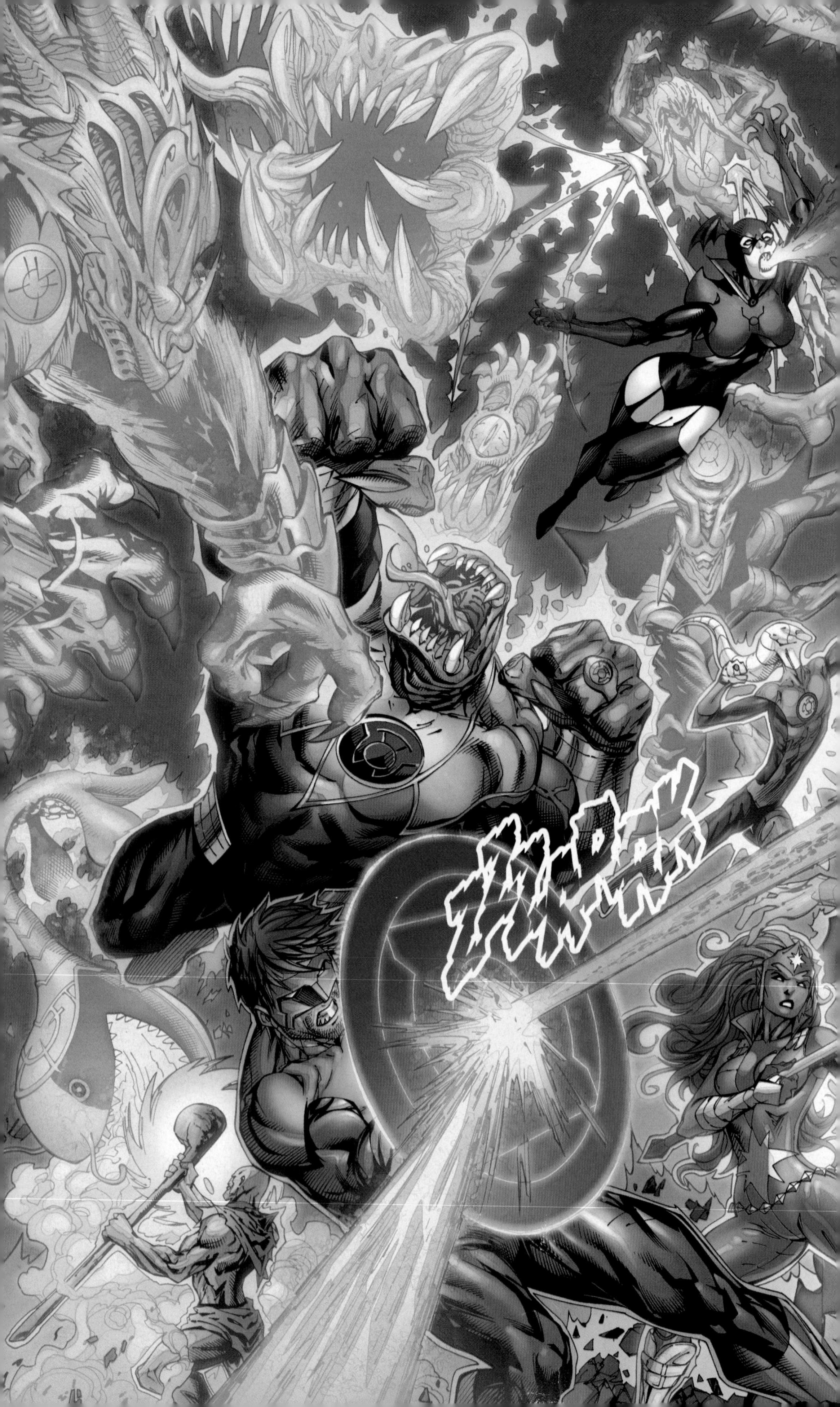
THOOK

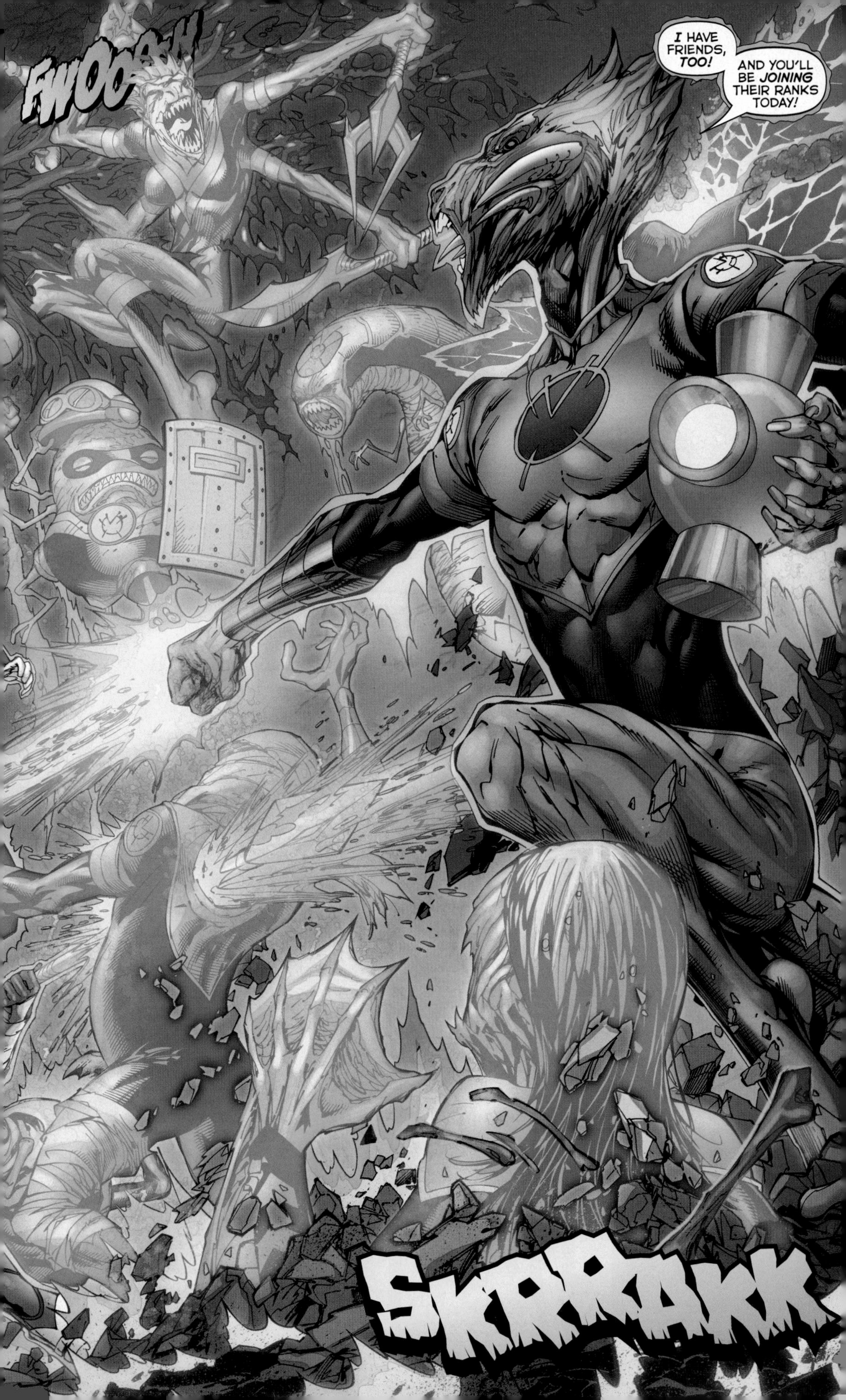
FWOOOSH
I HAVE FRIENDS, TOO!
AND YOU'LL BE JOINING THEIR RANKS TODAY!
SKRRAKK

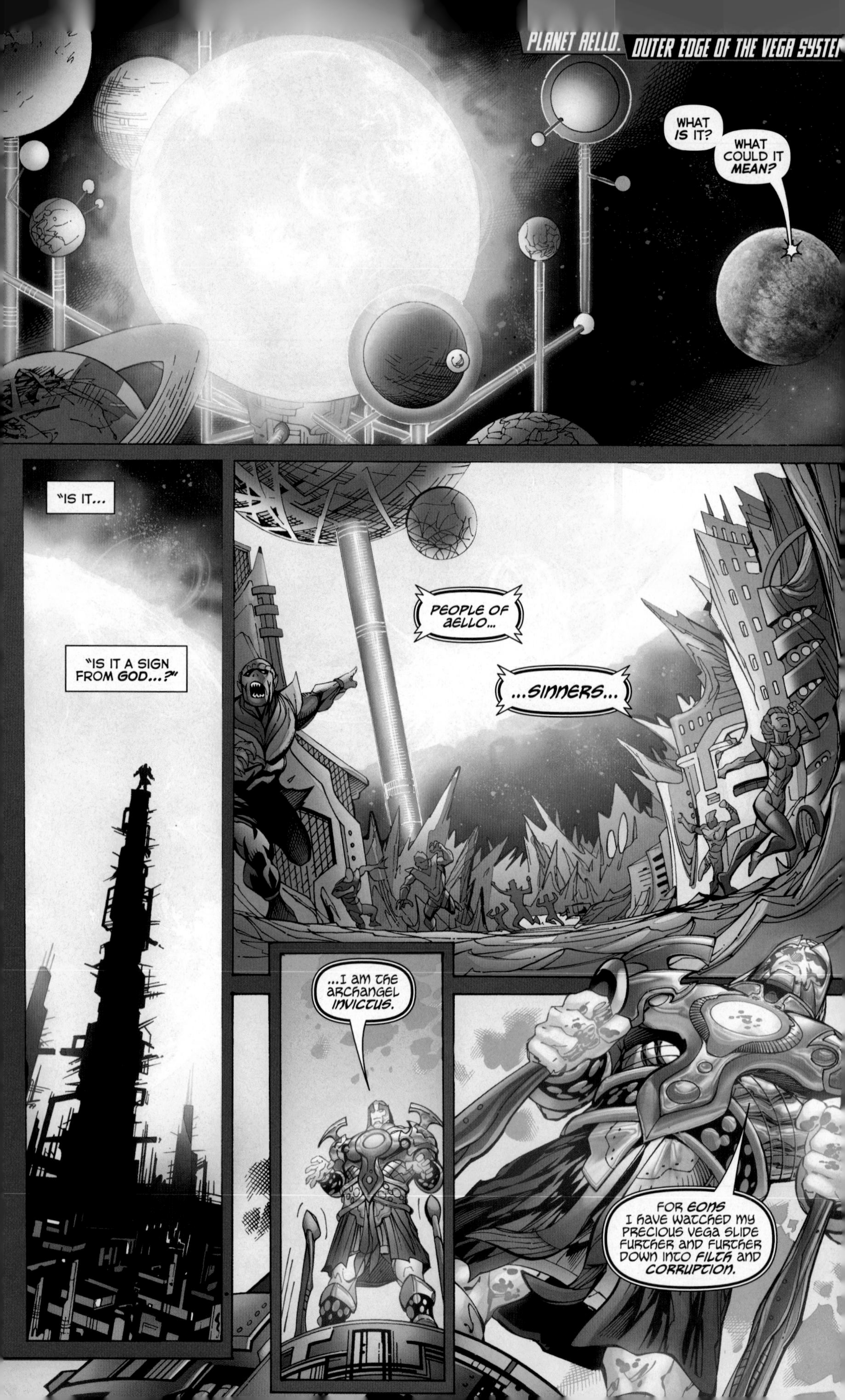
PLANET AELLO.
OUTER EDGE OF THE VEGA SYSTEM
WHAT IS IT?
WHAT COULD IT MEAN?
"IS IT...
"IS IT A SIGN FROM GOD...?"
PEOPLE OF AELLO...
...SINNERS...
...I AM THE ARCHANGEL INVICTUS.
FOR EONS I HAVE WATCHED MY PRECIOUS VEGA SLIDE FURTHER AND FURTHER DOWN INTO FILTH AND CORRUPTION.

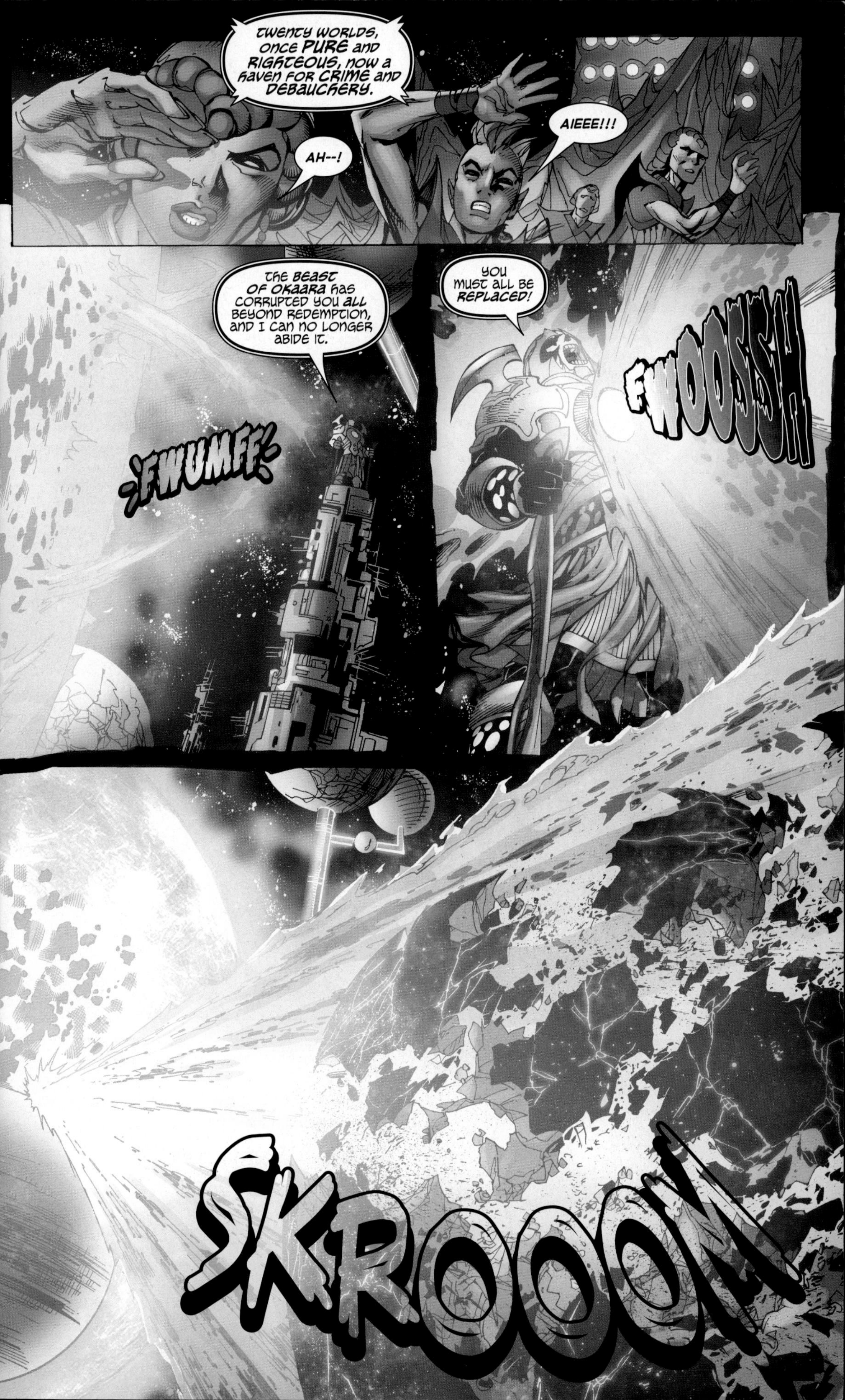
TWENTY WORLDS, ONCE PURE AND RIGHTEOUS, NOW A HAVEN FOR CRIME AND DEBAUCHERY.
AH--!
AIEEE!!!
THE BEAST OF OKAARA HAS CORRUPTED YOU ALL BEYOND REDEMPTION, AND I CAN NO LONGER ABIDE IT.
FWUMFF
YOU MUST ALL BE REPLACED!
FWOOSSH
SKROOOOM

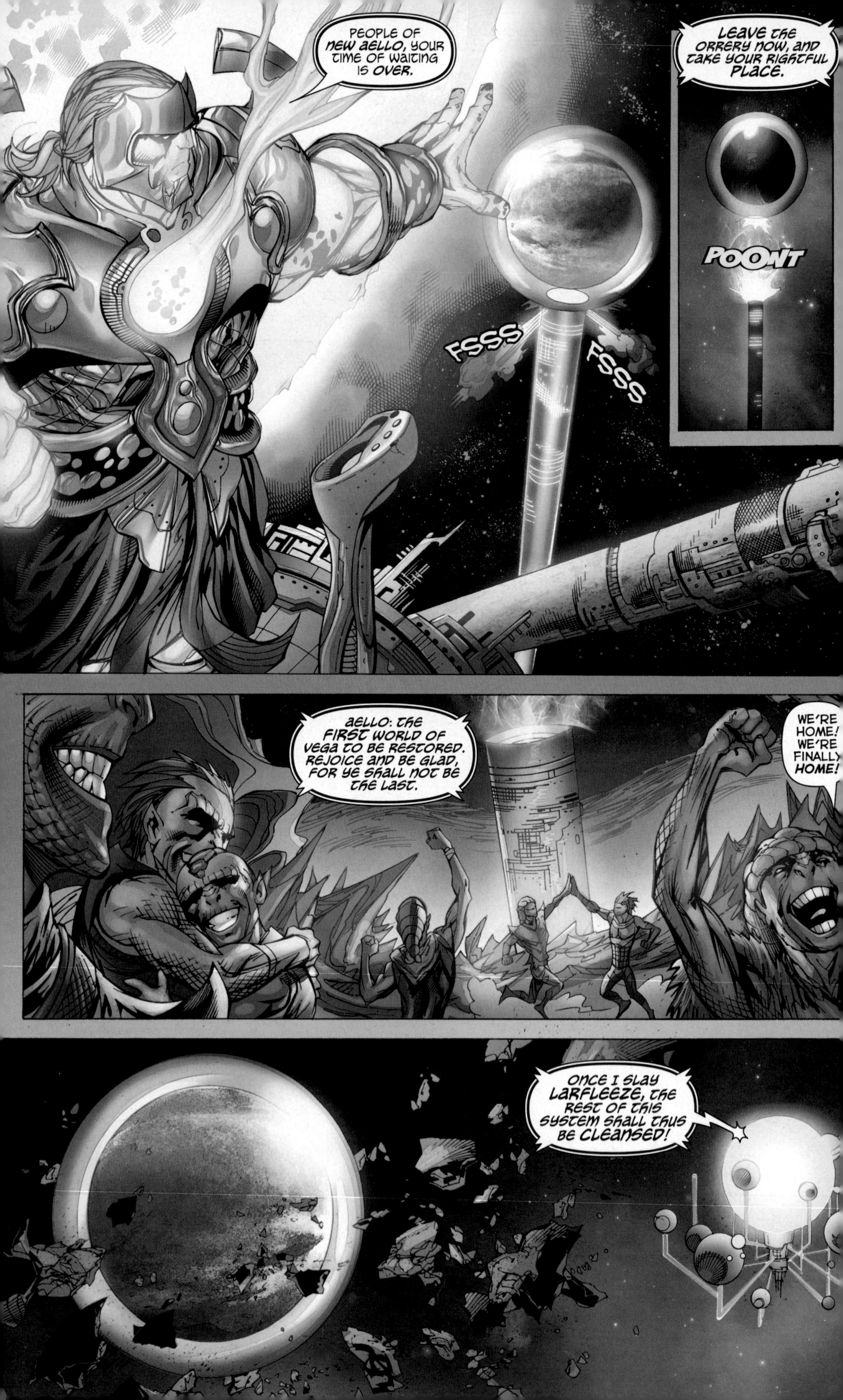
PEOPLE OF NEW AELLO, YOUR TIME OF WAITING IS OVER.
LEAVE THE ORRERY NOW, AND TAKE YOUR RIGHTFUL PLACE.
POONT
FSSS
FSSS
AELLO: THE FIRST WORLD OF VEGA TO BE RESTORED. REJOICE AND BE GLAD, FOR YE SHALL NOT BE THE LAST.
WE'RE HOME! WE'RE FINALLY HOME!
ONCE I SLAY LARFLEEZE, THE REST OF THIS SYSTEM SHALL THUS BE CLEANSED!

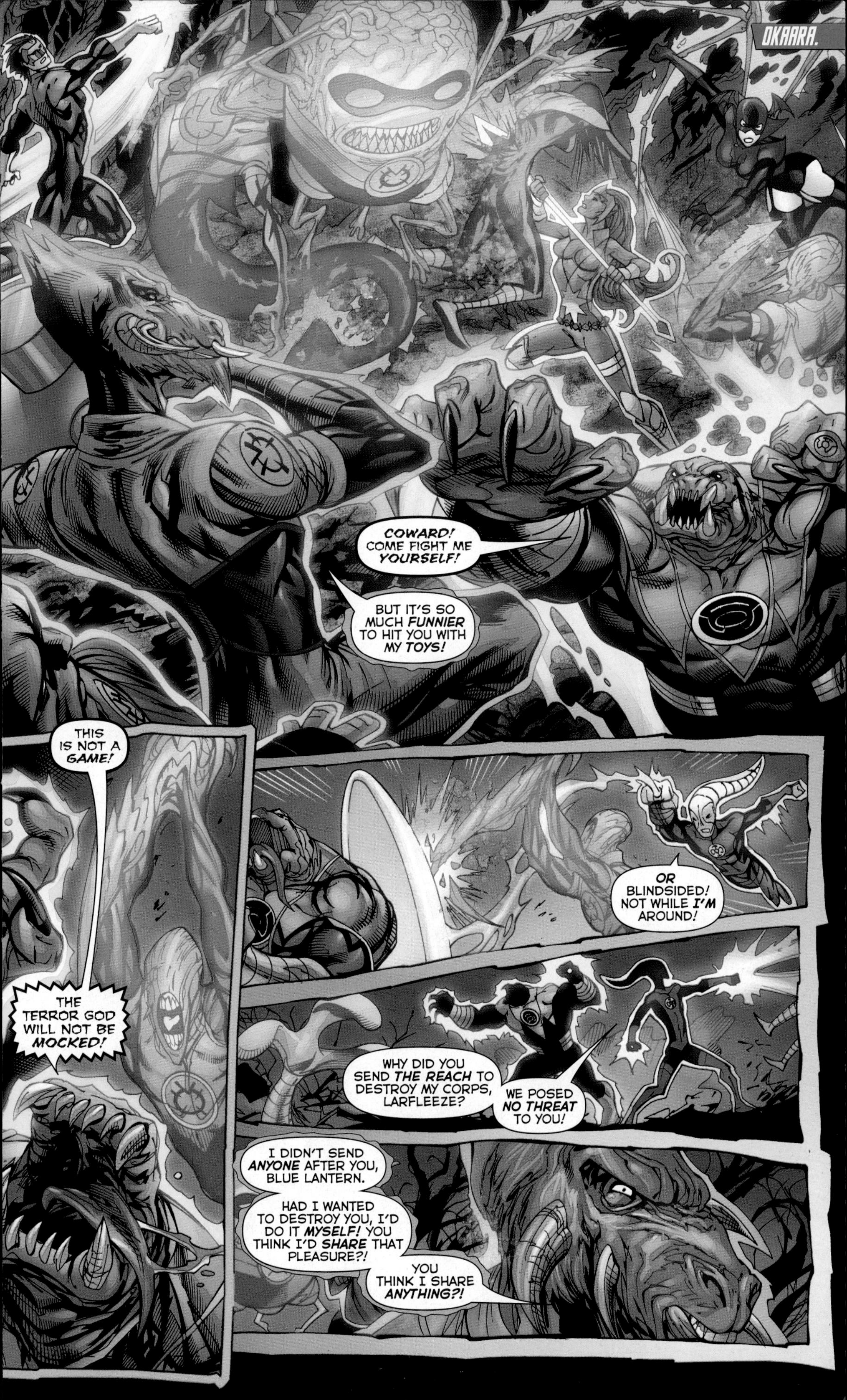
OKAARA.
COWARD! COME FIGHT ME YOURSELF!
BUT IT'S SO MUCH FUNNIER TO HIT YOU WITH MY TOYS!
THIS IS NOT A GAME!
THE TERROR GOD WILL NOT BE MOCKED!
OR BLINDSIDED! NOT WHILE I'M AROUND!
WHY DID YOU SEND THE REACH TO DESTROY MY CORPS, LARFLEEZE?
WE POSED NO THREAT TO YOU!
I DIDN'T SEND ANYONE AFTER YOU, BLUE LANTERN.
HAD I WANTED TO DESTROY YOU, I'D DO IT MYSELF! YOU THINK I'D SHARE THAT PLEASURE?!
YOU THINK I SHARE ANYTHING?!

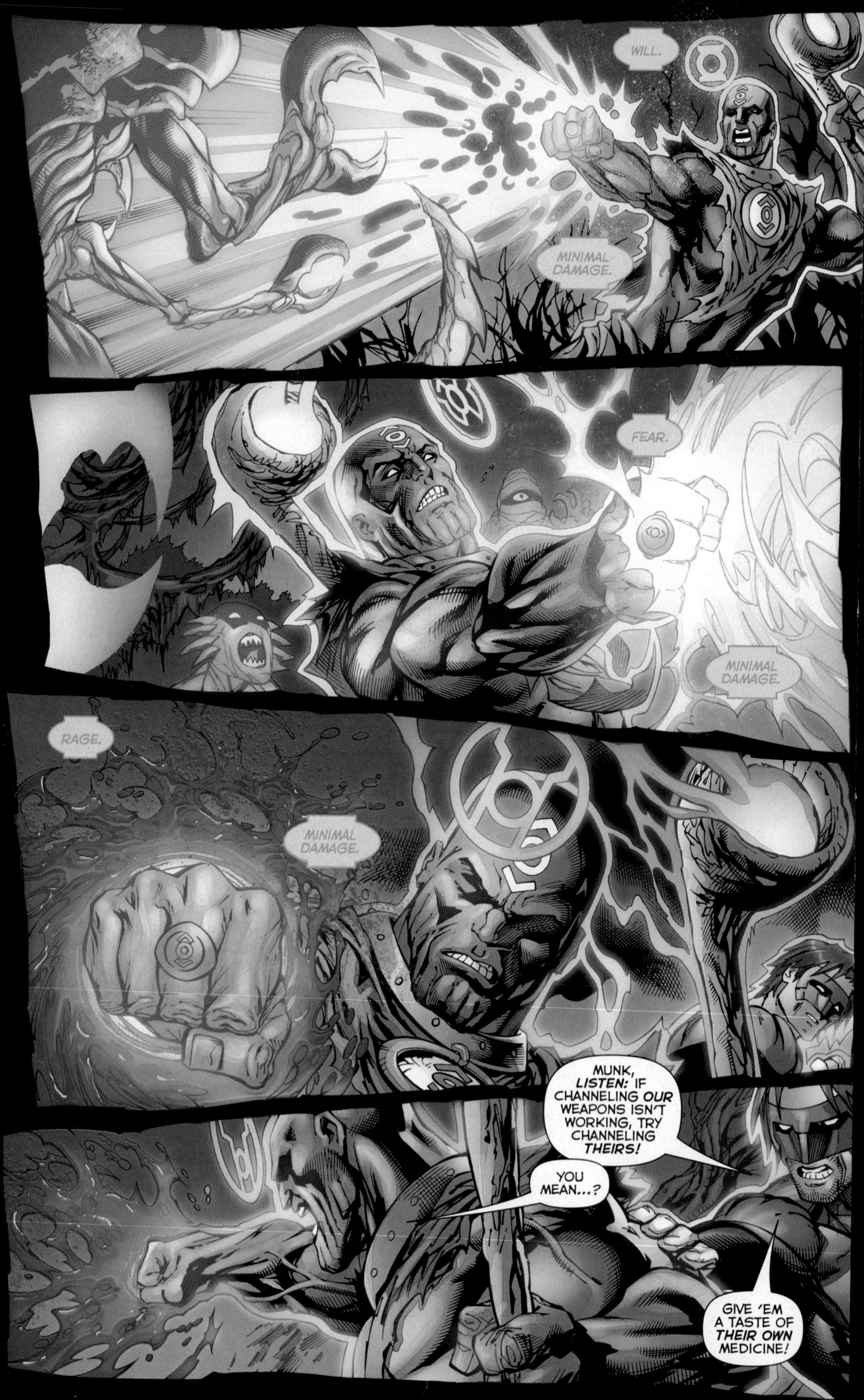
WILL.
MINIMAL DAMAGE.
FEAR.
MINIMAL DAMAGE.
RAGE.
MINIMAL DAMAGE.
MUNK, LISTEN: IF CHANNELING OUR WEAPONS ISN'T WORKING, TRY CHANNELING THEIRS!
YOU MEAN...?
GIVE 'EM A TASTE OF THEIR OWN MEDICINE!

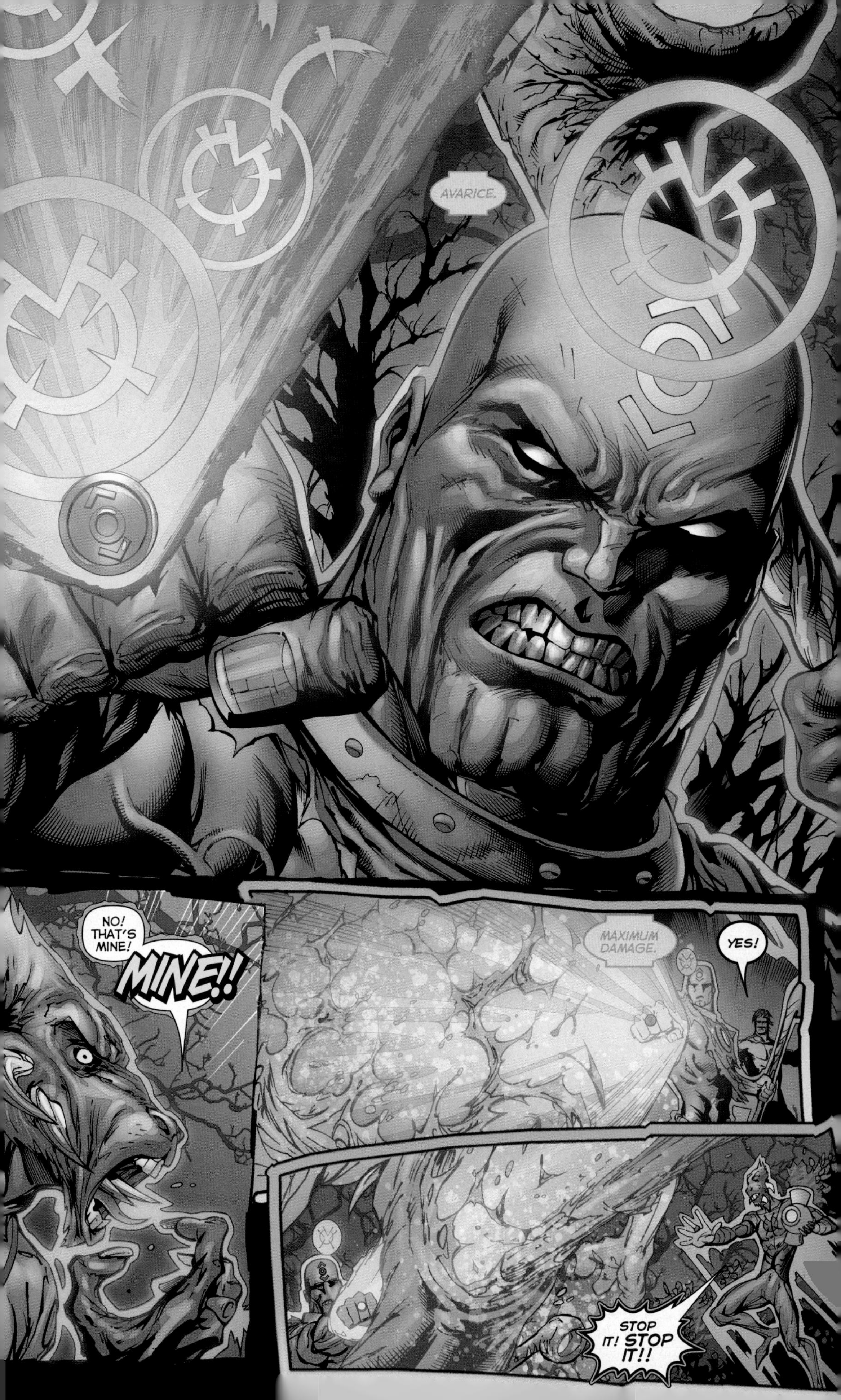
AVARICE.
NO! THAT'S MINE!
MINE!!
MAXIMUM DAMAGE.
YES!
STOP IT! STOP IT!!

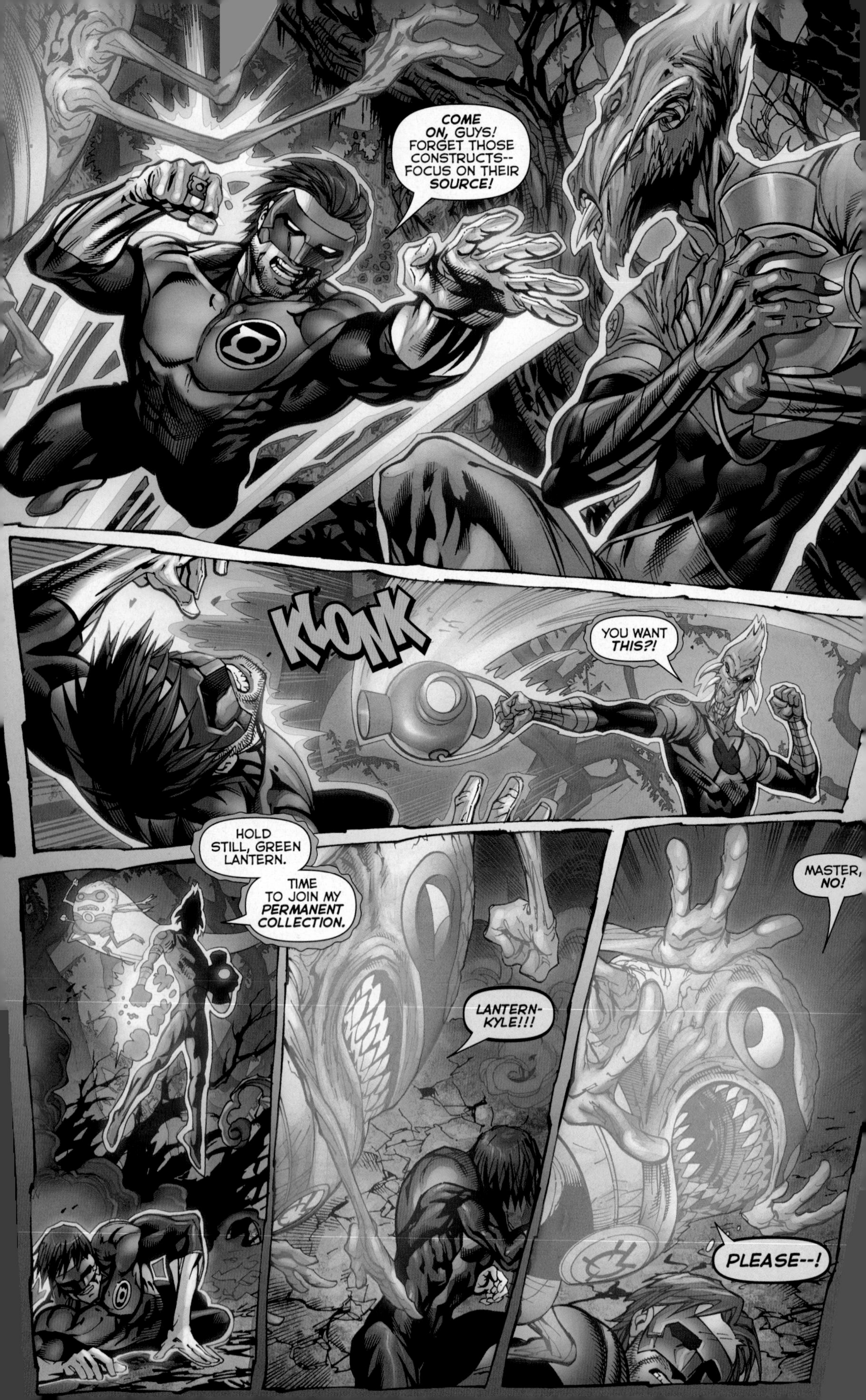
COME ON, GUYS! FORGET THOSE CONSTRUCTS-- FOCUS ON THEIR SOURCE!
KLONK
YOU WANT THIS?!
HOLD STILL, GREEN LANTERN.
TIME TO JOIN MY PERMANENT COLLECTION.
LANTERN-KYLE!!!
MASTER, NO!
PLEASE--!

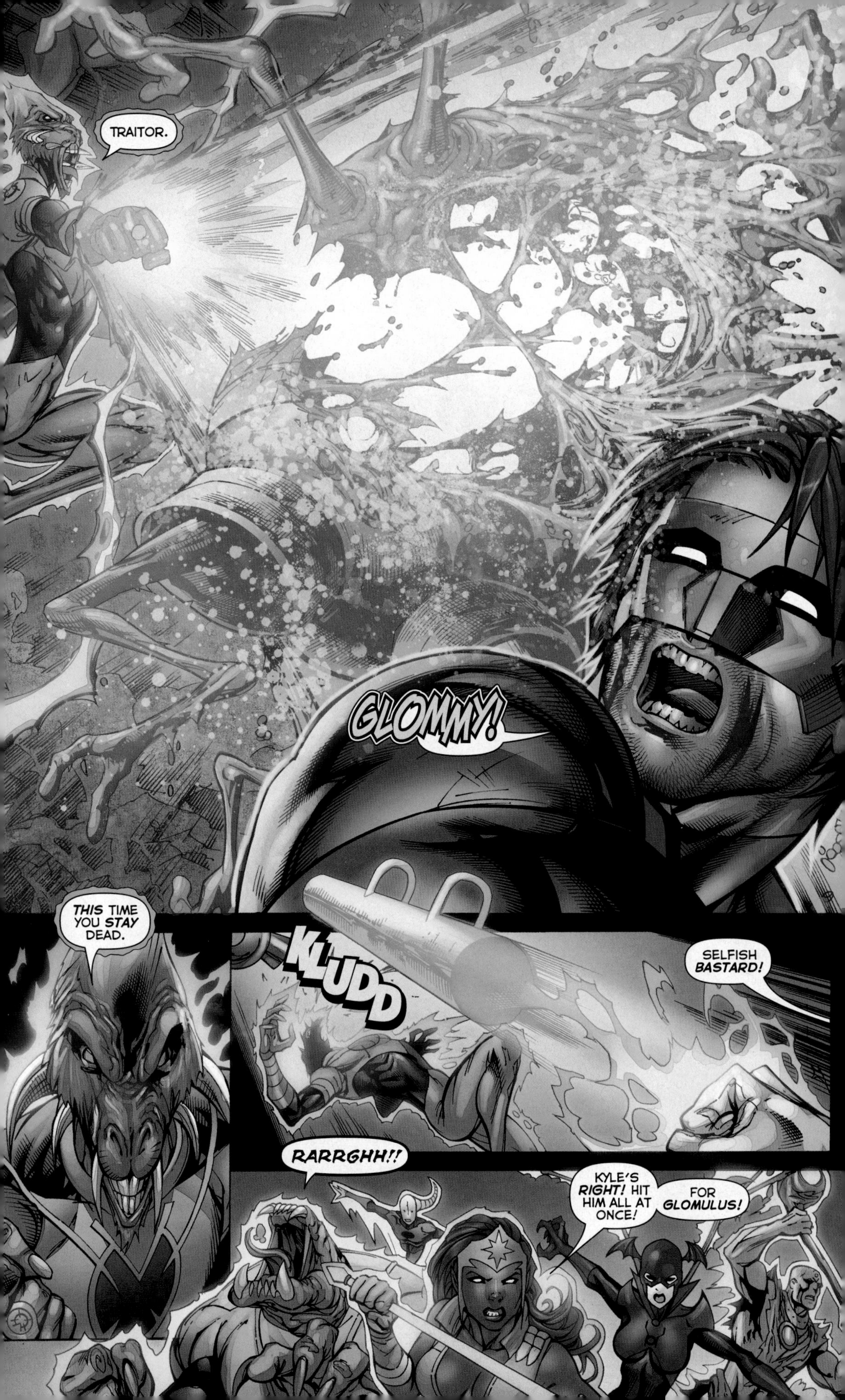
TRAITOR.
GLOMMY!
THIS TIME YOU STAY DEAD.
KLUDD
SELFISH BASTARD!
RARRGHH!!
KYLE'S RIGHT! HIT HIM ALL AT ONCE!
FOR GLOMULUS!

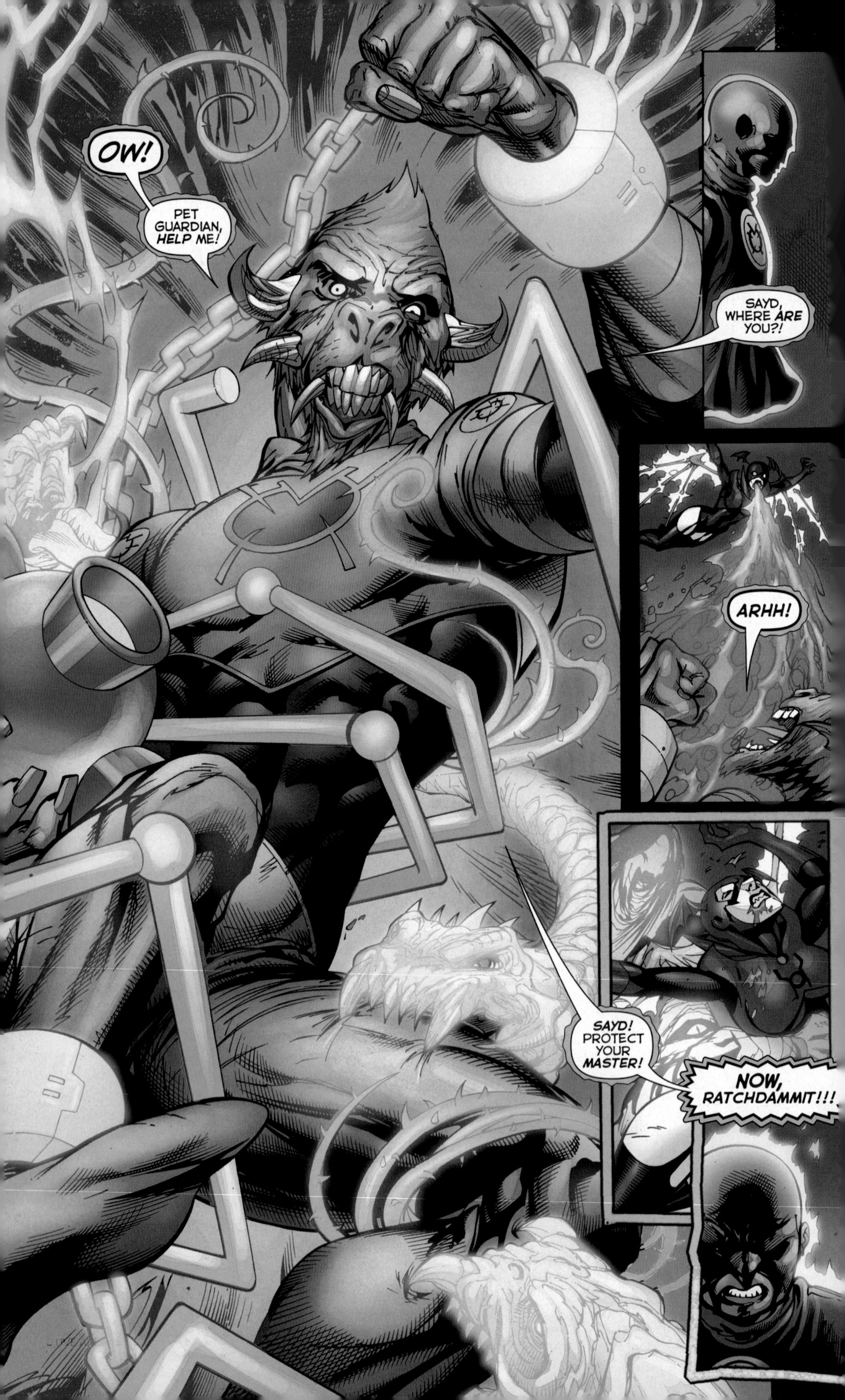

OW!
PET GUARDIAN, HELP ME!
SAYD, WHERE ARE YOU?!
ARHH!
SAYD! PROTECT YOUR MASTER!
NOW, RATCHDAMMIT!!!

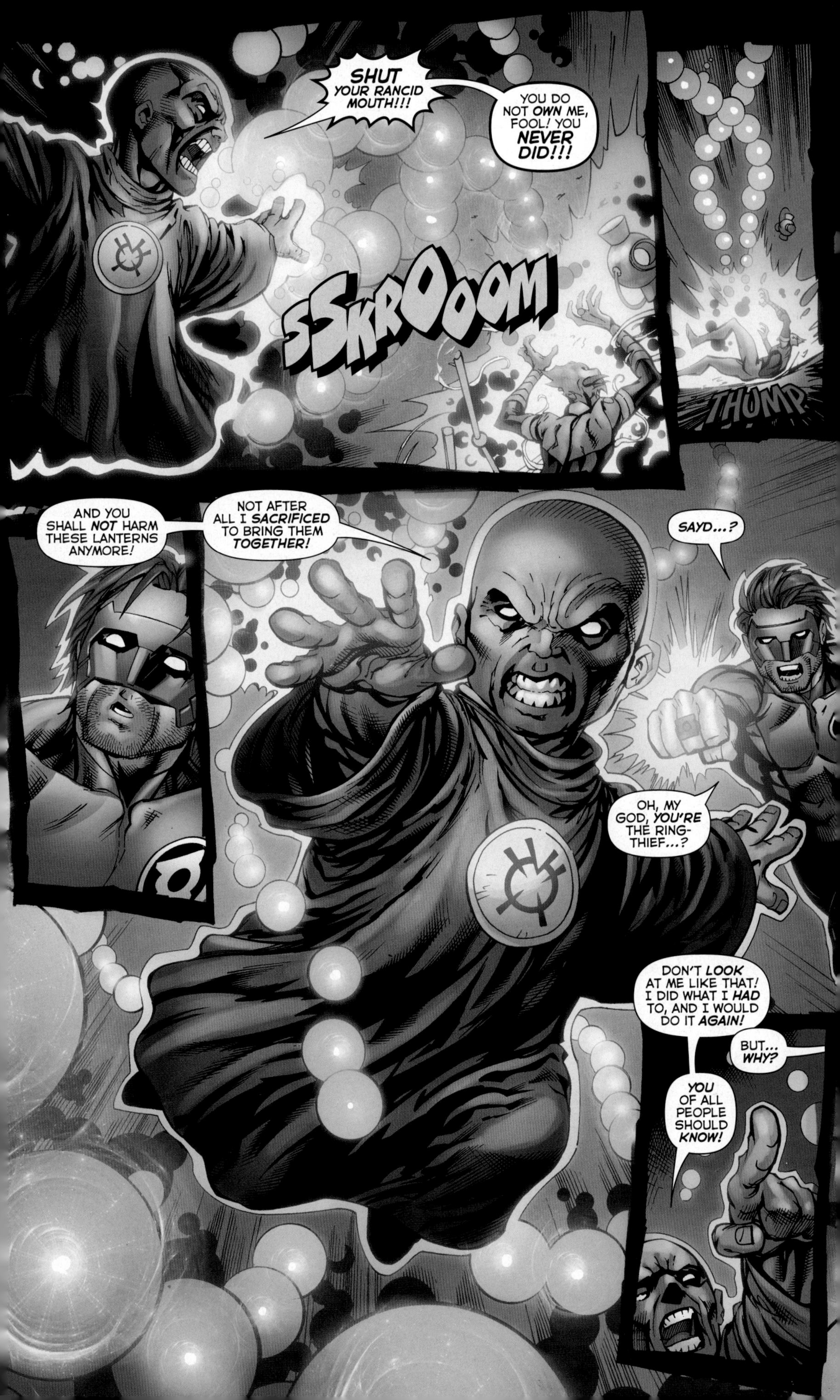
SHUT YOUR RANCID MOUTH!!!
YOU DO NOT OWN ME, FOOL! YOU NEVER DID!!!
SSKROOOOM
THUMP
AND YOU SHALL NOT HARM THESE LANTERNS ANYMORE!
NOT AFTER ALL I SACRIFICED TO BRING THEM TOGETHER!
SAYD...?
OH, MY GOD, YOU'RE THE RING-THIEF...?
DON'T LOOK AT ME LIKE THAT! I DID WHAT I HAD TO, AND I WOULD DO IT AGAIN!
BUT... WHY?
YOU OF ALL PEOPLE SHOULD KNOW!

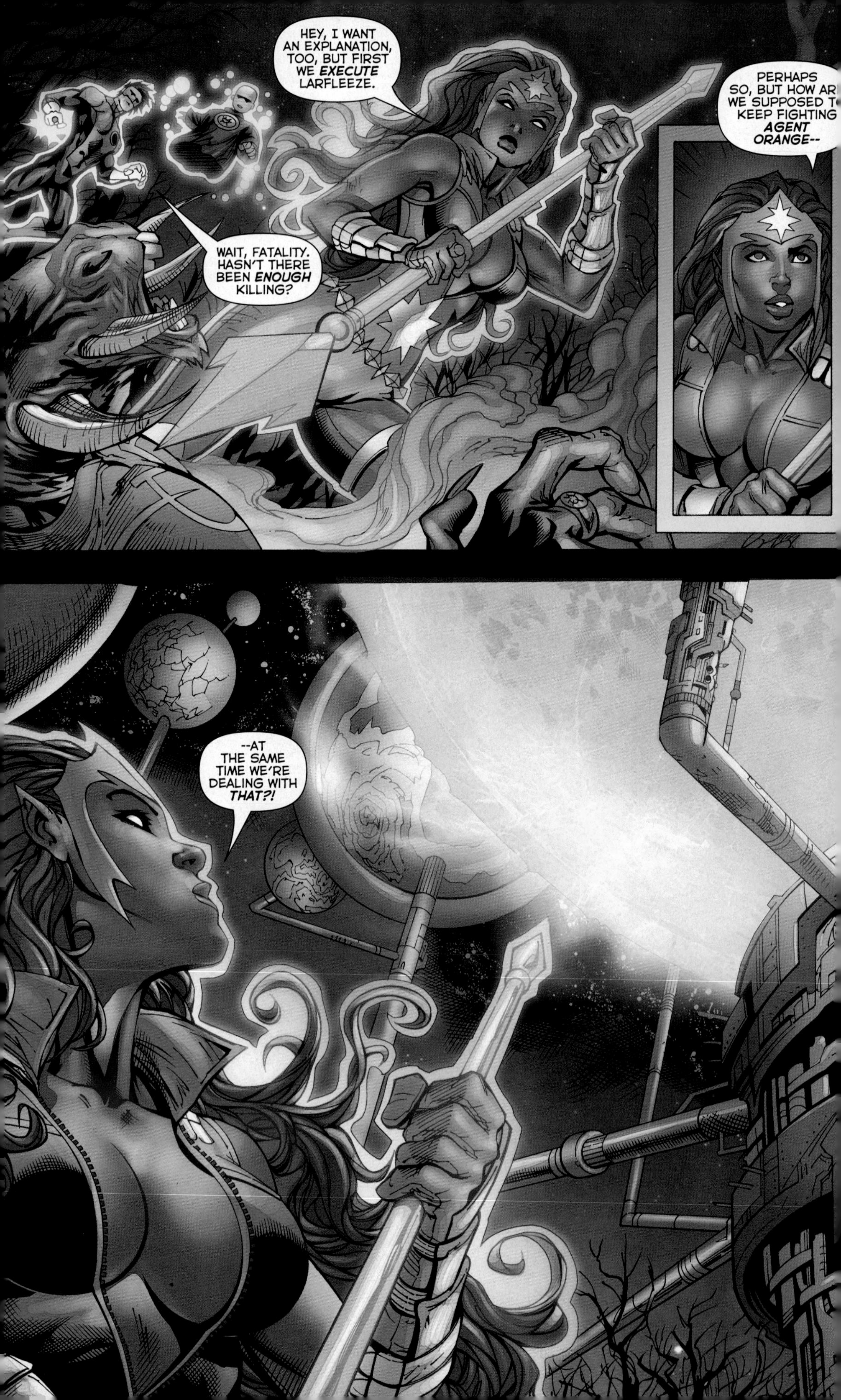
HEY, I WANT AN EXPLANATION, TOO, BUT FIRST WE EXECUTE LARFLEEZE.
WAIT, FATALITY. HASN'T THERE BEEN ENOUGH KILLING?
PERHAPS SO, BUT HOW AR WE SUPPOSED T KEEP FIGHTING AGENT ORANGE--
--AT THE SAME TIME WE'RE DEALING WITH THAT?!

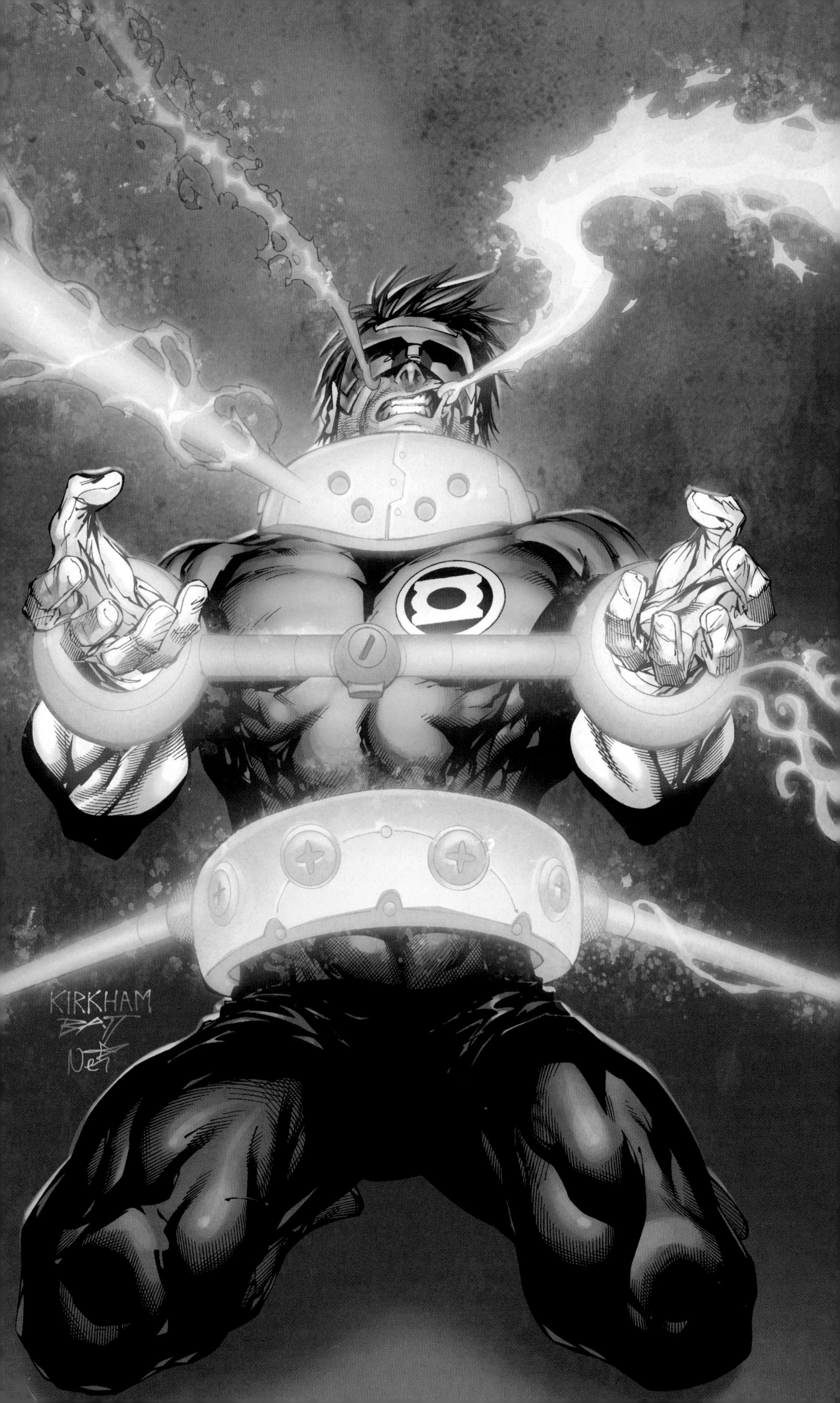
KIRKHAM

IN THE NAME OF LOVE

TONY BEDARD writer **TYLER KIRKHAM** penciller **BATT** inker cover by **TYLER KIRKHAM, BATT & NEI RUFFINO**

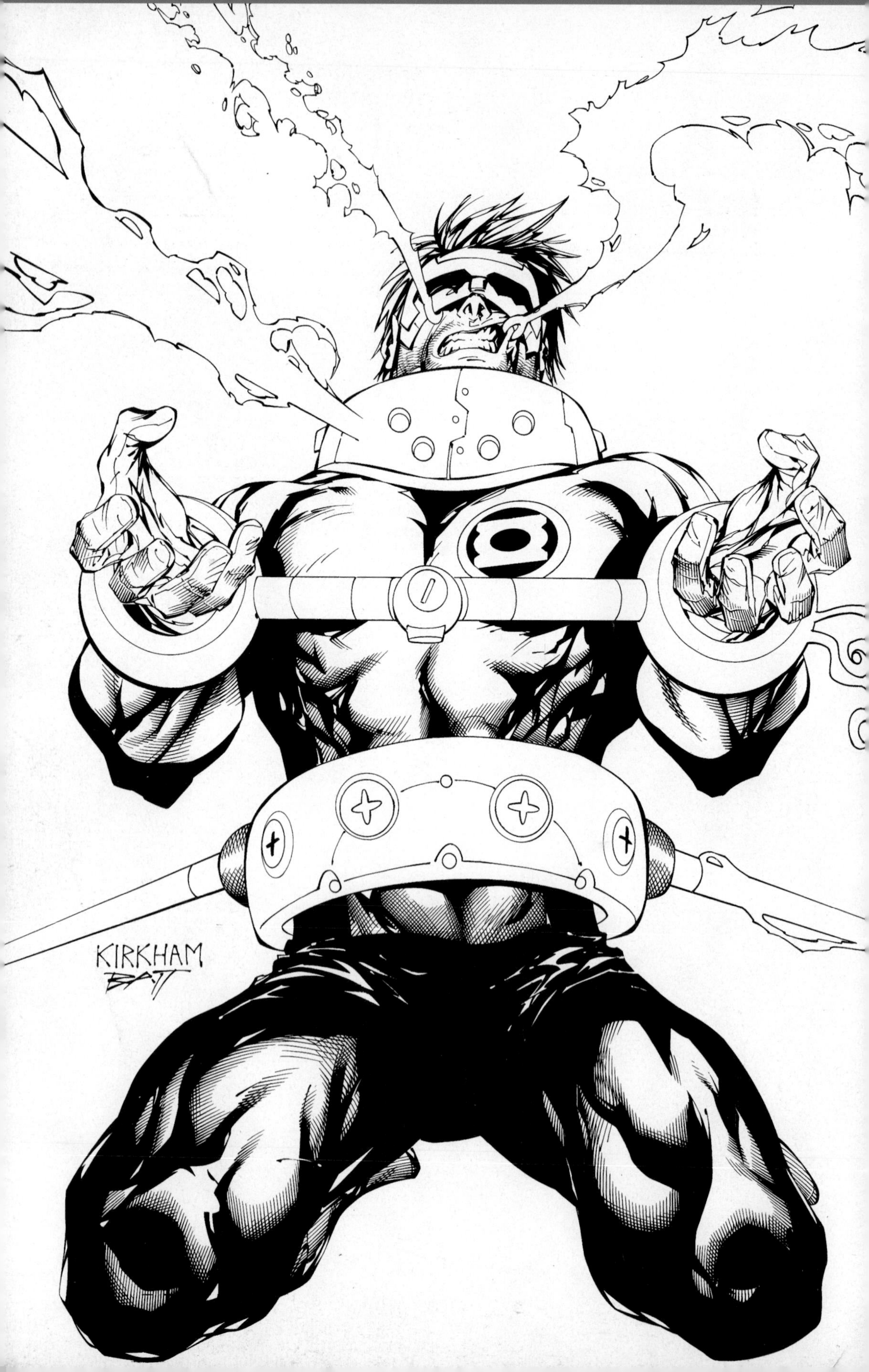
KIRKHAM
BATT

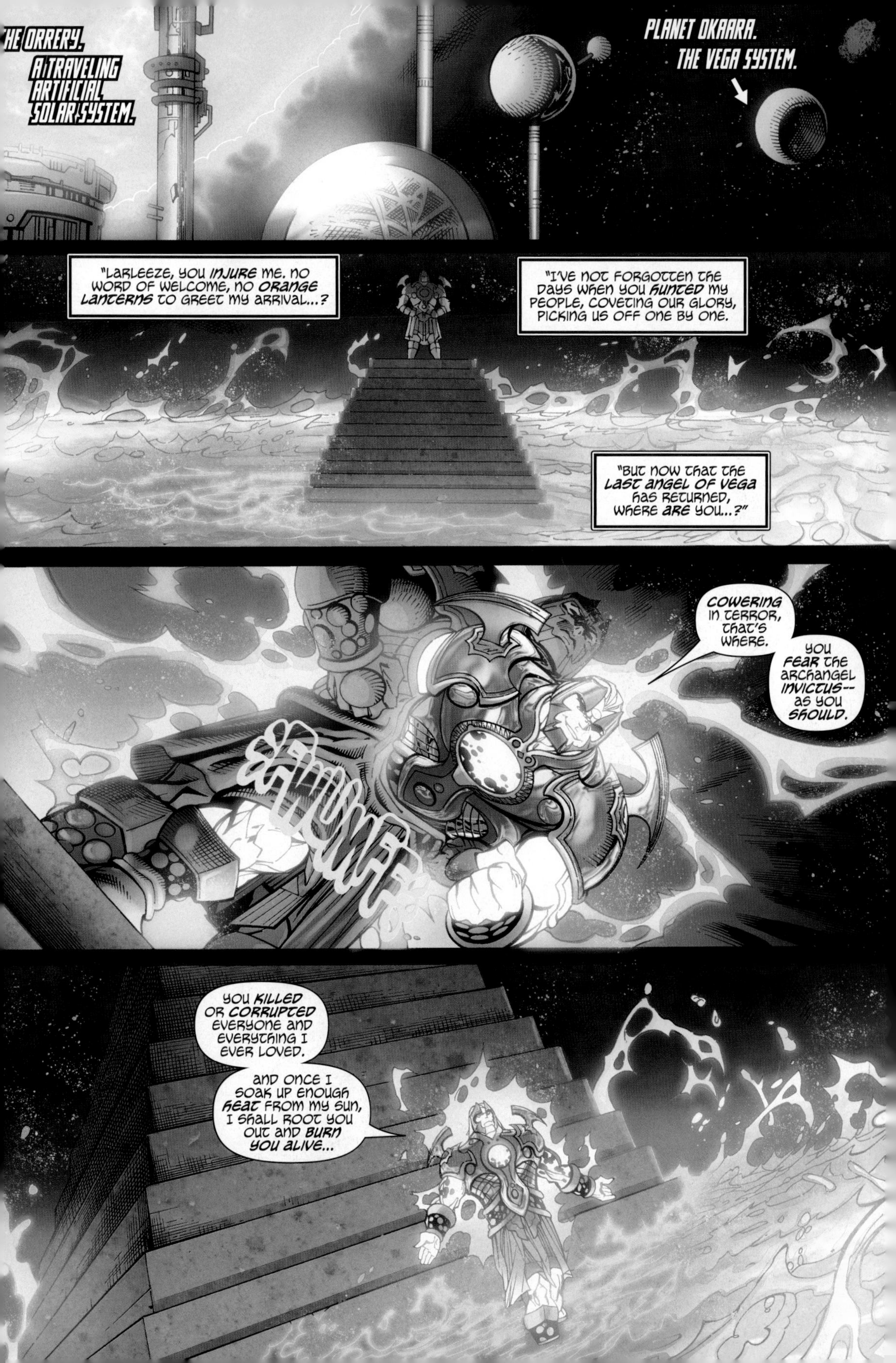
HE ORRERY.
A TRAVELING ARTIFICIAL SOLAR SYSTEM.
PLANET OKAARA. THE VEGA SYSTEM.
"LARLEEZE, YOU INJURE ME. NO WORD OF WELCOME, NO ORANGE LANTERNS TO GREET MY ARRIVAL...?
"I'VE NOT FORGOTTEN THE DAYS WHEN YOU HUNTED MY PEOPLE, COVETING OUR GLORY, PICKING US OFF ONE BY ONE.
"BUT NOW THAT THE LAST ANGEL OF VEGA HAS RETURNED, WHERE ARE YOU...?"
COWERING IN TERROR, THAT'S WHERE.
YOU FEAR THE ARCHANGEL INVICTUS-- AS YOU SHOULD.
YOU KILLED OR CORRUPTED EVERYONE AND EVERYTHING I EVER LOVED.
AND ONCE I SOAK UP ENOUGH HEAT FROM MY SUN, I SHALL ROOT YOU OUT AND BURN YOU ALIVE...

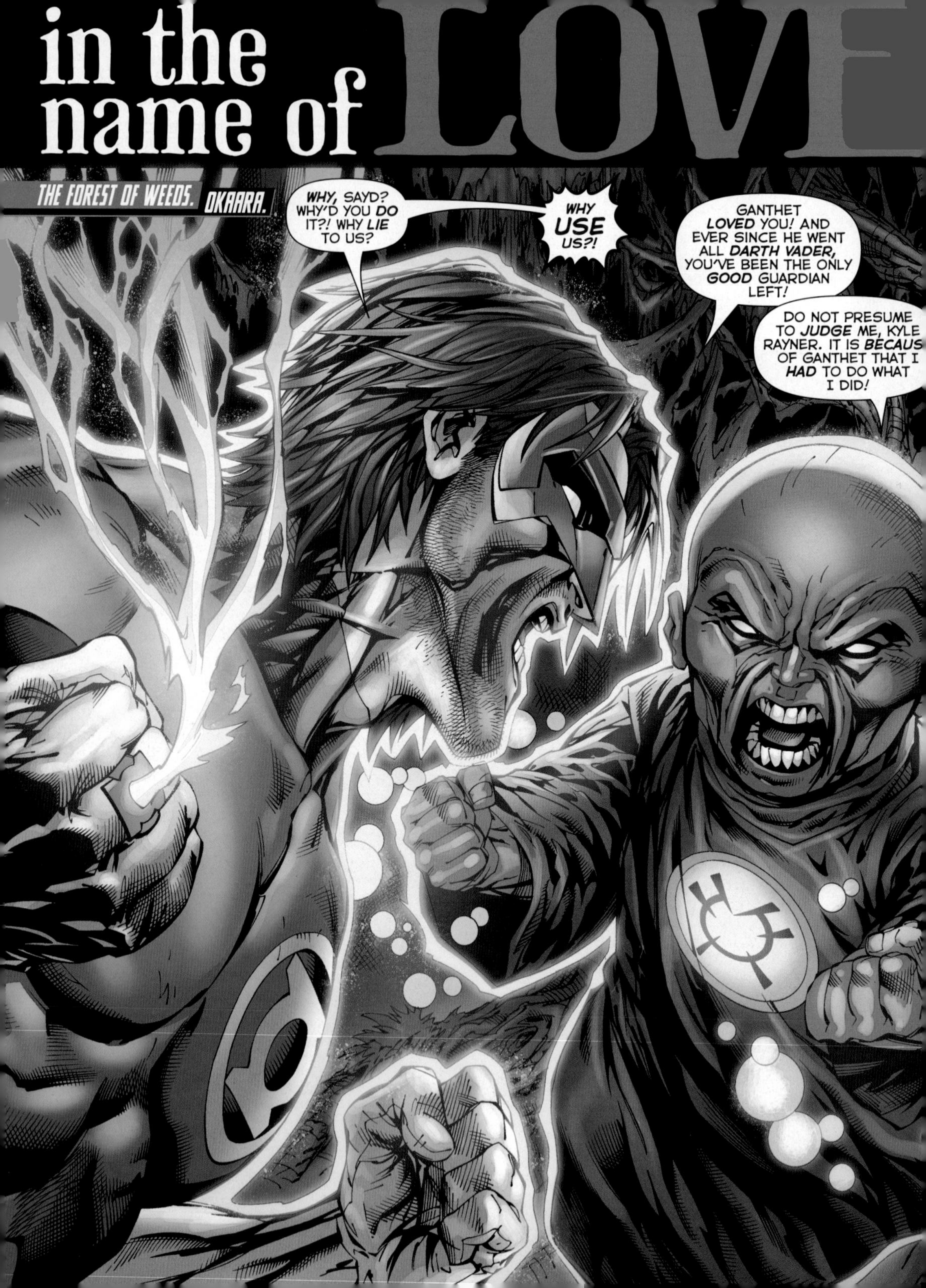
in the name of LOVE
THE FOREST OF WEEDS. OKAARA.
WHY, SAYD? WHY'D YOU DO IT?! WHY LIE TO US?
WHY USE US?!
GANTHET LOVED YOU! AND EVER SINCE HE WENT ALL DARTH VADER, YOU'VE BEEN THE ONLY GOOD GUARDIAN LEFT!
DO NOT PRESUME TO JUDGE ME, KYLE RAYNER. IT IS BECAUS OF GANTHET THAT I HAD TO DO WHAT I DID!

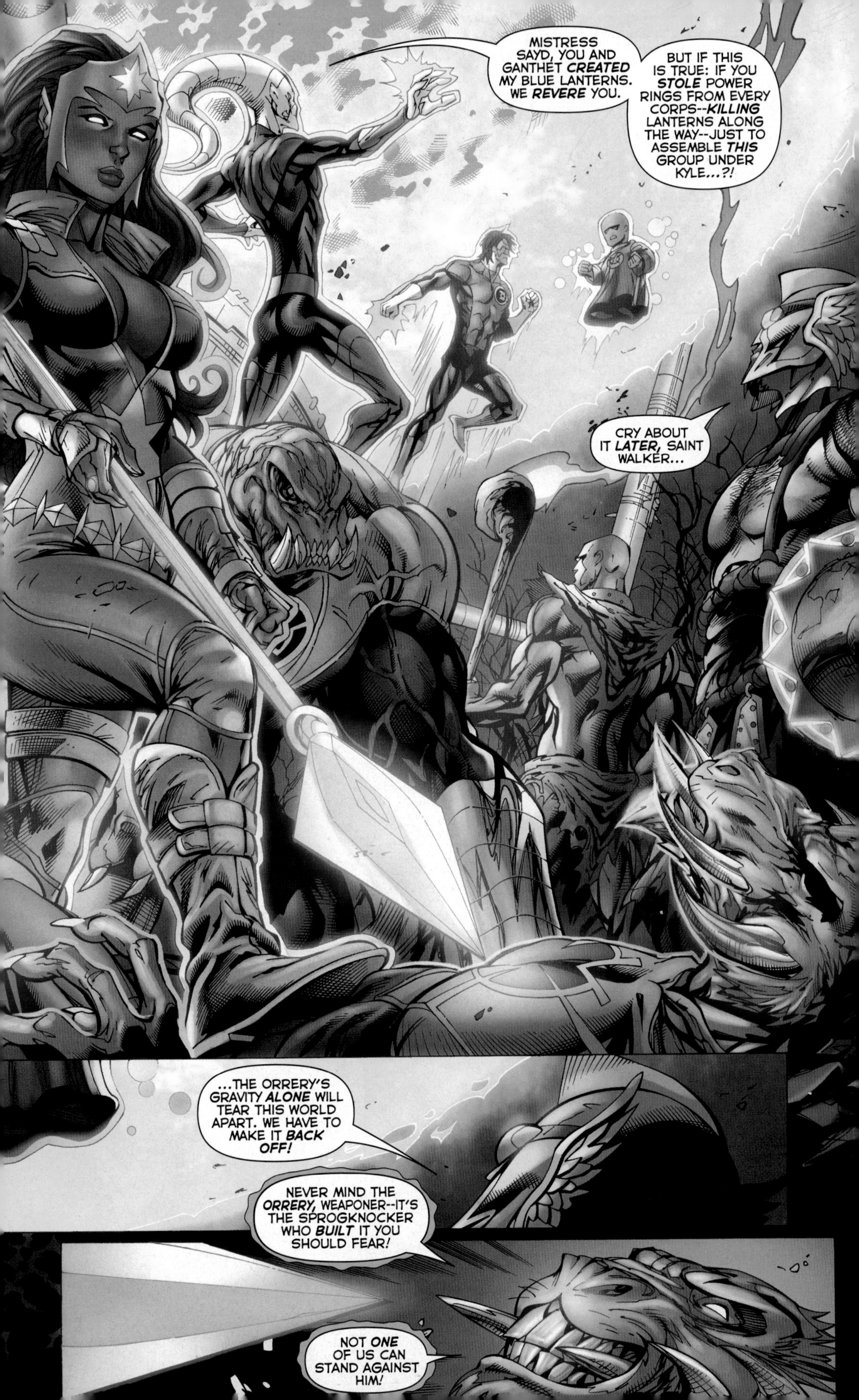
MISTRESS SAYD, YOU AND GANTHET *CREATED* MY BLUE LANTERNS. WE *REVERE* YOU.
BUT IF THIS IS TRUE: IF YOU *STOLE* POWER RINGS FROM EVERY CORPS--*KILLING* LANTERNS ALONG THE WAY--JUST TO ASSEMBLE *THIS* GROUP UNDER KYLE...?!
CRY ABOUT IT *LATER,* SAINT WALKER...
...THE ORRERY'S GRAVITY *ALONE* WILL TEAR THIS WORLD APART. WE HAVE TO MAKE IT *BACK OFF!*
NEVER MIND THE *ORRERY,* WEAPONER--IT'S THE SPROGKNOCKER WHO *BUILT* IT YOU SHOULD FEAR!
NOT *ONE* OF US CAN STAND AGAINST HIM!

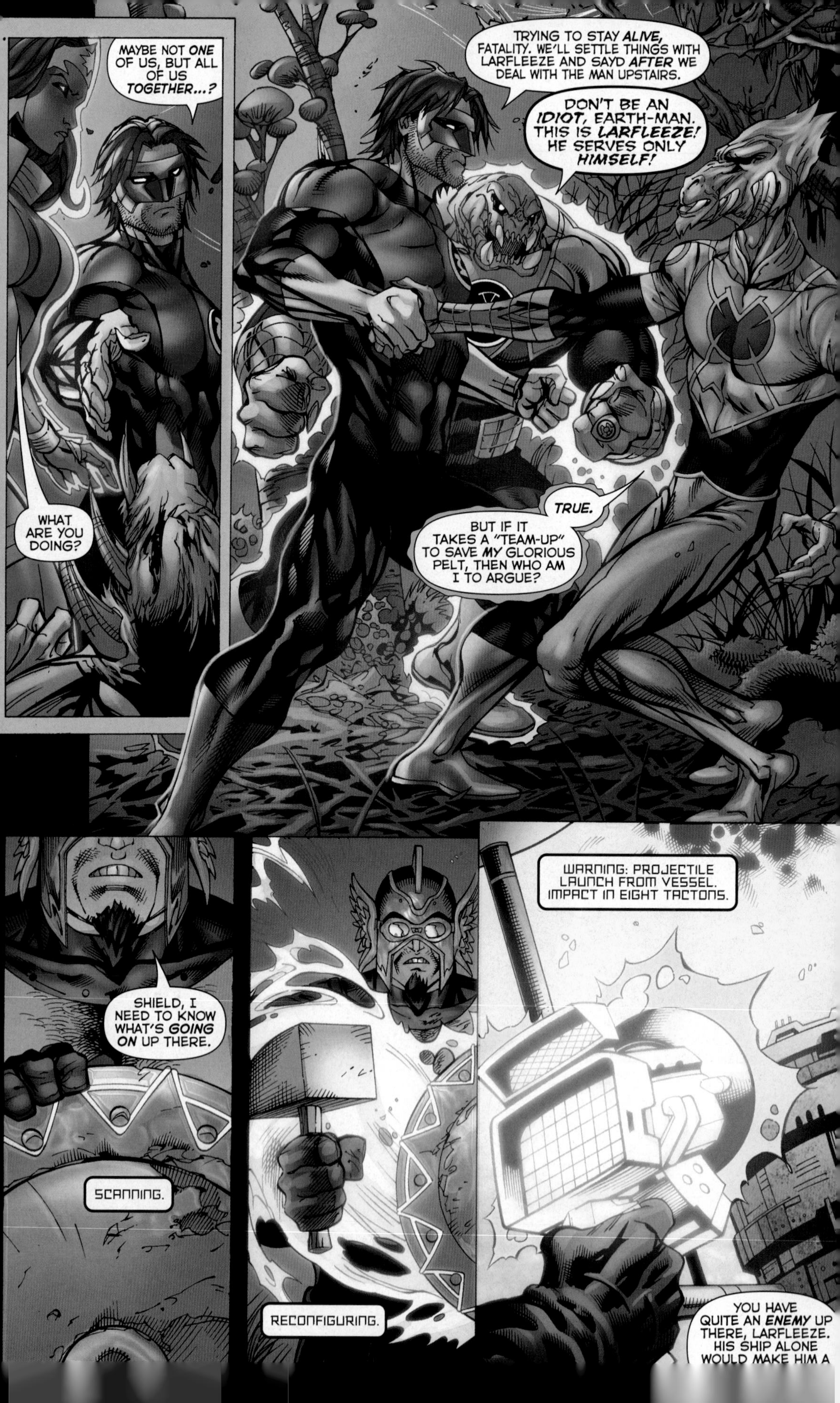
MAYBE NOT ONE OF US, BUT ALL OF US TOGETHER...?
TRYING TO STAY ALIVE, FATALITY. WE'LL SETTLE THINGS WITH LARFLEEZE AND SAYD AFTER WE DEAL WITH THE MAN UPSTAIRS.
DON'T BE AN IDIOT, EARTH-MAN. THIS IS LARFLEEZE! HE SERVES ONLY HIMSELF!
WHAT ARE YOU DOING?
TRUE.
BUT IF IT TAKES A "TEAM-UP" TO SAVE MY GLORIOUS PELT, THEN WHO AM I TO ARGUE?
SHIELD, I NEED TO KNOW WHAT'S GOING ON UP THERE.
SCANNING.
RECONFIGURING.
WARNING: PROJECTILE LAUNCH FROM VESSEL. IMPACT IN EIGHT TACTONS.
YOU HAVE QUITE AN ENEMY UP THERE, LARFLEEZE. HIS SHIP ALONE WOULD MAKE HIM A

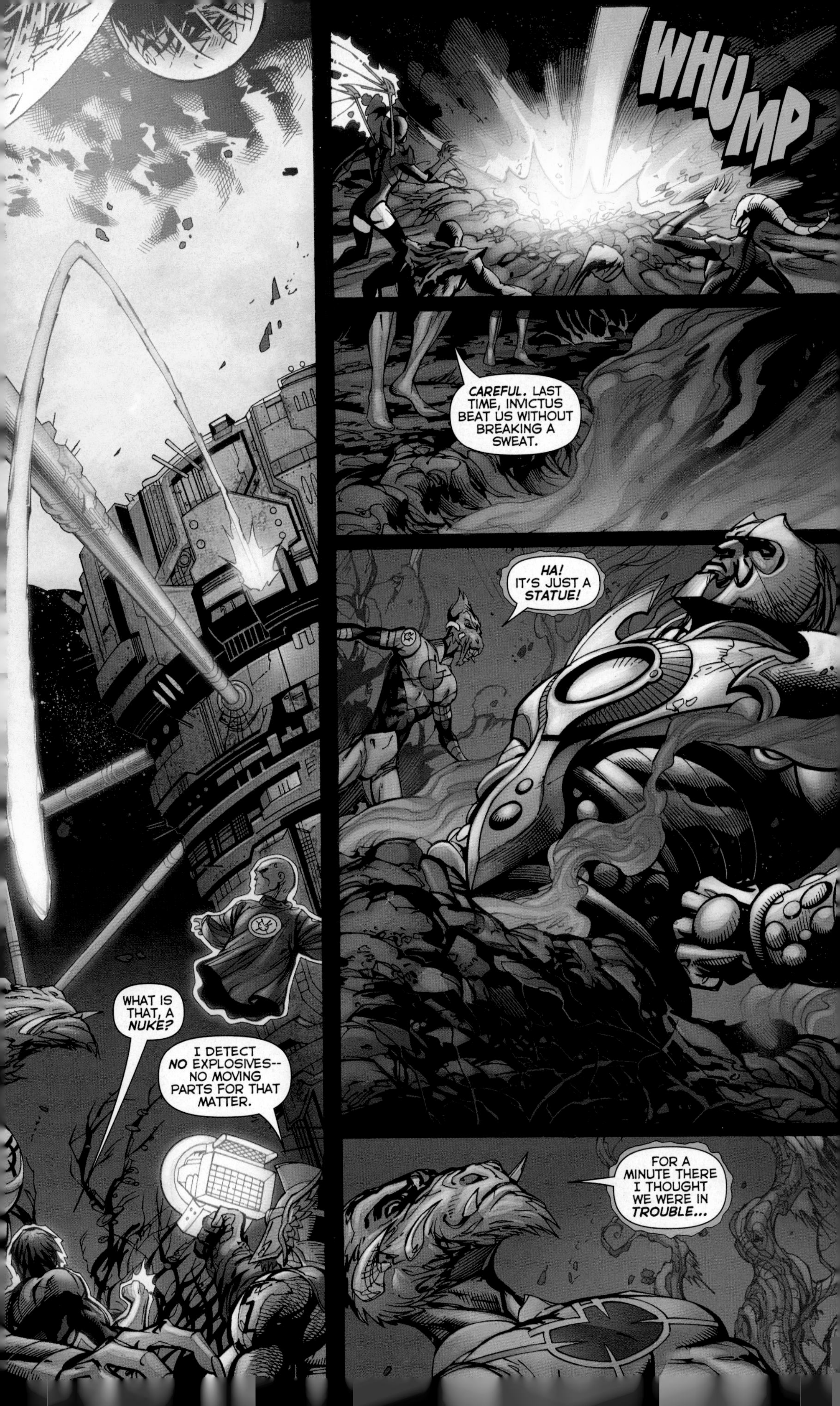

WHUMP
CAREFUL. LAST TIME, INVICTUS BEAT US WITHOUT BREAKING A SWEAT.
HA! IT'S JUST A STATUE!
WHAT IS THAT, A NUKE?
I DETECT NO EXPLOSIVES-- NO MOVING PARTS FOR THAT MATTER.
FOR A MINUTE THERE I THOUGHT WE WERE IN TROUBLE...

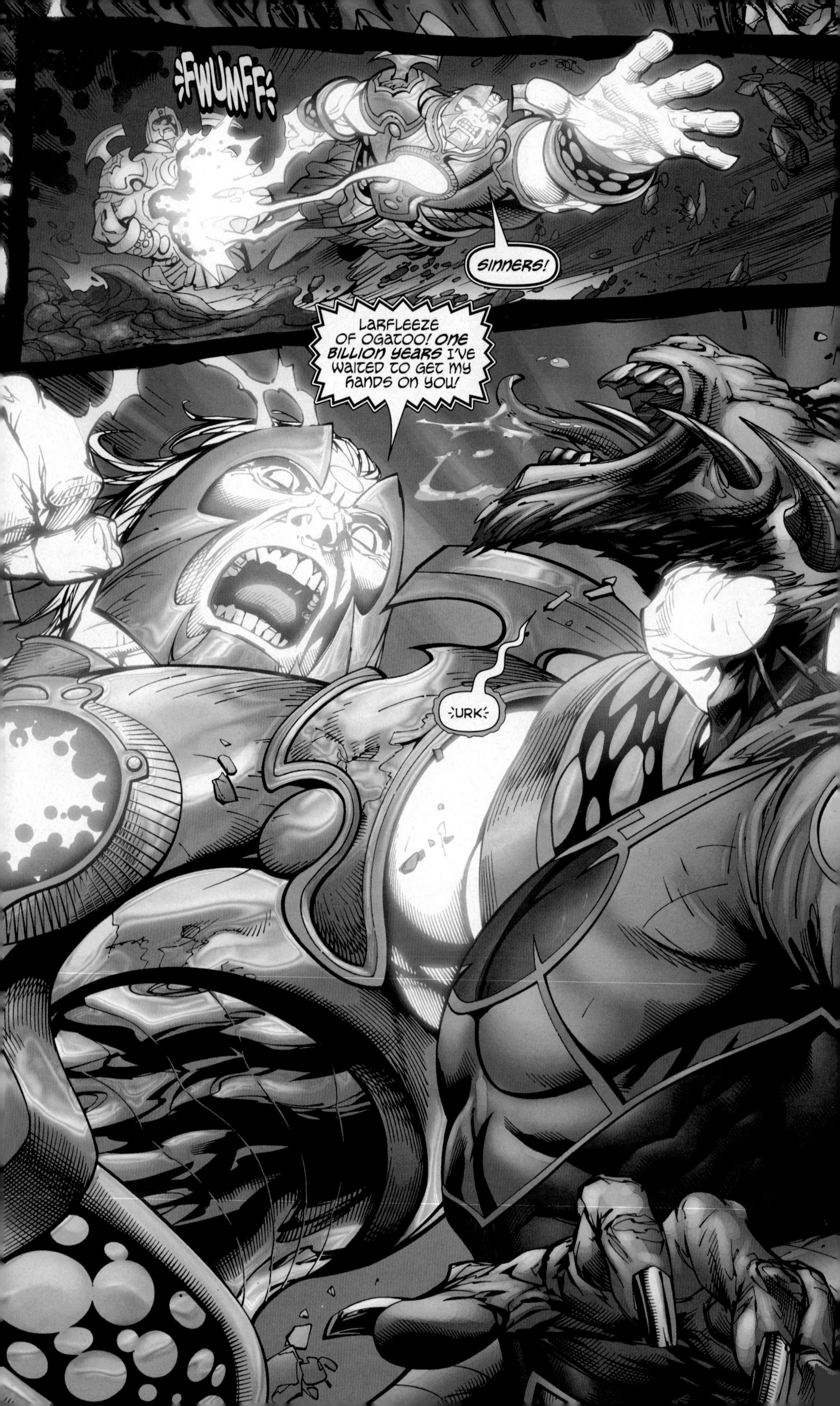
FWUMFF
SINNERS!
LARFLEEZE OF OGATOO! ONE BILLION YEARS I'VE WAITED TO GET MY HANDS ON YOU!
URK

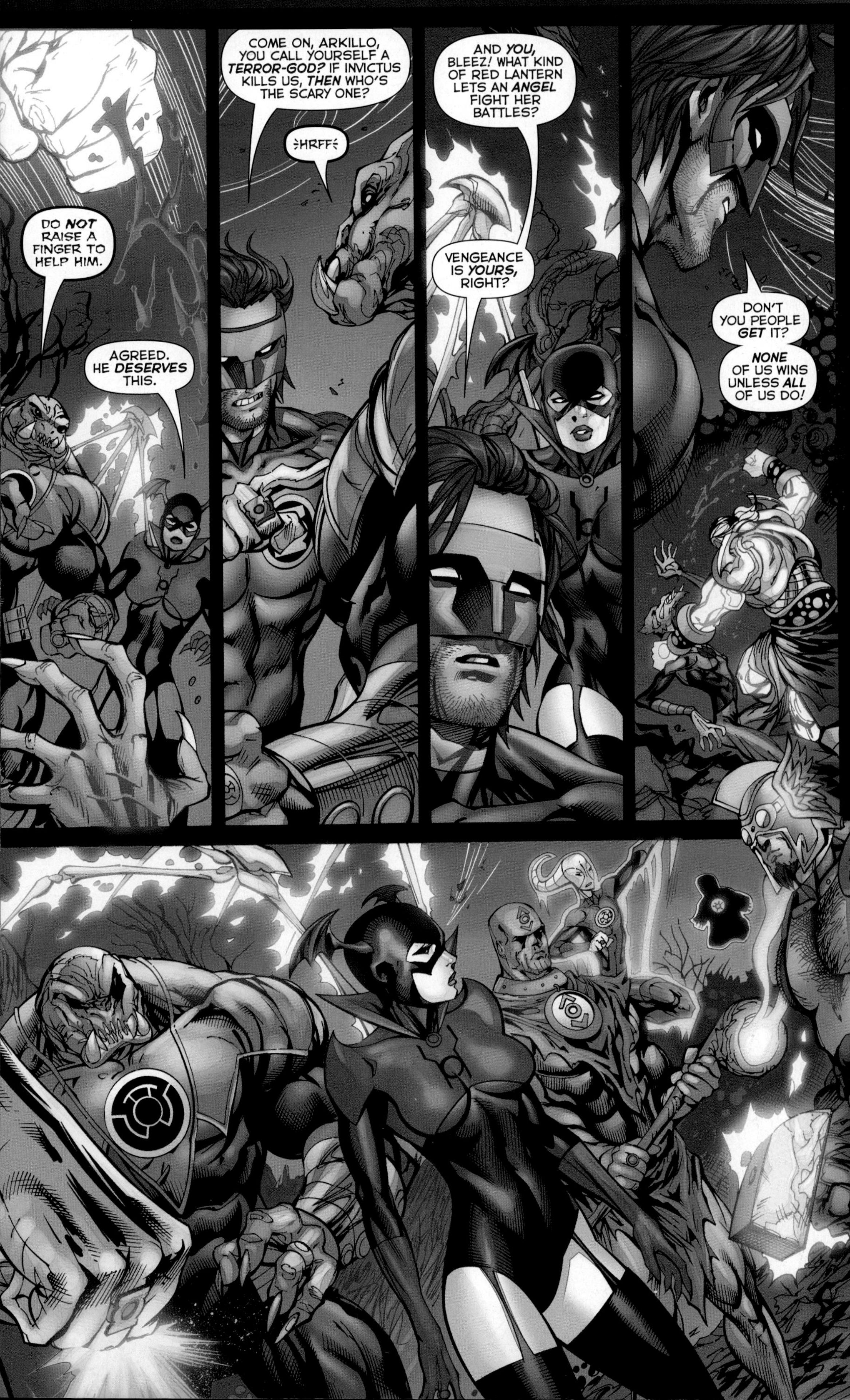
DO NOT RAISE A FINGER TO HELP HIM.
AGREED. HE DESERVES THIS.
COME ON, ARKILLO, YOU CALL YOURSELF A TERROR-GOD? IF INVICTUS KILLS US, THEN WHO'S THE SCARY ONE?
HRFF
AND YOU, BLEEZ! WHAT KIND OF RED LANTERN LETS AN ANGEL FIGHT HER BATTLES?
VENGEANCE IS YOURS, RIGHT?
DON'T YOU PEOPLE GET IT?
NONE OF US WINS UNLESS ALL OF US DO!

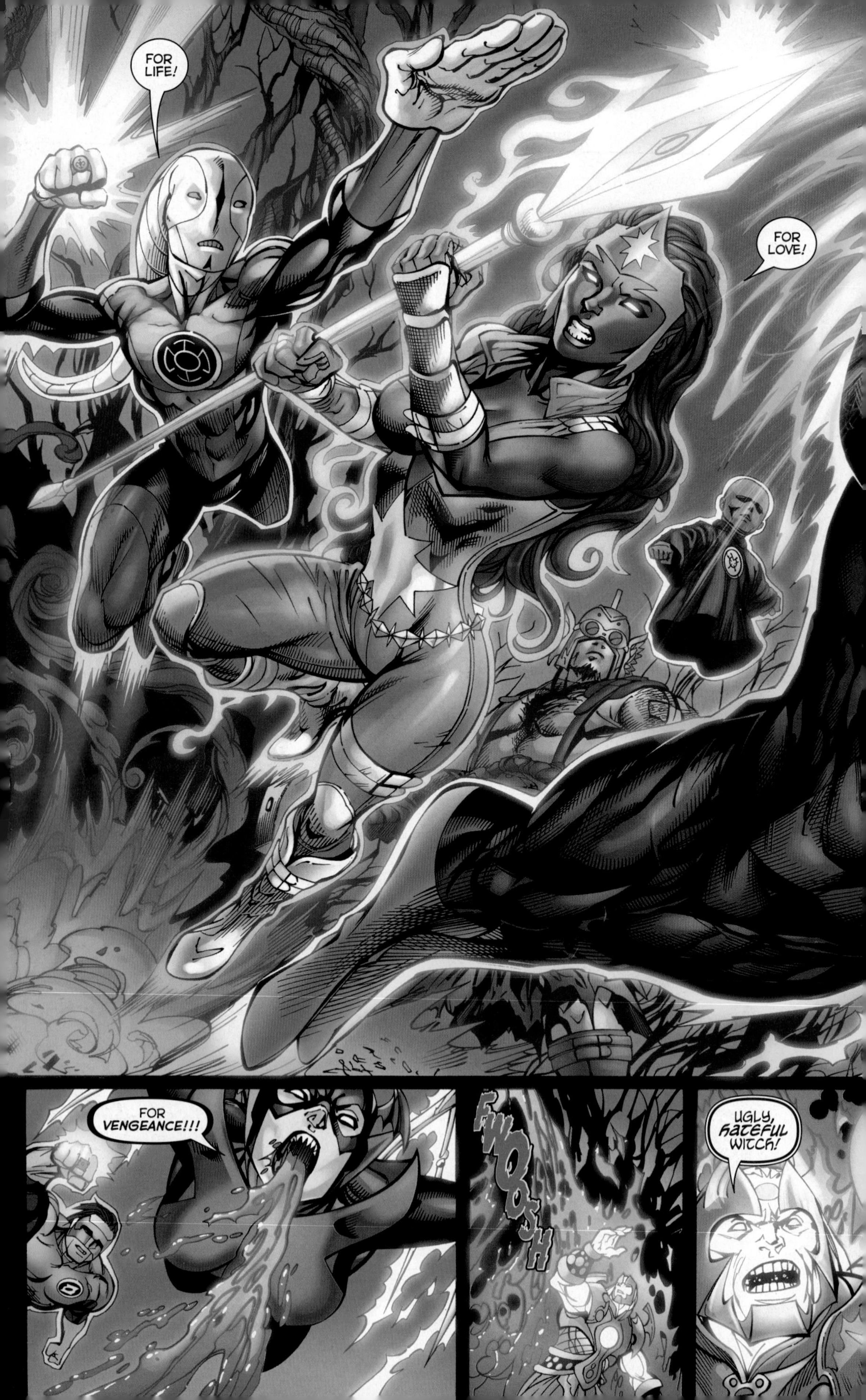
FOR LIFE!
FOR LOVE!
FOR VENGEANCE!!!
FWOOSH
UGLY, HATEFUL WITCH!

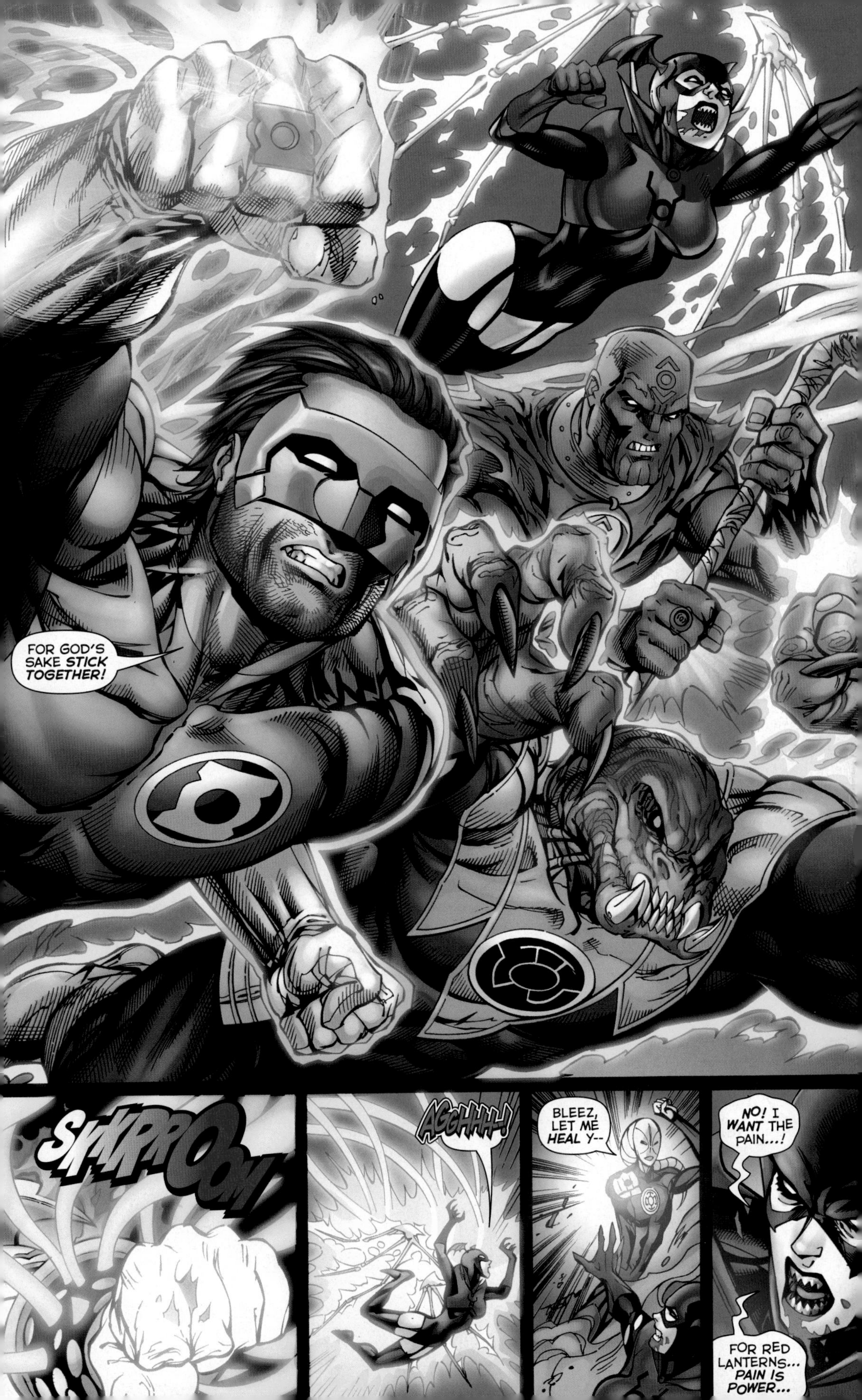
FOR GOD'S SAKE STICK TOGETHER!
SKKRROOM
AGGHHH!
BLEEZ, LET ME HEAL Y--
NO! I WANT THE PAIN...!
FOR RED LANTERNS... PAIN IS POWER...

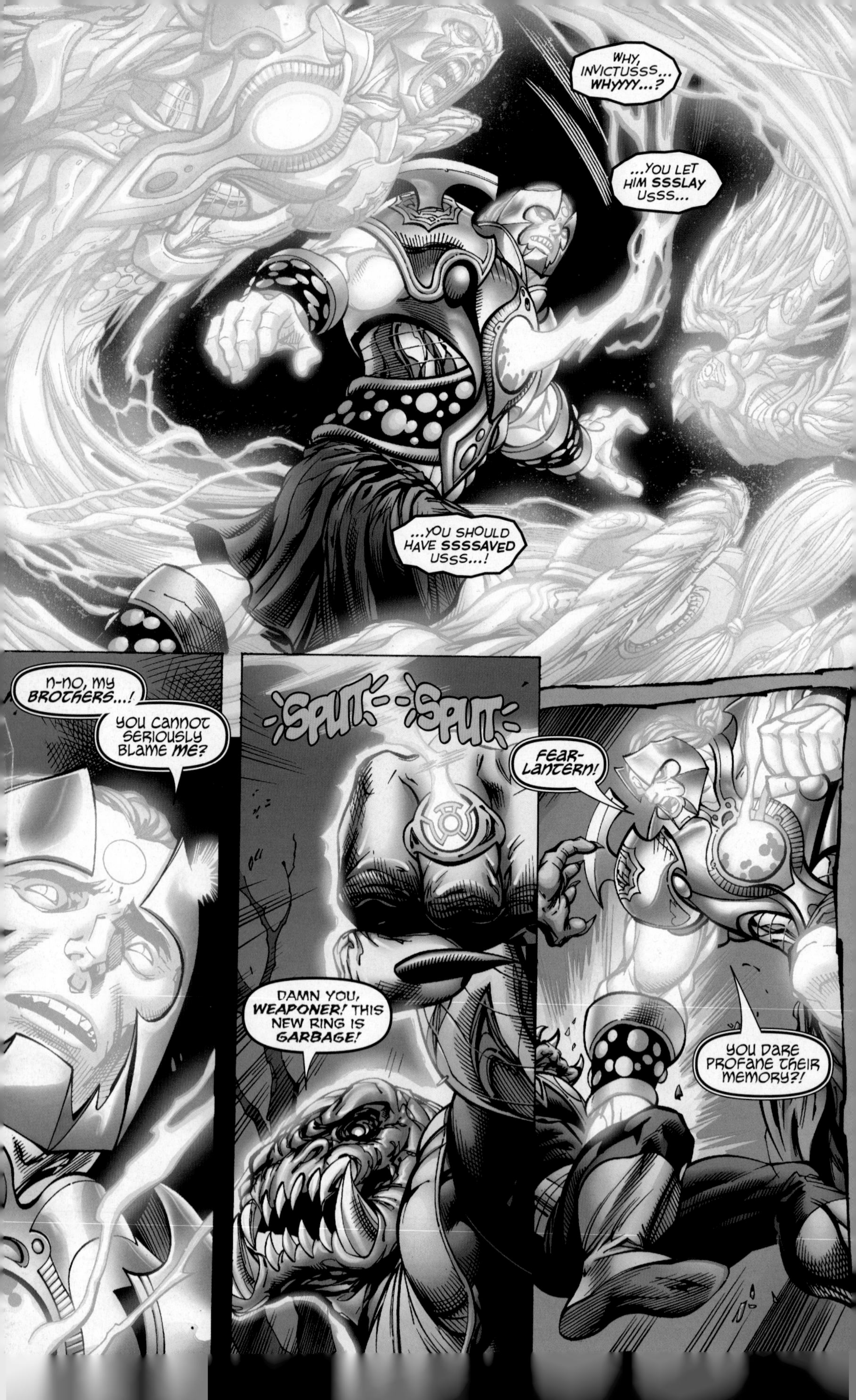
WHY, INVICTUSSS... WHYYYY...?
...YOU LET HIM SSSLAY USSS...
...YOU SHOULD HAVE SSSSAVED USSS...!
N-NO, MY BROTHERS...!
YOU CANNOT SERIOUSLY BLAME ME?
SPUT SPUT
FEAR-LANTERN!
DAMN YOU, WEAPONER! THIS NEW RING IS GARBAGE!
YOU DARE PROFANE THEIR MEMORY?!

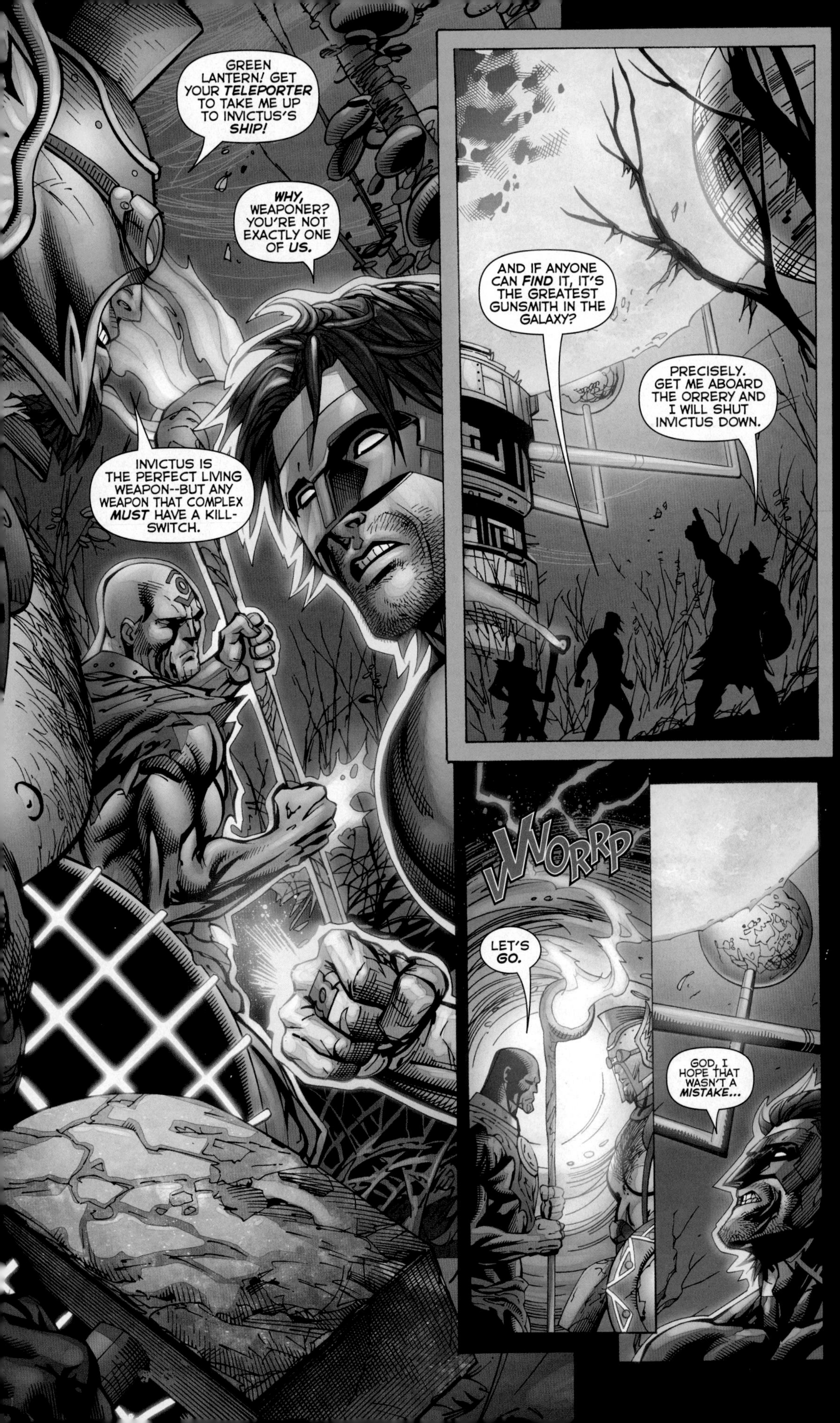
GREEN LANTERN! GET YOUR TELEPORTER TO TAKE ME UP TO INVICTUS'S SHIP!
WHY, WEAPONER? YOU'RE NOT EXACTLY ONE OF US.
INVICTUS IS THE PERFECT LIVING WEAPON--BUT ANY WEAPON THAT COMPLEX MUST HAVE A KILL-SWITCH.
AND IF ANYONE CAN FIND IT, IT'S THE GREATEST GUNSMITH IN THE GALAXY?
PRECISELY. GET ME ABOARD THE ORRERY AND I WILL SHUT INVICTUS DOWN.
VWORRP
LET'S GO.
GOD, I HOPE THAT WASN'T A MISTAKE...

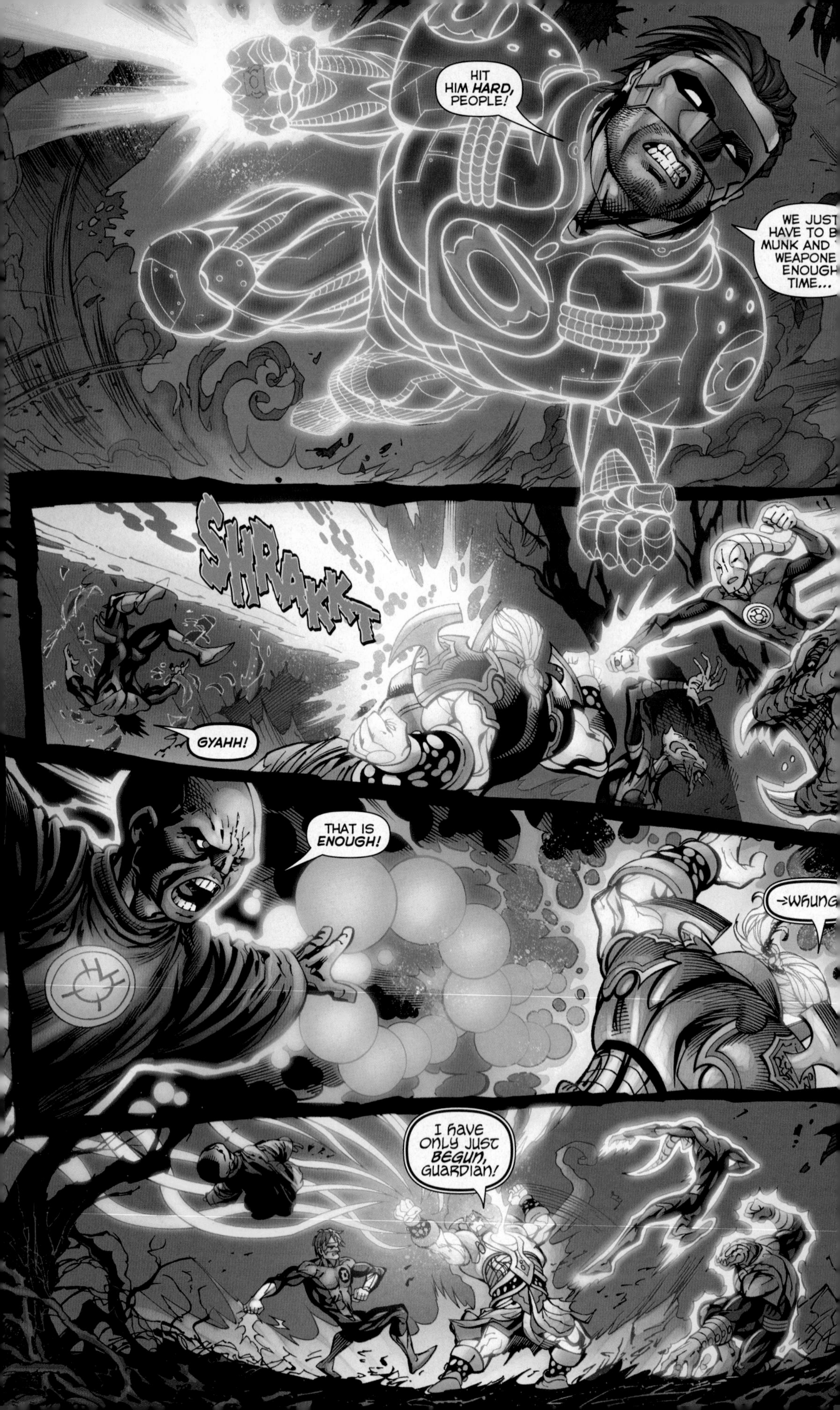
HIT HIM HARD, PEOPLE!
WE JUST HAVE TO B MUNK AND WEAPONE ENOUGH TIME...
SHRAKKT
GYAHH!
THAT IS ENOUGH!
WHUNG
I HAVE ONLY JUST BEGUN, GUARDIAN!

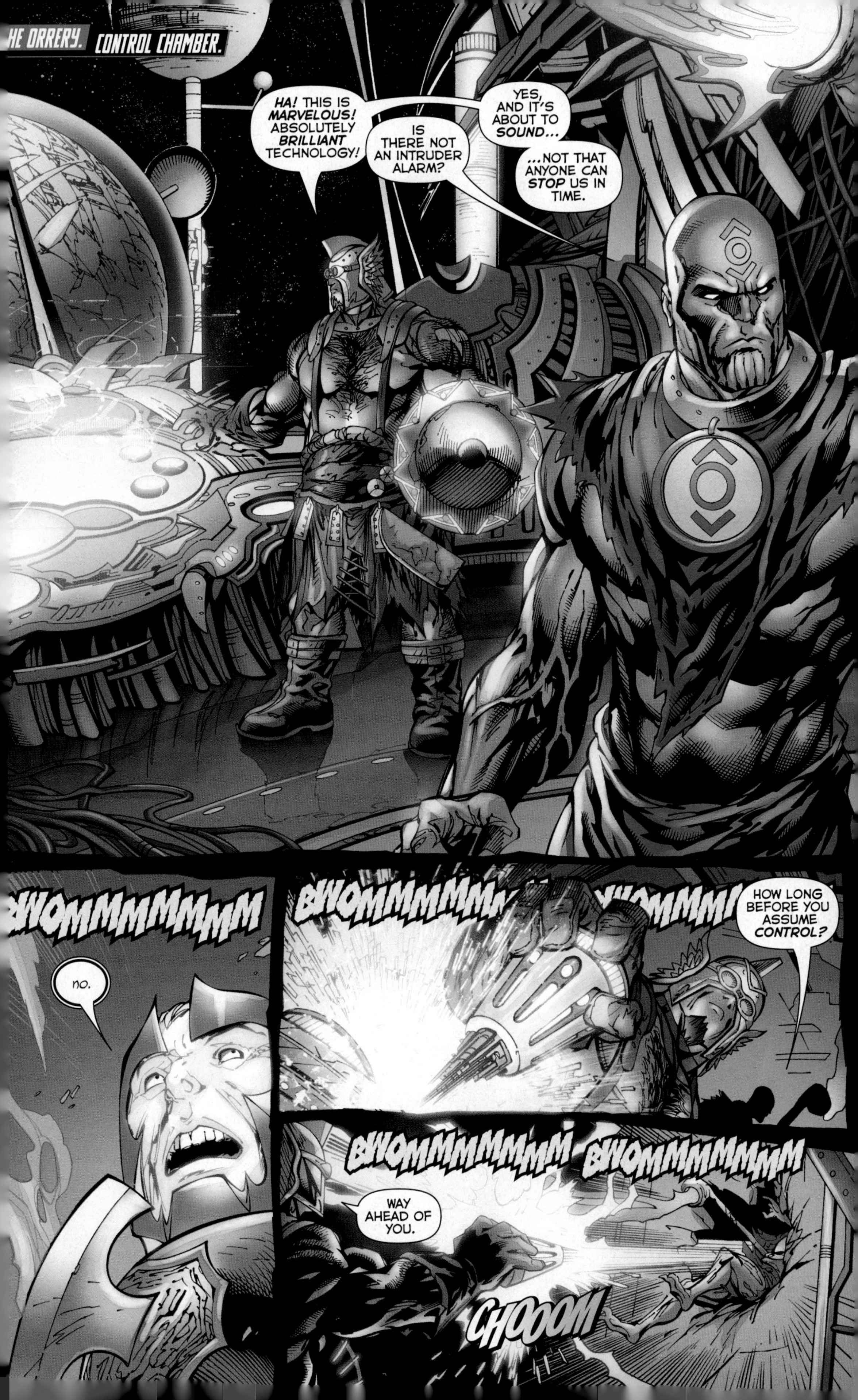
HE ORRERY. CONTROL CHAMBER.
HA! THIS IS MARVELOUS! ABSOLUTELY BRILLIANT TECHNOLOGY!
IS THERE NOT AN INTRUDER ALARM?
YES, AND IT'S ABOUT TO SOUND...
...NOT THAT ANYONE CAN STOP US IN TIME.
BWOMMMMMMMM
no.
BWOMMMMMM
BWOMMMM
HOW LONG BEFORE YOU ASSUME CONTROL?
BWOMMMMMMMM
BWOMMMMMMMM
WAY AHEAD OF YOU.
CHOOOM

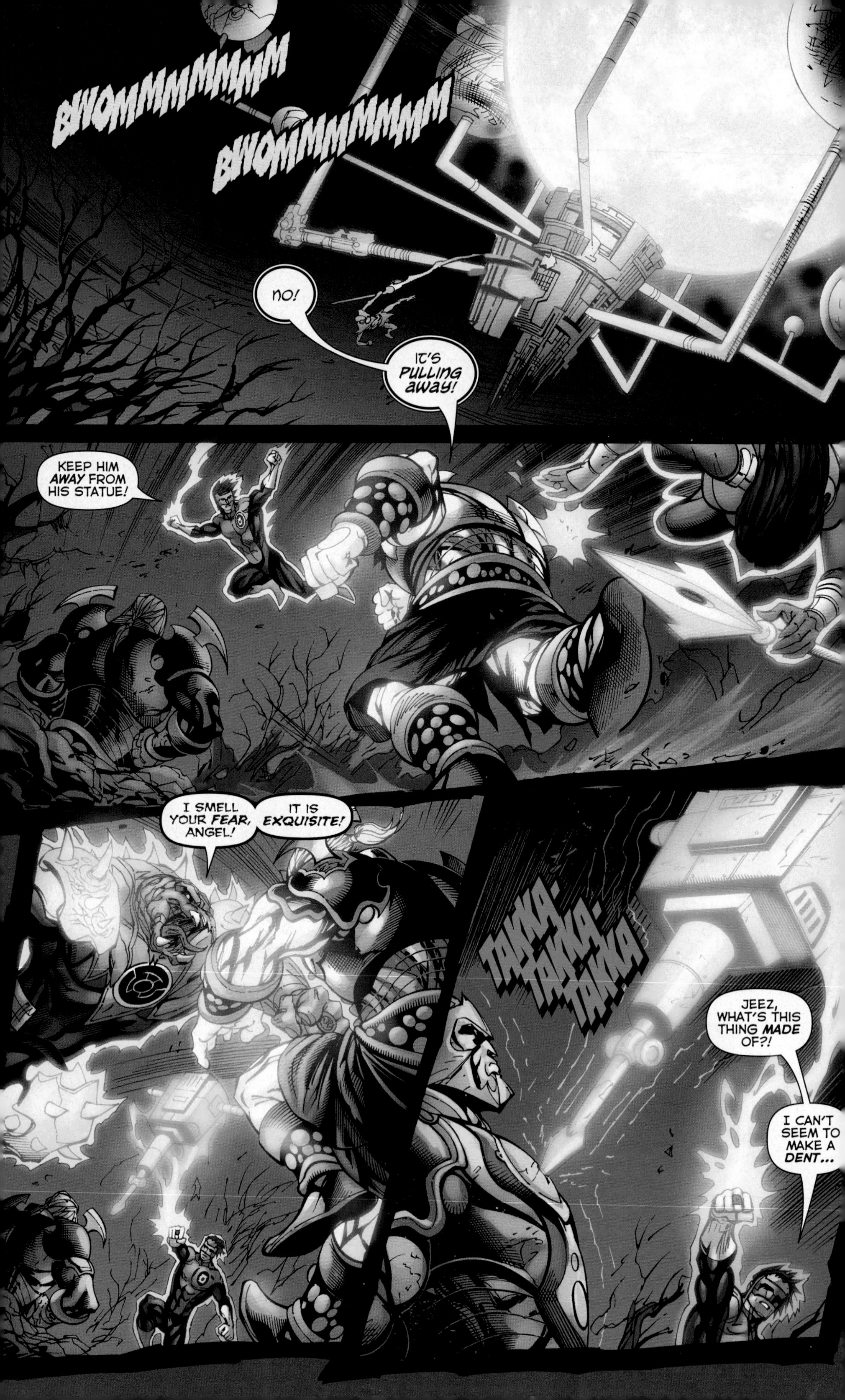
BWOMMMMMMM
BWOMMMMMMMM
no!
IT'S PULLING away!
KEEP HIM AWAY FROM HIS STATUE!
I SMELL YOUR FEAR, ANGEL!
IT IS EXQUISITE!
TAKKA-TAKKA-TAKKA
JEEZ, WHAT'S THIS THING MADE OF?!
I CAN'T SEEM TO MAKE A DENT...

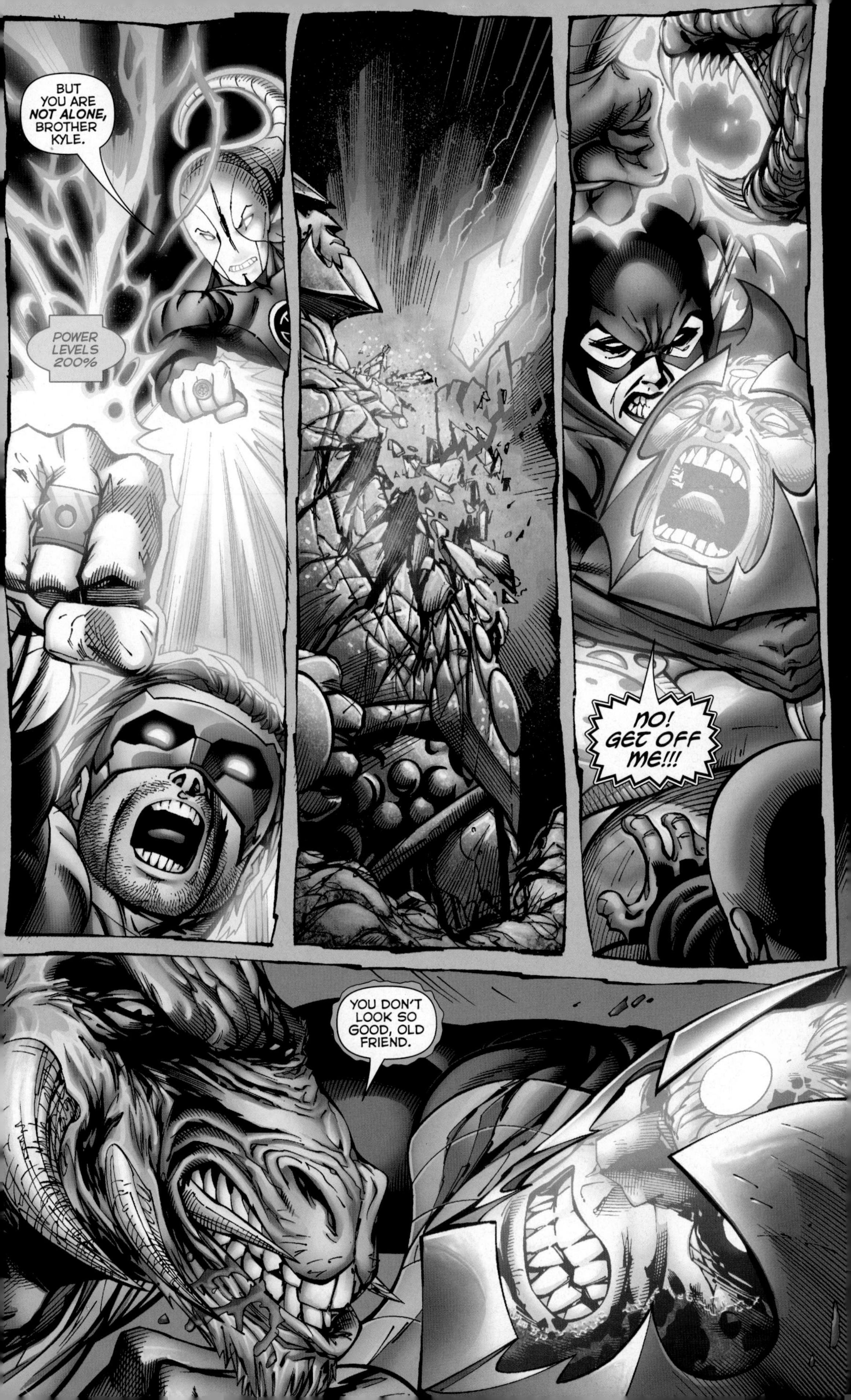
BUT YOU ARE NOT ALONE, BROTHER KYLE.
POWER LEVELS 200%
NO! GET OFF ME!!!
YOU DON'T LOOK SO GOOD, OLD FRIEND.

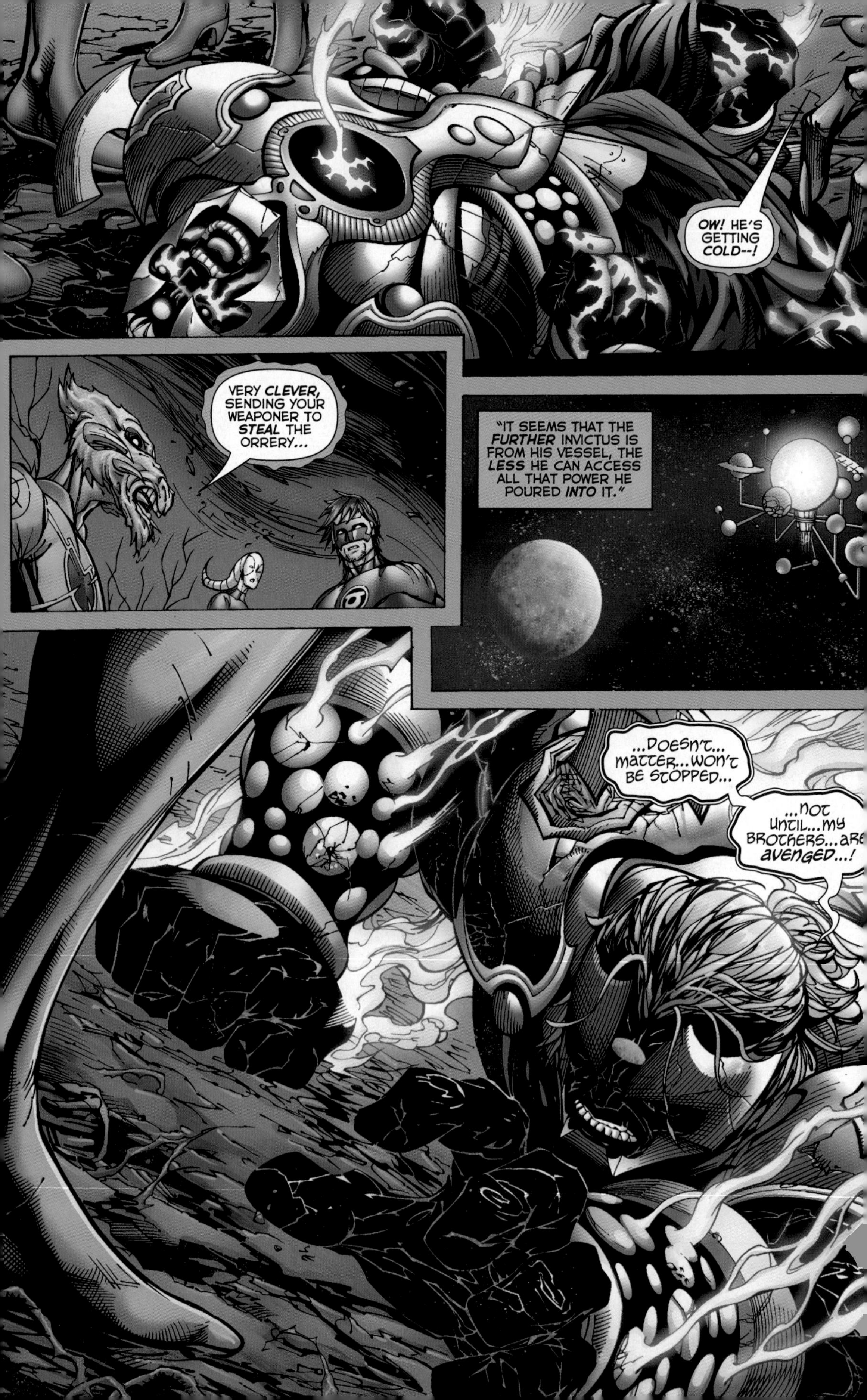
OW! HE'S GETTING COLD--!
VERY CLEVER, SENDING YOUR WEAPONER TO STEAL THE ORRERY...
"IT SEEMS THAT THE FURTHER INVICTUS IS FROM HIS VESSEL, THE LESS HE CAN ACCESS ALL THAT POWER HE POURED INTO IT."
...DOESN'T... MATTER...WON'T BE STOPPED...
...NOT UNTIL...MY BROTHERS...ARE AVENGED...!

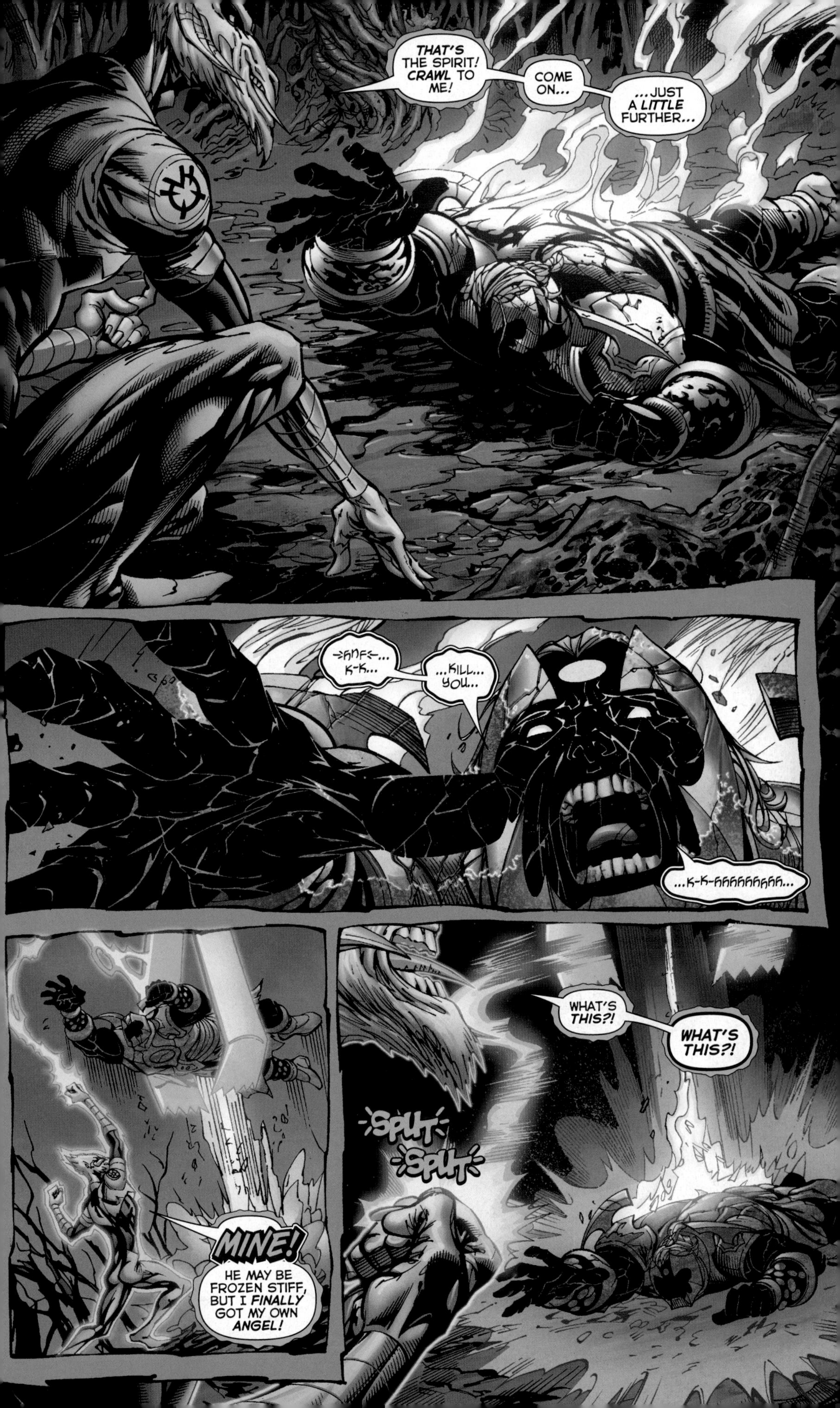
THAT'S THE SPIRIT! CRAWL TO ME!
COME ON...
...JUST A LITTLE FURTHER...
>ANF<... K-K...
...KILL... YOU...
...K-K-AAAAAAAAA...
MINE!
HE MAY BE FROZEN STIFF, BUT I FINALLY GOT MY OWN ANGEL!
WHAT'S THIS?!
WHAT'S THIS?!
SPUT
SPUT

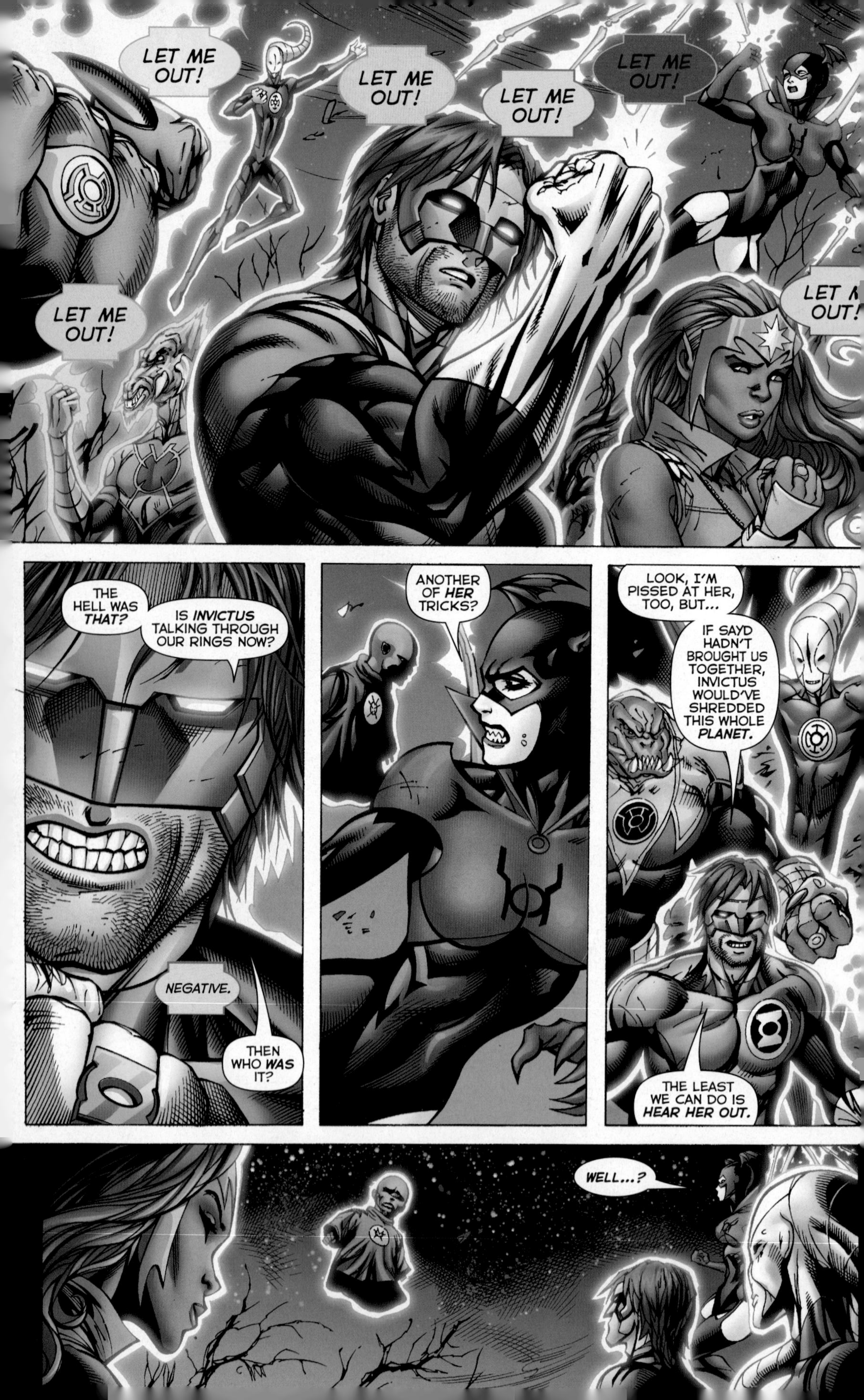

LET ME OUT!
LET ME OUT!
LET ME OUT!
LET ME OUT!
LET ME OUT!
THE HELL WAS THAT?
IS INVICTUS TALKING THROUGH OUR RINGS NOW?
NEGATIVE.
THEN WHO WAS IT?
ANOTHER OF HER TRICKS?
LOOK, I'M PISSED AT HER, TOO, BUT...
IF SAYD HADN'T BROUGHT US TOGETHER, INVICTUS WOULD'VE SHREDDED THIS WHOLE PLANET.
THE LEAST WE CAN DO IS HEAR HER OUT.
WELL...?

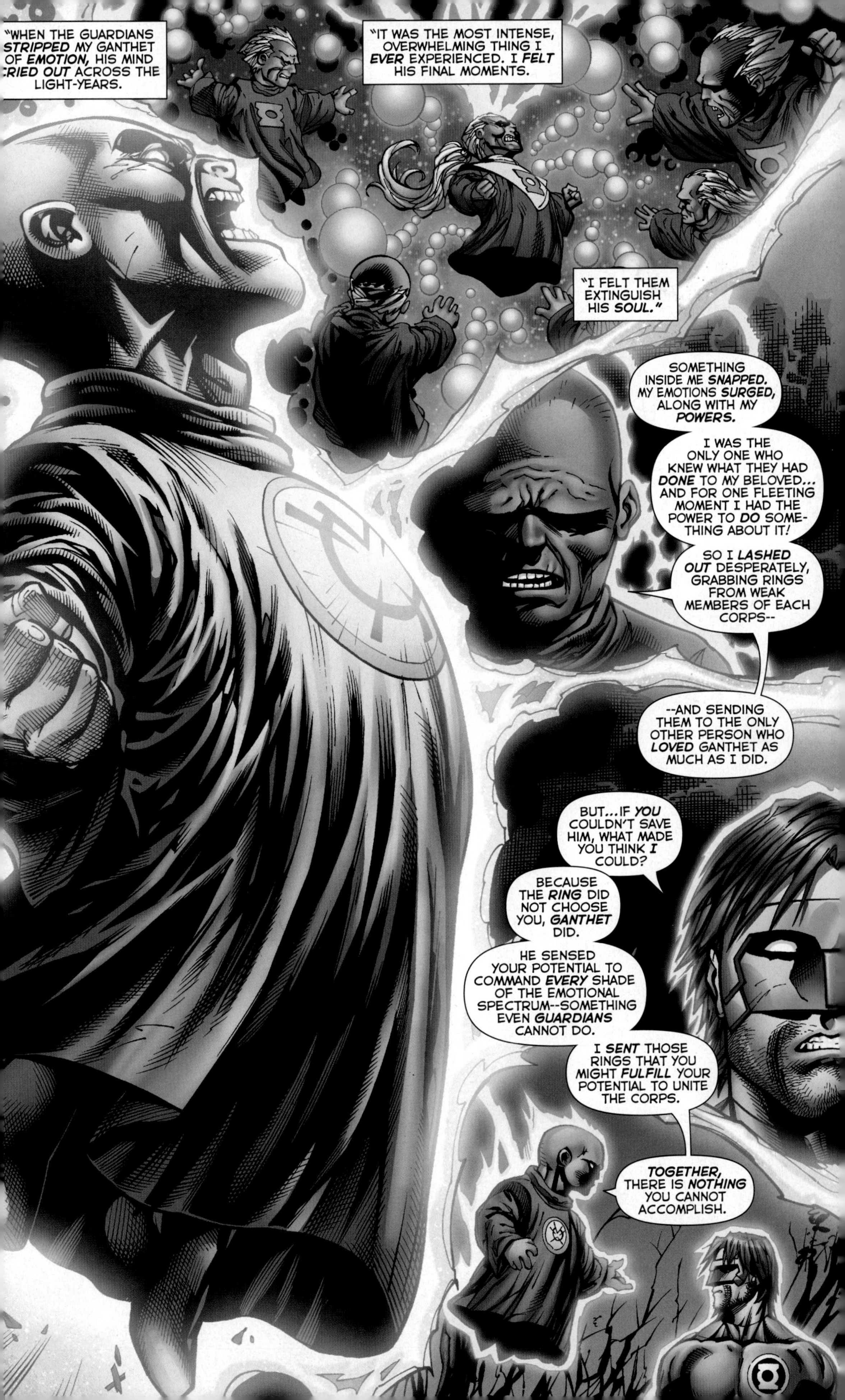
"WHEN THE GUARDIANS STRIPPED MY GANTHET OF EMOTION, HIS MIND CRIED OUT ACROSS THE LIGHT-YEARS.
"IT WAS THE MOST INTENSE, OVERWHELMING THING I EVER EXPERIENCED. I FELT HIS FINAL MOMENTS.
"I FELT THEM EXTINGUISH HIS SOUL."
SOMETHING INSIDE ME SNAPPED. MY EMOTIONS SURGED, ALONG WITH MY POWERS.
I WAS THE ONLY ONE WHO KNEW WHAT THEY HAD DONE TO MY BELOVED... AND FOR ONE FLEETING MOMENT I HAD THE POWER TO DO SOMETHING ABOUT IT!
SO I LASHED OUT DESPERATELY, GRABBING RINGS FROM WEAK MEMBERS OF EACH CORPS--
--AND SENDING THEM TO THE ONLY OTHER PERSON WHO LOVED GANTHET AS MUCH AS I DID.
BUT...IF YOU COULDN'T SAVE HIM, WHAT MADE YOU THINK I COULD?
BECAUSE THE RING DID NOT CHOOSE YOU, GANTHET DID.
HE SENSED YOUR POTENTIAL TO COMMAND EVERY SHADE OF THE EMOTIONAL SPECTRUM--SOMETHING EVEN GUARDIANS CANNOT DO.
I SENT THOSE RINGS THAT YOU MIGHT FULFILL YOUR POTENTIAL TO UNITE THE CORPS.
TOGETHER, THERE IS NOTHING YOU CANNOT ACCOMPLISH.

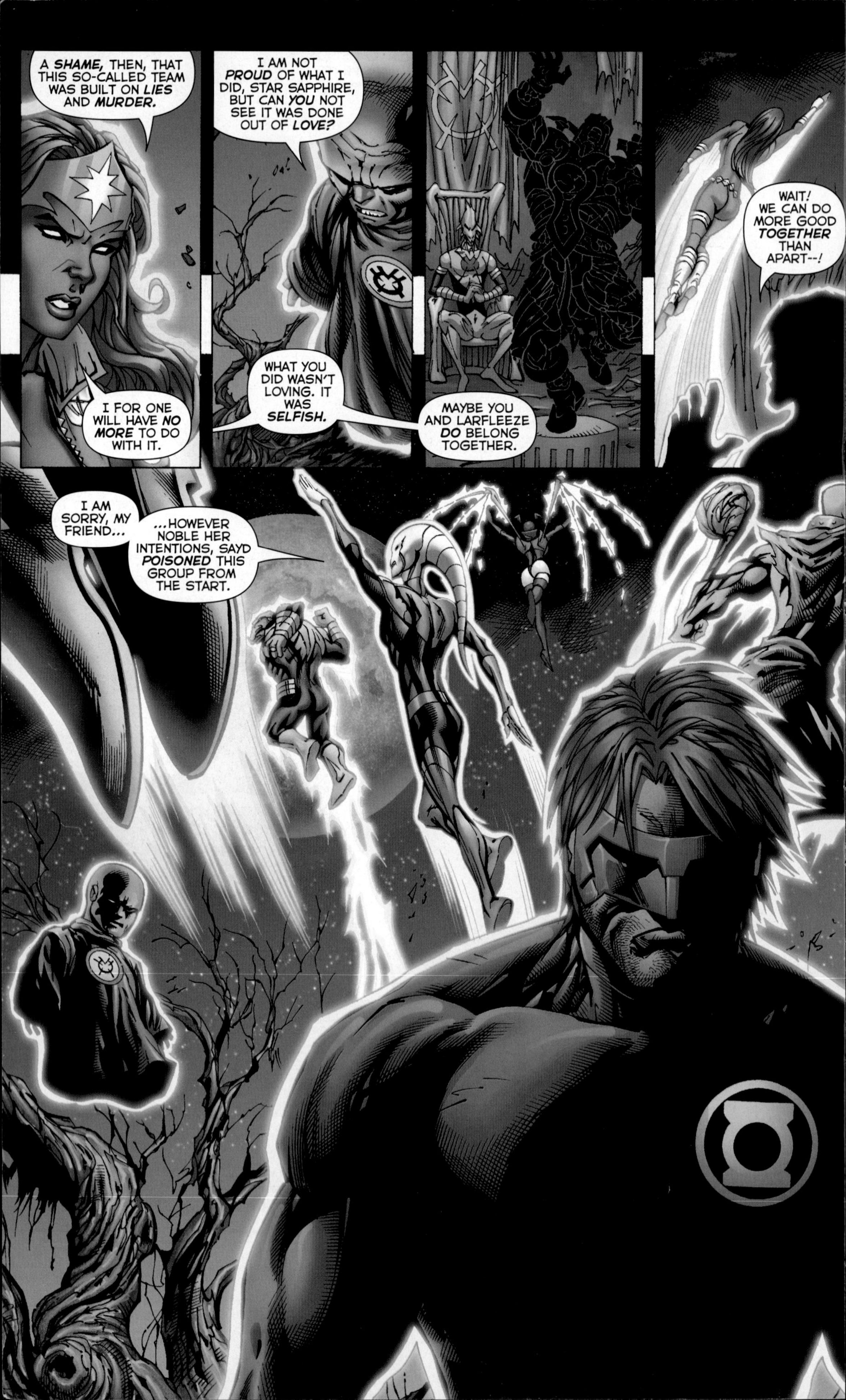
A SHAME, THEN, THAT THIS SO-CALLED TEAM WAS BUILT ON LIES AND MURDER.
I FOR ONE WILL HAVE NO MORE TO DO WITH IT.
I AM NOT PROUD OF WHAT I DID, STAR SAPPHIRE, BUT CAN YOU NOT SEE IT WAS DONE OUT OF LOVE?
WHAT YOU DID WASN'T LOVING. IT WAS SELFISH.
MAYBE YOU AND LARFLEEZE DO BELONG TOGETHER.
WAIT! WE CAN DO MORE GOOD TOGETHER THAN APART--!
I AM SORRY, MY FRIEND...
...HOWEVER NOBLE HER INTENTIONS, SAYD POISONED THIS GROUP FROM THE START.

GREEN LANTERN: NEW GUARDIANS
GLOMULUS CHARACTER SKETCH BY TYLER KIRKHAM

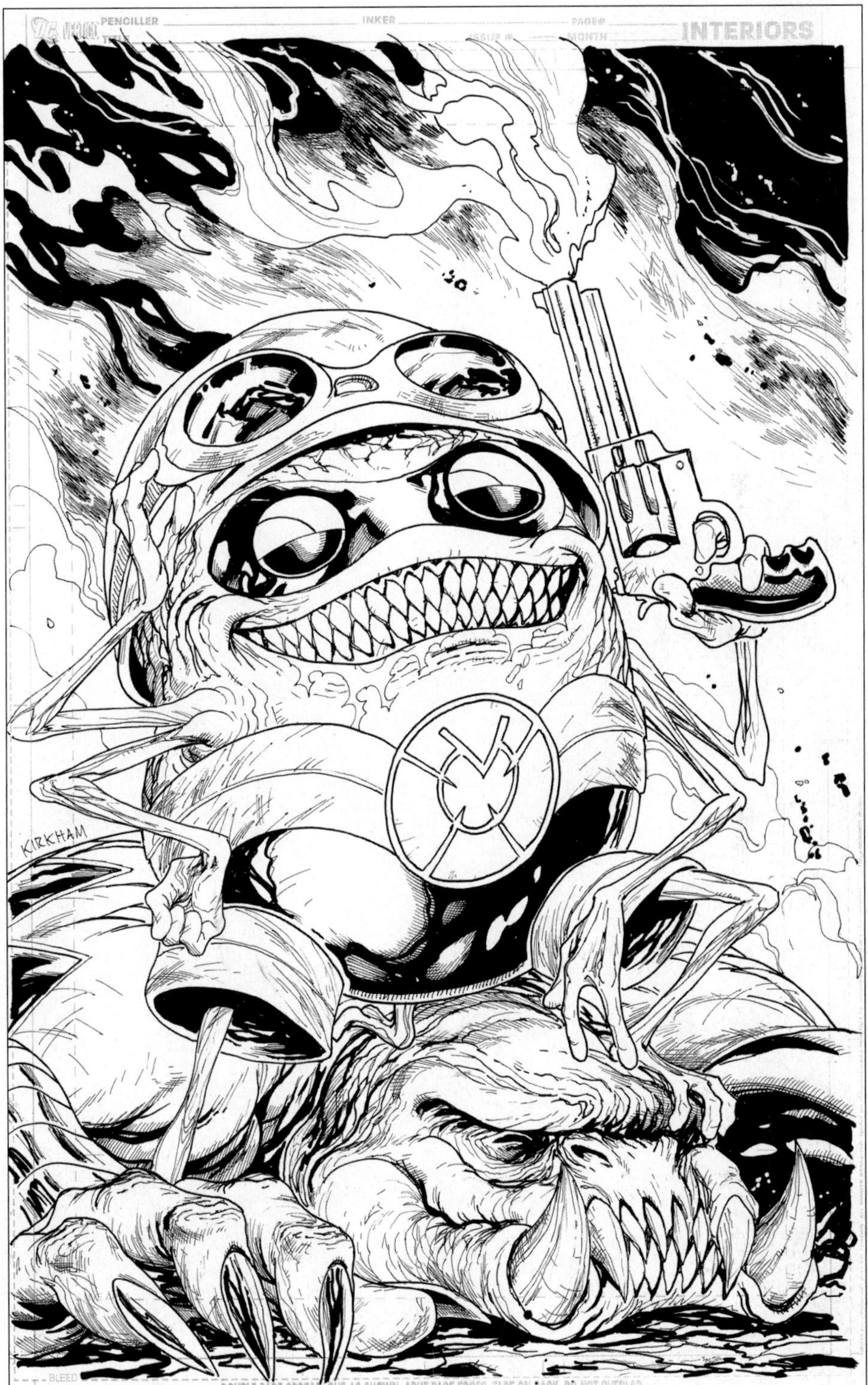
PENCILLER
INKER
PAGE#
ISSUE #
MONTH
INTERIORS
KIRKHAM
BLEED
CUT RIGHT-HAND PAGE AT THIS LINE
DOUBLE PAGE SPREAD: CUT AS SHOWN, ABUT PAGE EDGES, TAPE ON BACK, DO NOT OVERLAP
CUT LEFT HAND PAGE AT THIS LINE

GREEN LANTERN: NEW GUARDIANS
UNUSED COVER FOR ISSUE #10 BY TYLER KIRKHAM, BATT & NEI RUFFINO

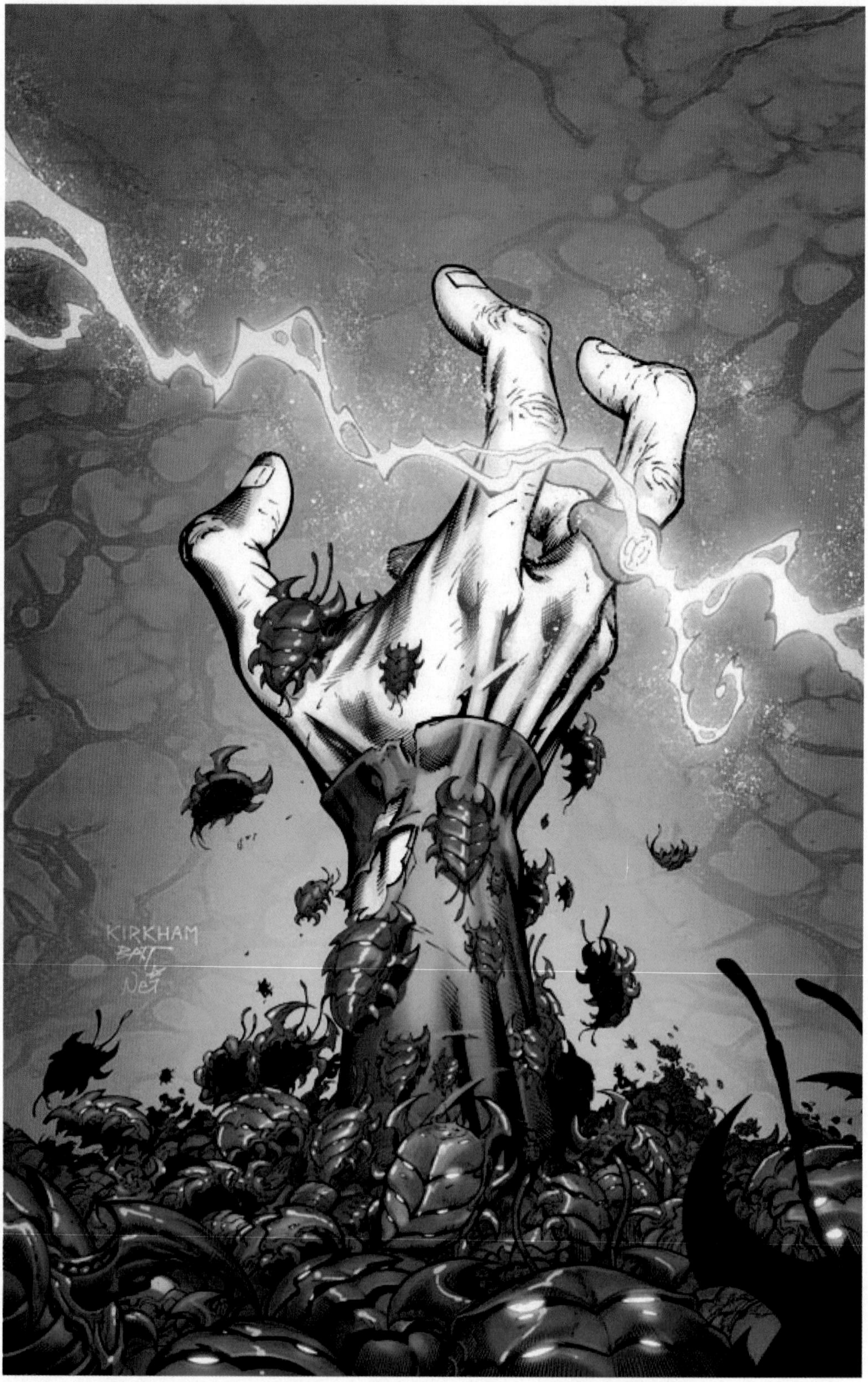

KIRKHAM
BATT
NEI

GREEN LANTERN: NEW GUARDIANS
KYLE RAYNER CHARACTER SKETCH BY TYLER KIRKHAM

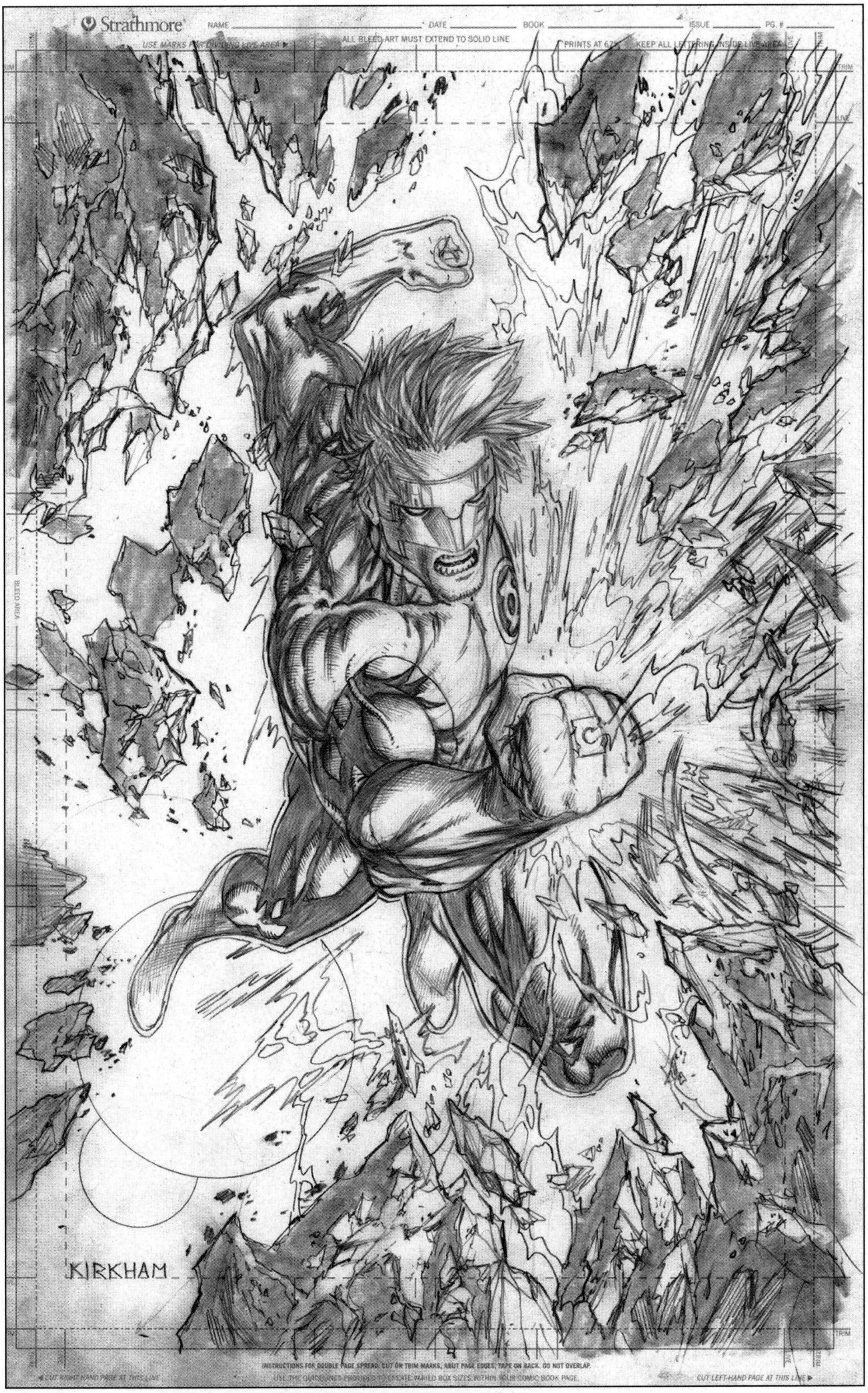

Strathmore
KIRKHAM

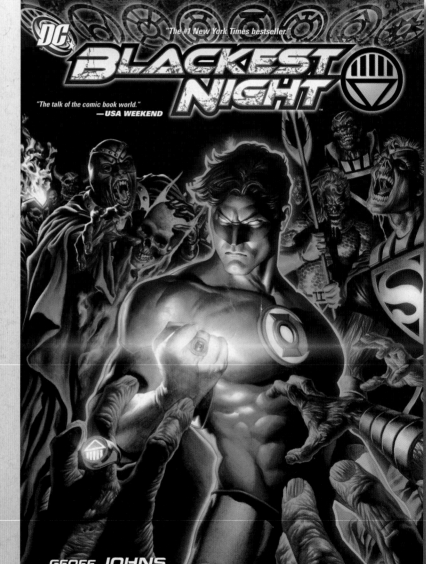